The Unanswered Self

Of the good in you I can speak, but not of the evil.
For what is evil but good tortured by its own hunger
and thirst?
Verily when good is hungry it seeks food even in dark
caves, and when it thirsts it drinks even of dead waters.

Kahlil Gibran, from The Prophet *(1923)*

The
Unanswered
Self

The Masterson
Approach to the
Healing of
Personality Disorders

Self

Candace
Orcutt

KARNAC

First published in 2021 by Karnac Books, an imprint of Confer Ltd

www.confer.uk.com

Registered office:
Brody House, Strype Street, London E1 7LQ

British Library Cataloguing in Publication Data
A catalogue record for this book is available from the British Library.

ISBN: 978-1-913494-32-2 (paperback)
ISBN: 978-1-913494-33-9 (ebook)

Typeset by Bespoke Publishing Ltd.
Printed in the UK by Ashford Colour Press.

Contents

Acknowledgments

My acknowledgments must open with further appreciation of the man who practiced within the evolving concept of personality disorder, even as he contributed to the growing definition of this concept. The work of James Masterson was always alive and continues to be: a process of therapeutic understanding and action continually subject to new discovery in the therapeutic encounter itself. As one of Masterson's associates, I will always value the way in which he also drew our own clinical discoveries into this process and gave them a forum. I hope to offer my thanks to Jim Masterson in continuing his work in this book – to carry forward his unique creative venture devoted to healing a fundamental human hurt.

Acknowledging the meaningful experience of the past forty years – especially the recognition of those who have brought companionship and insight to the undertaking – I can only partially find the right words of thanks. I hold valued recollection of the extra-Mastersonian teachers and supervisors I have learned from; the students – notably the supervisees – who taught me while I taught them; and the patients – who by necessity go unidentified – with whom I have shared a process of psychic growing-up.

Special appreciation is due to individual clinicians who maintain Masterson's teachings across the globe: Ralph Klein, M.D., former Clinical Director and Richard Fischer, Ph.D., associate, New York City, with whom I share memories of the beginning Institute; Judith Pearson, Ph.D., New York City, Director, the International Masterson Institute; Meral Aydin, Ph.D., Director, Masterson Institute Turkey; William Griffith, M.A., Director, Masterson Institute South Africa; Maggie Down, B. App. Sc., Director, Masterson Institute Australia; Caroline Andrews, M.A., M.A.P.S., and Elizabeth O'Brien, M.B.B.S., D.P.M., FRANZCP, Co-Directors, IMI Australia, in affiliation with the West Coast USA faculty; Loray Daws, Ph.D., British Columbia, Canada, former Co-Director, Masterson Institute South Africa, Masterson editor and ambassador at large; Louise Gaston, Ph.D., Director, Traumatys, and Monique Bessette,

Ph.D., Director, Victoria Institute, who both teach the Masterson Approach in Quebec, Canada; and Karla Clark, Ph.D., who provided a too-brief opportunity for a writing collaboration with one of the accomplished West Coast USA Mastersonians. Back on the East Coast USA, recognition is due to Diane Roberts Stoler, Ed.D., neuropsychologist, for her innovative work in trauma and hypnosis.

A special thanks must also go to Bradley (Baruch) Amins, Louise Gaston, Ph.D., and Loray Daws, Ph.D., with gratitude for their invaluable reviewing of the manuscript. Additionally, I extend my thanks for the support of two fellow writers, familiar with the nonverbal tyranny of words: Alice Schell and Maya Balakirsky Katz, Ph.D.

It also gives me pleasure to say thank you to Christina Wipf Perry, Publishing Director, Liz Wilson, Managing Editor, and copy-editor Nikky Twyman, at Karnac Books, whose expertise, organization, and warm encouragement have guided me through the birthing of this volume.

My acknowledgments would not be complete without the inclusion of my thanks to Patricia Masterson, with heartfelt appreciation of her kind thoughtfulness over many years.

Introduction

In *Psychotherapy of the Disorders of the Self* (Masterson and Klein 1989), reverently referred to by his associates as "The White Book" (the dust jacket served as our totem), James Masterson broadened his dynamic theoretical and clinical approach to include contributions by those he had trained and who worked with him:

> *For me, this volume marks an important stage in a professional journey that has had many turnings. Clinical concern and theoretical introspection evoke a wish to share, which led to writing and teaching. The deepening of this need to build a continuing community of ideas has impelled me to invite those who have learned from me to join me. This book represents their commitment and contribution to the Masterson Approach.*

(p. viii)

And, needless to say, "The White Book" marked an important stage in the careers of myself and the other associates, who also prized the clinical work, the writing, and the teaching, but had barely dreamed of being invited into a creative community with a leading mind in our field. "The White Book," and its companion volume, *Disorders of the Self: New Therapeutic Horizons – The Masterson Approach* (Masterson and Klein 1995), provided just that opportunity. It was an extraordinary "moment," for it not only marked our professional coming of age, but also exemplified Masterson's belief in us. "The White Book" and its companion volume not only welcomed us as part of a professional family, but also demonstrated Masterson's conviction that a living, growing society fosters new individual expression as essential for its scope and vitality.

Masterson's encouragement of the next generation of psychotherapists is not a fanciful family metaphor. In a substantial way he was the father figure, which is perhaps undervalued in this era of maternal emphasis. He brought disciplined structure and definition to our work with patients, and practical direction, through teaching and writing, to our interaction with the therapeutic world. Like the good-enough father, he did not praise unconditionally, but selectively encouraged in ways that supported individual accomplishment.

Masterson continued to incorporate writings of his associates in subsequent volumes. But "The White Book" and its companion volume are unusual in the opening of a master clinician's work to the creativity of those who have been in his training.

I was fortunate to have been invited to be part of the Masterson Group at its beginning in 1981 – this was the clinical arm of the Character Disorder Foundation, the forerunner of what is now the International Masterson Institute. There were three of us selected to join Dr. Masterson in his New York City office: Ralph Klein, M.D., who became Clinical Director after pioneering with Dr. Masterson at Payne Whitney Clinic, and Richard Fischer, Ph.D. and myself, associates. This original group was an egalitarian representation of clinicians: psychiatrist, psychologist, and social worker/psychoanalyst.

The following years were an exhilarating time of coming into being. Masterson himself was building an organization for postgraduate psychotherapeutic training and treatment, while expanding his concept of personality disorder in a field that was itself evolving new therapeutic perspectives. The rest of us accelerated to keep up – seeing patients and presenting at conferences with an understanding increased by ongoing supervision by Masterson and study of the books he steadily published. The Masterson Approach was forming even as we ourselves became teachers and writers and were joined in turn by new associates: an articulate group on the West Coast, and then colleagues abroad, in South Africa, Turkey, Australia, and Canada.

Self-individuation within the social context is the therapeutic aim of the Masterson Approach, and it was the professional goal set by Masterson for those he guided. Many of us, as we put into practice what we had studied, gained new insights from our experiences with our patients, and contributed our discoveries to the Approach. Masterson encouraged this participation, which added to the ongoing growth of ideas in the continuing synthesis he had undertaken and intended to pass along. For he showed us that theory, especially as it strives to understand and promote the growth of human personality, must itself grow and change.

The Masterson Approach has never been static. From the start, Masterson was unwilling to accept the status quo for the treatment of borderline adolescents. Refusing to follow a "wait and see" course of hospitalization that had little or no effect, and when the outcome of young lives was on the line, he steadily searched for ideas that could explain the dynamics driving his patients' repetitive, often contradictory, behavior, and lead to a new perspective on their treatment. This independent beginning was followed by the first of his characteristic syntheses: integration of object relations theory with the observations of child development studies. Two research projects and five books later, he had found a rationale and treatment for borderline personality disorder that worked for adults as well as adolescents, and had established himself as an authority in the field.

The synthesis continued. Work with borderline patients inevitably led to exploration of dynamic psychotherapy with personality disorder in general, and the possibility that different forms of personality disorder might follow a developmental process of their own (as reflected in *The Narcissistic and Borderline Disorders: An Integrated Developmental Approach*, Masterson 1981). At the same time, new schools of thought were evolving around the concept of personality, while contemporary psychoanalytic thinkers illuminated specific areas of pathology. Masterson steadily expanded his Approach to benefit from self psychology and advances in trauma theory and neurobiology. His treatment models for different personality disorders gained from the innovations of other pioneers. Just as Kernberg's theorizing concerning object relations informed Masterson's psychoanalytic psychotherapy of the borderline, so the Masterson Approach acknowledged the definitive ideas of Kohut in work with the narcissistic personality disorder, and the established but underappreciated writings of Fairbairn and Guntrip in work with the schizoid personality disorder. Finally, the culminating synthesis of the Approach – the borderline, narcissistic, and schizoid personality disorders grouped under the concept of disorders of the self – received a welcome affirmation from neurobiology and the insights of Allan Schore.

In 2005, Masterson brought out his last edited book: *The Personality Disorders Through the Lens of Attachment Theory and the Neurobiologic Development of the Self: A Clinical Integration*. This is a concise summation of his work, supported by detailed explorations by his associates, including a verbatim account of a supervision session (Masterson and Farley 2005). A significant addition to Masterson's model is cited in the contemporary attachment studies of Peter Fonagy and colleagues. The work of Fonagy, especially, is further elaborated in chapters contributed by Margot T. Beattie, Ph.D. (2005a, 2005b).

However, although Mahler is now reinstated as intrinsic to Masterson's theory, there is no attempt to review the Masterson Approach around the original developmental-object relation model. Consideration of schizoid personality disorder in conjunction with Mahler's differentiation sub-phase does not take place, to the loss, I believe, of both the understanding of that disorder and the integration of the Masterson Approach itself.

Masterson's synthesizing Approach, open to many new concepts but prioritizing clinical effectiveness, moved on so rapidly that possibilities of more painstaking elaboration at times were sacrificed for a broader view. One underdeveloped area was the exploration of a possible progression of types of personality disorder related to psychic arrest in the progressive developmental stages described by Mahler (Mahler, Pine, and Bergman 1975). It is a primary focus in this book to review more closely this specific building-block in the Masterson Approach in hopes of further demonstrating its persuasive clinical usefulness.

There is a vitality in Mahler's work that goes beyond the subject under observation and connects the reader to the living being. Originally, this association became an inspiration and a source of creative insight for Masterson. As he relates in his Prologue to "The White Book":

> *I immediately sensed that her work resonated with my own, and I was on the track she outlined like a bloodhound ... I put the two together, which led to the view that the borderline personality disorder was a developmental problem – a failure in separation-individuation or in development of the self.*

> (Masterson and Klein 1989, p. xv)

Nearly two decades later, this energy was renewed by "the explosion of knowledge from neurologic brain research," which supported child observation findings, including Mahler's. Specifically, Mahler's claim that maternal libidinal availability was essential for the infant's psychic growth was strengthened by Schore's conclusions: that mother-child "mutually-attuned synchronized interactions are fundamental to the ongoing affective development of the orbital prefrontal cortex, and, therefore, of the self" (Masterson 2005, pp. 9–11). Near the close of his work, and after occasional uncertainty as perspectives shifted in an era of intense theory-building, Masterson saw his Approach come full circle. He was to have the satisfaction (ruefully denied to Freud) of seeing his hypotheses scientifically validated.

A consistent correlation between Mahler's subphases of separation-individuation (the model of healthy maturation) and major types of personality disturbance (the pathological distortion of that model) is implicit in the Masterson Approach. Initially, Masterson drew a clear correspondence between borderline personality disorder and Mahler's rapprochement subphase of early childhood psychic growth. Later, as he explored narcissistic personality disorder, he speculated that this disorder related to a still-earlier subphase, probably the practicing subphase (Kohut is generally in agreement here). However, when Ralph Klein introduced the schizoid personality disorder into the Masterson Approach, Stern's new developmental model had taken the spotlight, and an analogy was not drawn between the differentiation subphase and that disorder (although Kernberg notes the connection, and Fairbairn and Winnicott's theorizing supports it). In this book, I aim to return to Masterson's original correlation of Mahler's developmental subphases and a shadow-side of corresponding disorders in personality. I hope to reinstate some of the lost effectiveness of the initial model by showing how the clinician's work is strengthened by an understanding of the healthy progression underlying the distortions of pathology.

I have found myself following this implicit schema in my work with patients. Perceiving the essence of the healthy child within the developmental distortion of the patient has seemed so clinically helpful that it has consistently shaped my understanding; moreover, relating that perception to a specific subphase of early development has significantly informed my diagnostic assessment and intervention. I think I can say that this guide has seemed so naturally true – as it presents evolving images of the early child frustrated by a normal developmental task that has somehow become a trap – that it has meaningfully shaped my perception and treatment of personality disorder. The true-to-life quality of the developmental model in my experience still evokes that insightful correspondence Masterson felt when Mahler's work first made sense of the misdirected energy of his adolescent patients. ("The White Book" includes a piece I wrote, based on modifications in clinical technique based on this schema; Masterson seemed open then to my keeping my assumption intact, and I hope he would now endorse my more explicit rounding out of the model [Orcutt 1989b, pp. 110–146].)

But still, why focus on this part of the Masterson Approach when linear models are minimized these days in favor of systemic, even spatial, concepts?

The linear model is clinically powerful. It speaks to the essence of dynamic psychotherapy: the patient's need to see his or her individual life as a meaningful progression, its parts interrelated and amenable to change. To accomplish this – held within the therapist's attentive presence – the patient finds the elusive words and feelings that complete the narrative and move it forward. The individual story – the beginning, the journey, the guiding intention – defines the patient's identity with the telling.

In 2005, in one of the last of Masterson's books, Judith Pearson, Ph.D., now Director of the IMI, reflects on narrative truth. Pearson speaks of "the shaping force of language," which from early childhood enables us to "tell" ourselves who we are, and to find validation in telling others of this discovery. Pearson's wonderfully inclusive piece reflects creatively on "The Analytic Quest for the Unnarrated Self" (2005, pp. 203–230), from its underlying strata in neurobiology, through the evolving conversation of mother–child attachment, through the primitive need to "sing up" a meaningful account of our environment, and ultimately to name the individual self. Her citations, which gather in a wide reading of scientific and creative literature, show how a complexity of thoughts about our being are contained in the linear narrative. Whether we are reminiscing on our birthday, or reclaiming lost parts of the story through the "talking cure," the narration of a linear journey through time shapes our sense of self. If the linear story we tell about selves is in part an illusion, it is the sort of illusion that Winnicott describes, and that we need to define our cultural "reality."

Pathology resists our attempts at theoretical and clinical taming. His Approach embodies Masterson's lifetime determination to draw together diverging sources of theoretical energy to better serve clinical demands. Masterson's therapeutic manner was directed by a passionate dedication that revealed itself in oblique ways. One way expressed itself through his involvement with the creative struggle of his favorite author, Thomas Wolfe (Masterson 1985, pp. 150–166). Another was symbolized in the bronze replica of *The Bronco Buster*, which he kept in his office. Remington's sculpture is described on the internet in these words: "[It] portrays a rugged Western frontier cowboy character fighting to stay aboard a rearing, plunging bronco, with a stirrup swinging free, a quirt in one hand and a fistful of mane and reins in the other."

Masterson's decades of defining and directing the treatment of personality disorder were often a wild ride. Especially in the case of borderline personality disorder, understanding the willfully oppositional and treating the supposedly untreatable became an achievable goal – a challenge to be met and then delegated to others who would value and continue this living accomplishment.

It is my hope to value, and to some degree strengthen and extend, the Masterson Approach, especially in regard to the clinical application of the developmental paradigm.

CHAPTER I

Overview: Personality Disorder and the Developmental Paradigm

The work of James Masterson is a synthesizing project left incomplete with unexplored possibilities for clinical application. It deserves an attempt at fulfillment not only because this may bring greater theoretical coherence to the evolving definition of personality disorder, but perhaps primarily because it offers guidance to clinical practice that is truly effective.

Masterson's fifteen books are as much a search as a discovery, and the search is still ongoing. It should be kept in mind that personality disorder is very much a contemporary concept, barely established now, and still just coming into being at the time of Masterson's first writings. Following the progress of Masterson's publications is itself a reliving of the growth of the concept of personality disorder: from the shift from the intrapsychic "character disorder" of drive theory, to the self-and-other-directed perspective of object relations and developmental studies, to the neurologically supported refocusing of self theory, to reaffirmation of the impact of maternal care on the infant's sense of being and resulting adaptation to individual personality style. Masterson's Approach has steadily gained from the ongoing formulation of personality disorder even while it has taken part in the creation of that definition.

Aside from his breakthrough volumes on the borderline, where he comes into his own in defense of his adolescent patients, Masterson is continually integrating new data from an expanding field and relating it to a coherent concept of personality disorder (increasing support from neurological findings must have been especially gratifying to his medical orientation). Above all, however, he is determined to keep his findings clinically pertinent. Although, I believe, he had acknowledged and incorporated information essential for defining his overview, the theoretical/

clinical synthesis of the Masterson Approach was still in its rounding-out state at the time of his death. Such a synthesis (I also believe) is a fundamental contribution to creating a curative clinical approach to contemporary personality disorder.

This book endeavors to follow Masterson's original direction: dynamic psychotherapy founded on the relational, developmental timeline of human psychic maturation. Historically, this viewpoint has been concerned, above all, with the growth of real children with their real mothers, and the application this has to the further psychic maturation of real patients of all ages with their interrelated therapists. The initial impact of Masterson's work was and still is derived from the unique effectiveness of this model in treating the borderline patient. It is the assertion here that the extension of the model – extensible by definition – not only facilitates treatment of other forms of personality disorder, but also it is proposed that a more inclusive perspective – a developmental, object relations, and self spectrum – provides a theoretical insight that renews that initial impact. Clinical action gains in persuasiveness, both for patient and for therapist, when the therapeutic process is perceived to be congruent with the process of human growth.

The Question of a Linear Approach

But why adhere to a linear, developmentally based approach, especially now, when the human mind is beginning to receive its due for all its networked, multidimensional, time-tricking, even illusional properties? Because the human psyche itself, I think, or at least the human psyche at present, requires the satisfaction of a linear overview. We both praise and lament the linear progress and change of things and of ourselves.

The linear model reflects the traditional view of the individual life experience: birth, childhood, youth, maturity, age, and death. We watch ourselves and others move and accomplish or relinquish along a temporal measure, and we primarily describe and judge our passage in those terms. Some parts of the story may predominate, be more vivid, but it is an evolving story with a beginning, middle, and end. Of course, this reflects the biologically governed, superficially observed movement of the self through clock time, but the telling of the "story" goes deeper.

The individual linear journey through time is perceived as just that: a progress toward self-definition, and the way in which we proceed (especially when we are tested) tends to characterize us. A primal pleasure, individual and communal, is to hear the story of an individual's struggle through obstacles to a conclusion (wrenching or edifying) of an ennobling sort. Even our dreams favor imagery of passage along paths, roadways, waterways, even through space, to report on our problematic passage through life. And, speaking of dreams, analysis itself was in part created to satisfy the patient's profound need for an emotionally complete self-narrative.

Narrative relies on spoken language, and the speaking and hearing of words continually shape human connection. The analytic dictum to "put it into words" suggests the expectation of an increasingly aware, intentional arranging of our ongoing experience in our lives and with others. Complexities increase from there, both inwardly and interpersonally, and again by happenstance, but the linear story we tell of ourselves forms a conscious mainstay of our identity – how we define, or hope to define, our personal being and its journey.

The Developmental Progression

In the following overview, the three "major dimensions" of personality disorder as defined by Masterson will be related to Mahler's subphases of separation-individuation in the order of infantile development. This overview reverses the order in which these dimensions were originally introduced to the Approach and, I believe, that now presenting them in maturational sequence contributes to the clarity of the model, and the logic of its clinical applications. Therefore, the schizoid condition will be described in terms of developmental arrest in the differentiation subphase, the narcissist, in terms of the practicing subphase; and the borderline, in terms of the rapprochement subphase.

Presenting these "major dimensions" in chronological order of psychic misdevelopment emphasizes why they can be considered "major." They can be seen as the consequence of characteristic distortions in the generally recognized nodal areas of early childhood growth, with a place, however misrepresented, in that sequence. These nodal points of childhood development have repeatedly attracted psychoanalytic thought as originating points of achievement or vulnerability, strength, or weakness, in the building of the mentally mature adult. Although various interpretations may attempt to define this growth, as Daniel Stern says, early human development goes forward in predictable "qualitative shifts":

> *Parents, pediatricians, psychologists, psychiatrists, and neuroscientists all agree that new integrations arrive in quantum leaps. Observers also concur that the periods between two and three months (and to a lesser degree between five and six months), between nine and twelve months, and around fifteen to eighteen months are epochs of great change. During these periods of change, there are quantum leaps in whatever level of organization one wishes to examine … Between these periods of rapid change are periods of relative quiescence, when the new integrations appear to consolidate.*

(Stern 1985, p. 8)

This developmental knowledge can strengthen treatment by guiding it in terms of normal maturational progress gone awry (essentially in affective, object-oriented ways), and in helping to shape therapeutic interventions accordingly. Understanding personality disorder in this way contributes to Freud's humanizing concept of mental illness: that psychopathology derives from distortion of normal mental processes, and contributes to our knowledge of them, albeit through an altered perspective. Additionally, just as Freud's understanding of healthy mental processes was increased by study of their pathological expression, so, conversely, seeing the healthy process at the core of pathology brings meaning to what at first may appear meaningless and therapeutically daunting. The often baffling, even maddening clinical work with personality disorder can find a more human anchorage when this perspective is maintained: when, within the schizoid's maneuverings, we see the persistent determination to protect the self; when the narcissist's self-aggrandizement can be traced to the exhilaration of equating self-expansion with self-affirmation; when the protests and contradictions of the borderline can be fundamentally recognized as the frustration and outright confusion of becoming one's own "holding environment" for opposing considerations.

A linear model is fundamentally unavoidable, to the extent that each developmental phase builds on the preceding phase(s) in order to construct the person. At the same time, chronological, linear description of human development is open to being called simplistic and rigid, and, if taken as all-defining, it surely would be so. Many influences have their effect, uniquely shaping individual development, and may be simultaneous, cumulative, modifying, and/or transformative, as well as sequential. As Sorenson says of Ogden:

> *he proposed synchronic dimensions of experience in which all components play enduringly vital roles, at once both negating and safeguarding the contexts for one another. Unchecked integration, containment and resolution … leads to stagnation, frozenness, and deadness.*

> (quoted by Bromberg 1998/2001, p. 272)

But all possibilities, viewed simultaneously, may lead to an impasse in both theoretical clarity and clinical directionality. An initial approach to treatment requires some prioritizing of focus.

The linear model can be used as other models (and often in conjunction with them) – as one guide for exploring how to proceed. The therapist must be constantly sensitive to the varied needs of the patient, and to what will carry the treatment forward.

The Differentiating Infant and the Schizoid Personality

The inclusion of the schizoid personality disorder as intrinsic to the Masterson Approach began as an invaluable addition by Ralph Klein, and was taken up by Masterson himself in his last three books. Although Masterson included the schizoid as "a third major dimension of psychopathology" (Masterson and Klein 1995, p. ix), he did not attempt to explicitly integrate this diagnosis with Mahler's developmental spectrum. I believe that understanding the schizoid within Masterson's framework not only strengthens the Approach theoretically, but contributes substantially to clinical effectiveness with the schizoid patient.

The contemporaneous and sometimes mutually acknowledging the-orizing of Mahler and the independent object relationists is basically in agreement in their observations concerning the first year of the mother–child relationship. Exploration of this topic consequently tends to sup-port Masterson's original developmental–object relations hypothesis. Especially now that this direction appears to be reinforced by neurolog-ical findings, return to Masterson's first model is rewarding because we can now see via neurology how a new psyche is first shaped together with another psyche, and later can be reshaped by other psyches – notably in the clinical relationship.

It is hard to imagine why Masterson, together with the mental health field in general, should have been slow to accept understand-ing of the schizoid personality – especially since the concept has long been with us, and since it represents a uniquely modern state of mind and personality. In 1960, Khan definitively places the schizoid on the psychic map, noting this is "a new type of patient that has come into prominence in the last two decades" (1974, p. 13) and referring back to Fairbairn's assertion in 1941 that "schizoid conditions constitute the most deep-seated of all psycho-pathological states … capable of trans-ference to a remarkable degree, and present[ing] unexpectedly favoura-ble therapeutic possibilities" (Khan, 1974, pp. 13, 14). It seems puzzling to say that the independent object relationists, who put forward and developed the concept of the schizoid, were regarded (or disregarded) until recently as rather auxiliary analytic figures.

Even now, there persists a disinclination to see Fairbairn, Guntrip, Winnicott, and Khan as an unproclaimed school in themselves: focused in thought, if not formally, and impelled by subjectively motivated in-quiry into the nature of the schizoid state. One possible explanation for this, pertinent here, rests on the supposition that it takes a specialized state of mind to most effectively comprehend and communicate with the schizoid patient. This is the state of mind, advocated by Freud, that can let go its conscious and logical inclination, and enter into the "free" associative language of the unconscious. Only, in this instance, there is a significant shift in technical balance. Freud's analyst remained a detached observer, noting patterns of association in the patient, while remaining scientifically apart and personally unaffected. The analyst of the schizoid also retains anchorage in conscious reasoning, but at the same time allows for a receptivity that facilitates a degree of subjective mental, emotional, even physical, experiencing of the patient's inner life. This is especially pertinent, as these patients characteristically project their problematic inner experience into the psyche of the analyst. It is likely that many dynamic psychotherapists, although highly intuitive, may favor a pragmatic stance inclined toward verbalized structuring and interpreting rather than acknowledging the nonverbal and mutual experiencing – they may tend toward work with pathologies originating in later developmental stages.

I am inclined to believe that Masterson is more this latter style of clinician (as is Kernberg), which gives him his special strength in working with the borderline. The borderline is to some degree caught at the juncture of mental development where consciousness and reasoning begin to predominate, and needs clinical guidance in finding right- and left-hemispheric balance. The mental world of the schizoid, which may require for entrance a greater intuitive receptivity toward altered states of consciousness, may have seemed less congenial for Masterson. By 2005, however, Masterson seems to be well on his way to finding the theoretical location for the schizoid within his Approach. Unquestionably, I expect, the neuropsychological language of Allan Schore made the schizoid more accessible to Masterson's medical mindset, and it probably indicates the more exactly systemized scientific route that theory of the schizoid must take to find a more general understanding in the field. By 2005, Masterson had found this orientation amply supported by the implementation of attachment theory by Fonagy, Gergely, Jurist, and Target, and its application to "borderline" personality disorder, and had subsequently incorporated Fonagy's work in his therapeutic synthesis.

In the meantime, some common comprehension of the modern schizoid patient's quandary is forming in the popular mind. Schizoid *anomie* is captured in the caricature of the electronics genius whose brilliance is only matched by his social incomprehension, or in the image of the untethered astronaut floating helplessly in outer space. Concern is growing around what seems a generation of young people absorbed in an isolated world of computer games in the basement.

The infant of Mahler's differentiation subphase of separation-individuation (approximately four to nine months of age) is observably developing out of "total bodily dependence" within a vaguely experienced "dual unity" with mother. This psychological emergence is visibly witnessed in the infant's "hatched look," or evidence of a beginning perception that there is more to be discovered. The infant begins to explore accumulating discoveries of difference, especially between infant and not-infant, while the mother provides the necessary organization and continuation of things. Mahler describes how the determined curiosity of the differentiating infant is excitingly supported by an increasing capacity to move – to reach out and push back – and to perceive – not just to touch and taste, but to see as well as hear over a distance. A reciprocal sensitivity between infant and mother ("mutual cueing") assures a safe, ongoing feedback that supports the infant's growth, while to a degree shaping it (for safety and cultural character) to the limits set by the mother.

Mahler, Winnicott, and Bowlby agree upon the importance of the mother's attuned, consistent presence, supporting the wakening, increasingly active curiosity of her infant. Winnicott speaks of how the "good-enough" mother supports the "going-on-being" of her infant, "holding" its "spontaneous impulse" of self "through time" (these terms are now becoming ingrained in the analytic language). The mother's "impingement" on her infant's spontaneity is minimal, and the undisputed message of the differentiation subphase is that it is safe and acceptable to *be*, and will continue so.

The problem of the schizoid begins when this message goes awry. Then things are reversed: the infant's needs are no longer primary in the relationship with the mother, but are secondary to her needs. This maternal "impingement" (Winnicott) encourages the development of an infant personality congruent with the emotional needs of the other at the cost of the emotional needs of the self. Exploring the mother's face, of much importance at this time, now assumes distorted emphasis, shifting value from exhilarated curiosity in everything to scrutiny on the mother. The reciprocal "mirroring" so poignantly described by Fonagy is curtailed, and with it the infant's ability to form an increasingly defined sense of self through the mother's receptivity. Instead, with the schizoid, the sense of self is inhibited in order to be congruent with the mother's degree of "acceptance." In Khan's words, "reactivity" supplants "authenticity." Because relationship now requires compliance in place of spontaneous expression, interaction for the schizoid will begin to assume some degree of detached calculation (aware or unaware). In future relationships, the other party may perceive a lack of emotional connection, while the schizoid will be troubled not only by that, but by an inability, in itself, to connect.

Going beyond Mahler's study, the independent object relationists theorize that the world of the early infant is composed of fragmented (Fairbairn), or "ununified" (Winnicott), perceptions of the self. The one-year-old relies on the continuity provided by the mother to connect his or her perceptions. Gradually, increasing experience and capacity for memory will enable the child to assume a more flowing sense of things. Unfortunately, the mother of the schizoid-to-be curtails the infant's wide and spontaneous exploring of self and surroundings by her disinterest, or perhaps by anxiety disproportionately aroused by this activity. The infant then learns to minimize or even dissociate such activity, developing a reactive personal style reliant on the mother's approval. Discrete self-states remain detached from each other, though they may later on come into focus (voluntarily or involuntarily) when briefly useful (they tend not to be sustainable) or when "triggered" by specific circumstances. "Switching" states frequently occurs as a means of managing emotion. In the more healthy process of things, the average person simply identifies the otherwise integrated residue of self-states as quirks in an otherwise consistent sense of self: "I wasn't myself when I said that"; or "Tonight I'm going to put on my party hat"; or "I act like a jerk around authority figures"; or "Holidays bring out the little kid in me." The schizoid personality, though, automatically shifts from self-state to self-state more or less persuaded that each position momentarily represents the whole self. This can be painful when, typically, the schizoid involuntarily distances in interpersonal situations. Or, more adaptively, the schizoid may have learned to call upon partial aspects of the self to comply (à la Guntrip's "compromise") within certain socially receptive situations (the actor's performance, the appearance of the debutante or model, etc.).

Winnicott describes an overarching partial state – the "False Self" – that is constructed by the schizoid to provide superficial compliance with others. Probably formed on the residue of the socially adaptive aspect of the self, the false self acts as protector for the "True Self," whose "unacceptable" impulses must be kept hidden. Detached from a unified sense of self, the false self is experienced less as a variation of the schizoid's being and more like a protective mask. An important patient resistance is found in the fear that, if the "mask" is removed, there will be no face behind it. Masterson's

"Real" self requires, primarily, the building of the patient's sense of authenticity within the therapeutic relationship, so that the disconnected aspects of being (including the "false" interface with others) find a place within the sense of self as a whole – integrated, not rejected.

The dynamic understanding of the independent object relationists is indispensable for guidance in establishing a therapeutic alliance with the schizoid patient. A counseling approach clearly is not productive: schizoid pathology has been formed on the substitution of injunctions of what and how to perform, in place of acknowledgment of who one *is*. Counseling may be perceived as just more of the same, and may invite the merely compliant response that has supported the patient's "false," chameleon-like social adaptation. Although the therapist's prolonged receptivity (including protracted silences) is crucial, the "receptivity" is compromised if the patient has been compliantly saying what he or she thought he or she was expected to say. That first year or so of treatment, in many ways a tentative, experimental monologue on the part of the schizoid patient, needs to have increasing validity as a shared dialogue, and not serve as camouflage for a hidden self.

The treatment model of the schizoid patient follows the developmental model of the "environment-mother" (Winnicott), who herself is able to experience her child as an entirety, intuitively "holding" the infant while the infant begins to discover itself. This process, if inadequately experienced in the first year of life of the schizoid patient, forms the core of the therapeutic treatment. I have suggested that this might be referred to as the "environmental transference" – the initial establishing of collaboration as the pre-object "facilitating environment" described by Winnicott.

As Winnicott explains: "What there is of therapeutics in this work lies, I think, in the fact that the *full course of an experience is allowed*" (1941, p. 67). The patient who, as an infant "has had no one person to gather his bits together starts with a handicap in his own self-integrating task." The therapeutic environment allows the patient "to feel integrated at least in the person of the analyst." He continues:

An example of unintegration phenomena is provided by the very common experience of the patient who proceeds to give every detail of the weekend and feels contented at the end if everything has been said, though the analyst feels that no analytic work has been done. Sometimes we must interpret this as the patient's need to be known in all his bits and pieces by one person, the analyst.

(Winnicott 1945, p. 150)

Elsewhere, he adds: "In the world I am describing, the setting becomes more important than the interpretation" (Winnicott 1955, p. 297).

Here, Winnicott's concept of transitional space is clinically vital. In that beginning time of mostly undirected talk, the patient will have touched upon a topic of special personal significance. This may have been a brief mention, seemingly insignificant (rock climbing, stamp collecting), but the listener's interest has evoked an unexpected gleam of patient anticipation, and perhaps an accounting of detail. This is likely to be the schizoid patient's transitional area, under the control of his or her expertise, where the other is allowed to enter, is even welcomed, while engaged but unintrusive. The analogy to play therapy (which Winnicott makes) is apt. The patient arranges very personal "toys" in very personal ways, as an indirect expression of an enthusiasm questionably acceptable to another. When the other expresses uncritical interest, a connection is formed that may lead to more explicit communication. For the child patient, the toys may be blocks; for the adolescent, computer games; for the adult patient, words describing interests. The schizoid patient uses this trial space to test the interpersonal environment: if this is promising, the next step can be considered – otherwise, it was only a game.

Ralph Klein devotes detailed study to short-term and ongoing therapeutic process with the schizoid patient. His perceptive and invaluable guidelines focus on the working-through of Guntrip's "schizoid dilemma" (not too far, but not too close), and the ultimate facing of the Mastersonian abandonment depression ("dread of cosmic aloneness," Masterson and Klein 1995, p. 59). Especially at the beginning of treatment, Klein advises that "The schizoid patient has to know where the therapist stands," and that place will not feel safe to the patient unless it seems "at a safe distance, one that is predictable, stable, and nonintrusive" (1995, p. 70).

Dynamic treatment of the schizoid personality disorder relies on the patient's gradual but steady attainment of a sure, consistent sense of self within "safe" relational interaction. The positive experience of interpersonal give and take counterbalances the anxieties that had become ingrained in association with spontaneous reaching out to another and its consequences. The self can now begin to incorporate this experience of consensual interchange (see Ralph Klein's "consensus matching," Klein 1995, p. 100) – to use as a base for an increasingly complex and feeling therapeutic relationship.

The Practicing Child and the Narcissistic Personality

The infant who has substantially mastered the developmental tasks of the first year impresses us with an increasingly defined individual presence. He or she is now increasingly upright, traveling, and more often referred to as "child" rather than "baby." This junior toddler now freely accepts physical distance from mother as long as the distance can remain pleasurably maintained by "checking back" (Mahler, then Bowlby) to her approving presence. Increased separation remains a delighted discovery of new perceptions as long as some "refueling" (Fuhrer) from the familiar attunement with mother is available. That the junior toddler still evokes a symbiotic sense of oneness with the other is reflected in Freud's observation that the child's narcissistic pleasure calls up the residue of our own narcissistic childhood experience, as we join in the delight of "his majesty, the baby." Both in present time and in memory, we share that "moment" when discovery of the world is simply an exhilarating extension of our own existence.

For the practicing child (approximately nine to fifteen months of age), the repeating of new experiences is encouraged by their pleasurable nature, and the positive expectation gained and approval won open the way to further exploration of the unfamiliar. The negative side of things is an inconsequential obstacle; it gains acknowledgment only insofar as the predominance of the positive is not dislodged or, if too troublesome, is then rejected. Successful passage through the practicing subphase relies on the forming of a positive base to support further psychic growth. In Mastersonian terms, it might be said that the practicing child relies on the secure establishing of the rewarding unit (good part-self/good part-object) as necessary for the eventual consideration of the possible existence of a negative unit (bad part-self/bad part-object). Delayed readiness to process too-unpleasant perceptions and feelings actually strengthens that readiness, and is not the same as being stuck in that process, with its pathological outcome.

Like the practicing subphase child, the narcissistic personality thrives on a relationship that perpetuates the loop of reciprocal good feeling. The persuasiveness of this phenomenon is observable in many charismatic public figures whose magnetism also calls forth its complement in the unswerving devotion of idealizing followers: the polarities of "manifest" and "closet" narcissism feed off each other.

The narcissistic patient tries to replicate this reassuring loop in the therapy. The empathic therapist allows this to happen to a degree – not as a regressive humoring of the patient, but as validation of the patient's feeling, which is an expression of an insufficiently validated need. As Kohut established, the analyst does not deal with the factual account of an episode, but acknowledges the feeling involved in what occurred. Thus, the therapist does not attempt to correct the patient's perception or behavior (Therapist: "Do you think if you had done it differently, your boss would have been less critical?"), but responds in keeping with the patient's feelings (Therapist: "It must have hurt to be spoken to in that way"). As the therapist will rapidly discover, attempts to introduce a more interpretive point of view are flatly rejected (Patient: "You don't even listen to what I tell you") or are perceived as a critical attack, which is then met with a counterattack (Patient: "Are you telling me there's something wrong with me? Well, maybe there's something wrong with you!"). The maintaining of mutually harmonious feeling provides the empathic relationship in the therapy – a way of relating that the patient will eventually internalize as the basis for a "cohesive" self (Kohut).

The increasing inner sense of confidence and solidarity will, in turn, begin to slowly admit more negative feeling and recognition of a non-symbiotic other. This is a natural process that takes place at its own pace, unless unduly hurried along or discouraged. With the narcissistic patient, there may be a countertransference pull to replicate the early mother's wish to speed up her child's progress or, conversely, to hold it back. In the parallel process of treatment, premature forcing of separateness or acknowledgment of "bad" feelings may overwhelm the newly cohesive sense of self with a fear of "fragmentation" (Kohut). On the other hand, overprotection from the inevitable faulty starts and dissatisfactions of a practicing relationship may tend to entrench solicitousness and preservation of the status quo over encouragement and exploration. The therapist of the narcissistic patient neither pushes the patient toward insight ("You need to think past your sensitivity if you want to get things done"), nor protects the patient from realistic expectations ("Others should really understand your sensitivity to what they do"). Instead, the therapist consistently validates feeling ("It can be hard going when others don't seem to know what matters to you").

While Masterson's understanding of the narcissist has compatibility with Kohut's, his clinical approach seems more adapted to work with a personality whose capacity for self-observation is further along developmentally. Masterson's semi-interpretive formula of "pain-self-defense" (Therapist: "My disagreement with you causes you pain, so you defend yourself by rejecting what I just said") is more likely to evoke further defense rather than introspection (Patient: "Why should I listen to you? You don't understand me at all"). In my opinion, this intervention is premature for the narcissistic patient newly entrusting him- or herself to therapy, and willing to experience emotional pain only within the context of an acknowledging other. Instead, an empathic intervention is needed to reinforce the validity of the patient's feeling response within the relationship (Therapist: "I am concerned that my personal comment took away from our appreciating your point of view"). However, Masterson's intervention, I propose, applies to a more advanced stage of therapy also addressed by Kohut. It addresses the psychically maturing narcissist who has achieved sufficient self-cohesiveness and observing distance (strengthened ego/self) to consider the dimension of "no" as well as "yes." Masterson's narcissist seems analogous to Kohut's narcissist in the second phase of treatment, where "optimal frustration" (Kohut) is a desirable addition to the pure "mirroring" necessary to establish a cohesive base for the self.

To a great extent, the practicing subphase is a time of consistency and consolidation, but it is a time when the Mastersonian narcissist must begin to face the anxiety of possible fragmentation brought on by venturing beyond this reassurance. The Masterson narcissist balances on this developmental edge, tentatively testing a positive sense of selfhood with a trial of the negative, and with it the possibility of separate selfhood. Meeting this challenge occupies the next developmental subphase of the growing child.

The Rapprochement Child and the Borderline Personality

As any parent of a two-year-old will attest, the transition from a world of "yes" to a reality containing both "yes" and "no" is a place of contention, especially when "yes" and "no" cannot be neatly divided from each other. How bewildering this can be may be seen (when no response seems to fit) in the parental frustration often accompanying that of the child, and the parallel exasperation often felt by the therapist of the borderline patient.

The two-year-old of the rapprochement subphase (approximately fifteen to twenty-four months of age) is negotiating a time of major psychic transition. A full field of differentiated elements (good/bad, self/other) will now have to be affirmed and held within an ever-integrating consideration, balancing and rebalancing as a shifting basis for further thought and action. Dissociation will decreasingly determine the basic patterning of relationship in response to the significant other (to "disappear" what one is not yet prepared for or willing to handle). The guiding patterns will have been unconsciously set, with dissociation remaining only as one of various defenses protecting these patterns, while an increasingly conscious mind explores the adaptive possibilities of modification, compromise, and choice. Importantly, with the increasing primacy of the left hemisphere, there is spoken language – the distance modality that allows us to communicate our subjective position to separate others once symbiotic attunement is no longer the dominant mode of communication. And this ability to maintain, logically consider, and resolve opposing concepts (the essential basis for defining and managing conflict) is supported by the developing prefrontal cortex, with its maturing capacity for judgment and impulse control.

In a course parallel (and intertwined with) the physical evolution from the mother, the psychological birth of the infant accompanies the growth of the self from a personhood almost a specialized reverberation of the mother, to an independent but interactive contributor to a system of social beings. The directing principle for this process, maintained by the object relationists in a major analytic paradigm shift, is our human need for each other. The developmental "moment" facing the two-year-old focuses this transformational shift of responsibility to the individual, first shaped within the relational matrix, and then more consciously evolving within the interrelational context of human society.

The distinctive developmental challenge is learning to consider self and other as separate and individual, while each evokes a mixture of good and bad feelings. It was even intriguing to discover self and other as physically apart, as long as harmonious good feelings governed that experience. Bad feelings next might be entertained, but as a discovery that could be withdrawn from or rejected. Next, good and bad might both find representation if both were kept oscillating in perception. However, to "disappear" one side of a potential conflict, or to assign sides to alternating opposition, no longer works. Antitheses are now complex and contain bits and pieces of each other.

For instance, the toddler will cling to a dependent position because this has been associated with good feelings. However, the urge and capacity for independence also feels good. Dependency is acquiring some unwelcome feelings of personal limitation. The toddler therefore acts oppositionally, in search of the new good feelings, even rejecting once-welcome comforts. Soon enough, however, the reassuring feelings of dependency are missed, and clinging is sought again. For a while, the old either/or solution will be applied to the situation: independent urges will be dismissed in favor of the comfort of clinging, or the restraints of clinging will be rejected for the appeal of free exploration. But the either/or solution does not seem to adequately address the new problem: dissatisfaction is to be found in both satisfactions. Is oscillation no longer the answer? Switching alternatives before dissatisfaction can catch up with things? The toddler hectically shifts dependent and independent positions, pursuing the enduring feeling of uncompromised "good" familiar to the earlier developmental stages, and protesting its elusiveness. This is Freud's "anal ambivalence," or the commonly recognized "terrible twos": developmental dissatisfaction in attempting to control a contradictory reality. The toddler's mother (and, later, the therapist of the borderline caught in this developmental "moment") will have the trying responsibility of modeling how to stay steady in an inconsistent world. Mother and therapist alike must demonstrate how mixed feelings are evoked in most situations, and must be acknowledged, however conflictual, until they can be inclusively considered in terms of reality as well as pleasure.

The maturational acceptance of the mixed good and bad in human nature characterizes what Melanie Klein describes as the depressive position. This marks the relinquishing of the idealization of the mother–child relationship, and is resisted out of the fear that acceptance of the bad will harm the good, which then cannot be repaired. Similarly, Freud speaks of our need to mourn the loss of our idealization of important relationships if we are not to remain "melancholy" about the necessary acceptance of disillusionment intrinsic to the human condition. This transition for the two-year-old is aptly described by Kavaler-Adler as "developmental mourning" (2014, p. xxvii). The achievement of a conscious, independent, self-observing, and self-correcting self can now maintain crucial human relationship through a new capacity to perceive both self and others within their own complex contexts, and clarify and enrich that perception with the exchange of words. But this reality of choice and interaction is only achievable if we relinquish the idealization that still holds us to an oversimplified time we have outgrown.

The mother of the two-year-old is challenged to remain consistent – but consistent in what way? Human nature seeks a reduced, stable resolution of things, especially one that feels and seems good. The discovery that such a state is best approximated through the balancing of complex, contradictory, and changing realities is not the sort of consistency that was hoped for. Developmental mourning is involved in the insight that living itself is a complex, often paradoxical process, rather than an inevitable passage toward an ideal goal.

The mother of the irreconcilable toddler maintains a patient consistency of attitude supported by an adult perspective already present in the mother's psyche. She provides a model as well as a support for managing this bewildering time. She holds steady for the child's contradictory moods and moves toward independence, then dependence, then back again. In addition, mother and child now have words to help express and sort out the confusion. Mother can say: "Come sit on my lap!" Junior can answer: "No, I won't!" Mother then can reflect: "Sometimes you like this, sometimes you don't. You don't always feel the same" or "You can choose one now, and save the other for later." The mother has words as well as steady tone to hold the comings and goings in a continuum of sorts. She models acknowledgment of this first significant experience of conflict: the containing of coexisting opposites in an unresolved emotional context without losing emotional stability.

The mother contains her child's indecision without interfering with the child's frustrated but improving capacity to manage it. This means that the mother does not complicate the situation further by associating healthy experimentation with parental reactivity: Mother: "Come back! Don't you love me anymore?" Or "Grown-up children don't want to sit on mother's lap all the time!" The mother relinquishes the adventuresome child freely (within the limits of safety), and accepts him or her back with equal warmth. The learning itself, with mother's interest and support, is up to the child. For the mother to hold on too tightly, or let go indiscriminately (reinforcing preference with the giving or withholding of affection or approval), may set up a dysfunctional pattern in the learning process.

Mastery of this subphase gains the child the beginning capacity to tolerate impulses that may involve mixed personal and interpersonal feelings. Rapprochement initiates the sorting, modifying, and compromising required to get along in a world of choices and decisions – especially a social world. The either/or tendency to oversimplify is tenacious: Child: "If I just hold close to Mother, I will feel good, she will feel good, and nothing will ever feel bad again." Letting go that expectation surely calls for a maturational need for mourning at this juncture in the developmental passage.

The borderline patient is commonly recognized by a changeable, contrary style essentially alternating between clinging and then contention to the point of problematic acting out (interminable phone calls, then missed sessions, unpaid fees). Although inclined toward an independent attitude, the borderline seems often to have learned to associate independence with disapproval by the other. Consequently, a positive direction on the patient's part somehow is twisted into a matter for transferential dispute. There is a countertransferential pull for the therapist to repeat the early mother's reluctance, or disapproval, of her child's developmental urge to meet life on his or her own terms. The therapist (unlike the early mother) must "hold center stage" (Masterson) by maintaining the perplexities of the situation in the same field of observation: "I see a complication here. You want to be in charge of what you are doing, but you also seem to expect me to give you a hard time over it." Patient: "So what?" Therapist: "Why not hold on a minute and check me out? Maybe it's all okay!" At this point, the patient may shift to the other polarity: adopting the dependent attitude that mollified the early mother's anxiety over her child's increasing self-sufficiency. Here, the therapist must resist the countertransference pull toward false supportiveness, paralleling the early mother's relief at her child's compliance (and perhaps the therapist's appreciation of a seeming truce in the process). Instead, the therapist continues to hold the inclusive observing field: "How come a short time ago all you wanted was to move into your own place, but now you insist that nothing could be better than staying home?" Patient: "You didn't think it was a good idea." Therapist: "Are you saying you'll give up any plan of yours that doesn't have my hundred percent support?" Patient: "What do I know? You're the therapist." Therapist: "Does this mean you're coming here so I can make all your decisions for you?" Patient: "Of course not! What are you talking about?" Therapist: "I'm calling to your attention how you're making it all you or all me, all right or all wrong, when we could work on this together, with each of us having some of the pieces."

Masterson's therapeutic aim is to "confront" the complexity contained in both the dependent and independent stance ("Seems you feel two ways about this"), and then in turn confront how resorting to an acting out, either/or solution avoids the intrinsic dilemma ("So you keep your appointments, but you're always late. Could be you want to be here and also you don't?"). The eventual confrontation suggests juxtaposing both stances: "Why don't you just tell me how part of you doesn't want to be here even when part of you does?" It is at this stage that the treatment begins to engage with the core dilemma: the fear that the healthy assertion of self will lead to loss of the mother's love, her presence, or survival itself.

As Masterson again points out, in the pathological context, on the rapprochement level the achievement of each developmental step forward carries the implied threat of the loss of the mother's love: the abandonment depression. What he could have added is that this characterological malaise is intensified by the distress brought about by a significant shift in healthy maturation itself. "Borderline" is a well-chosen description, in that failure to meet the developmental task of the rapprochement subphase additionally leaves the individual unable to cross the division between a still-unformed and an essentially integrated psyche. A comprehension of whole self and other, each with mixed positive and negative qualities and a capacity to understand the reciprocal effects, must be integrated in order to facilitate the mourning that accompanies psychic maturity. Without sufficient achievement of separation and individuation, there cannot be enough definition in psychic interplay to permit the experiencing of the guilt and reparation described by Melanie Klein or the oedipal resolution described by Freud. Mastery of rapprochement, according to Mahler, introduces the next and no doubt ongoing subphase of "on the way to object constancy," which leads from childhood to latency and beyond, or in pathology marks the "borderline" between personality disorder and neurosis. The "borderline" patient must find the determination not only to face the intense fear of not being able to survive without the mother's love (which once was a real threat but is now a fantasy), but also to build the psychic strength to accept a loss of the ideal in the inner world that accompanies the transformation of psychic birth.

Overall Consideration: Technique

There is a natural progression in child development that can be shadowed in the clouded reflection of pathological personality misdevelopment. In spontaneous growth, the wide-ranging curiosity of the one-year-old begins to find personal and emotional definition within the good feeling of the fifteen-month-old, then must meet the two-year-old challenge of reconciling opposing feelings and comprehensions. In parallel, the schizoid relinquishes spontaneous outreach for cautious compliance, the narcissist limits emotion and relationship to mutual good feeling, and the borderline keeps the contradictions of a complex world in separate boxes. The striking feature of personality disorder is the almost staccato interruption, at critical points, of the steadily inclusive flow of the process of psychic growth. In the therapeutic work, pathology is recognizable in places that are set or even unapproachable (notably emotionally and/or interpersonally) in what otherwise may be a relatively flexible personality. The patient behaves in accordance with largely automatic assumptions that are held so basic to functioning that a vigilant anxiety guards even their questioning. These assumptions, we are coming to believe, include patterns for social survival established in the earliest of human interreliance and are only subject to change in later situations approaching a similar degree of mutual trust. No wonder terrible anxieties concerning abandonment or nonexistence are called up by the relinquishing of these assumptions/patterns, even when they are maladaptive in present reality.

Classical analysis, by Freud's definition, is directed toward the patient whose mind has defined self and other and their relationship and can talk about it. Work with personality disorder, based on the mind still caught in places of significant growth and communication, cannot rely on the spoken word in the same way. The further back the personality disorder is based in childhood development, the more the healing process must relate to intuitive, nonverbal experience. This has a definitive effect on technique: words carry the manifest message, but are not necessarily received in their dictionary sense so much as by their implication. Do words convey interest, acknowledgment, alignment, questioning, opposition, correction? This is the latent communication. Importantly, does the latent "tone" of the words assure a consistent and attentive presence?

As technical communication is different between the neurotic and the patient with personality disorder, so it varies from one personality disorder to another. For the schizoid patient, whose struggle begins with the fundamentally nonverbal acceptance of being, silence in itself may communicate both receptiveness and a need for safe distance. The therapist's response may simply accept this as a possible foundation for taking a second step:

Both: (Prolonged silence).

Pt.:   Am I supposed to be saying something?

Th.:   I thought you might be thinking.

Pt.:   Shouldn't I say what I'm thinking?

Th.:   Sure, but that's up to you.

Pt.:   (With a possible hint of potential playfulness) This gives me something to think about.

The still predominantly nonverbal communication with the narcissistic patient may seem more superficially interactive, but requires the one-note reinforcement that is needed to strengthen and maintain the basically positive view of relationship needed to move forward:

Pt.:   They know I'm their best for years, and now they give the award to the new guy.

Th.:	After all that time, that must hurt.
Pt.:	Yes! He's a flash in the pan! So what if sales are up!
Th.:	You'd expect they'd recognize your longtime achievement.
Pt.:	Year after year I gave them what they wanted.
Th.:	You've proven your value.
Pt.:	So why do the bastards give the award to the new guy?
Th.:	It doesn't seem fair – you stay the distance, he gets the prize.
Pt.:	You know, you're pretty understanding. But maybe you should consider how times can change.

The shift in personality state, although it may increasingly benefit from insight, takes place because of a shift in perspective – a shift that occurs under conditions of diminished anxiety in an increasingly trusting relationship. The pathological limitation on seeing is widened, but first, looking around takes priority over looking within.

The borderline, in ways, is the most challenging to define in terms of technique, because the therapist's position must hold steady while containing the malleable view of the patient. It is useful to recall that the borderline, like the two-year-old, requires a steadying and verbalized "adult" perspective while trying to reduce a contradictory reality to manageable terms.

The pre-object world is a world of absolutes. At its most evolved, it is a place of either/or, reversing self and other, and good opposite bad. It understands resolution in terms of win or lose – truce is not moderation, but a pause in contention. There is success or failure, or – worse – love or loss. Self and other pick sides, and subjugation of one by the other establishes what is good – at least for now. This is the formulaic guidance of the right brain, which determines survival behavior and drives it by emotion.

The mind of the two-year-old is transforming in accord with left-hemisphere contribution and domination: the newly exercised ability to reason things through. This is not something that can readily be explained to a toddler, or to the borderline, who will have to take time to live through the experience. Now there is a need for a specialized kind of "holding" that Masterson called "confrontation" in order to form a bridge toward greater exercise of the activity of the conscious mind.

The following dialogue demonstrates the balancing act involved in maintaining an overall point of view while the borderline vacillates between partial explanations for the whole:

Pt.:	This is the man I will give my life to.
Th.:	Okay. But do you keep in mind he's still dating his ex-wife?
Pt.:	You never want me to do things my way.
Th.:	Just hoping you're thinking of everything.
Pt.:	You just want to make my choices for me.
Th.:	How do my concerns take away your choices? Your choices are yours to choose.
Pt.:	You'd leave me stranded like this? You used to give me good advice.
Th.:	You seem to think that if I respect your right to choose, I won't support you.
Pt.:	But what should I do?
Th.:	Did you come here for me to make your decisions for you?
Pt.:	Of course not. Why are you arguing with me?
Th.:	Sounds more like the argument is going on in you – maybe you wonder if you can do it your way and still count on my support even if I question you.
Pt.:	I guess I never thought of it that way.

Unless the supposedly irreconcilable opposites can find reasonable consideration within the therapist's all-inclusive field, there will be no model for new possibilities of arrangement. This "confrontational" interchange will have to be repeated many times before it takes form – not only as a growing capacity in the patient for a more complex point of view, but also as a maturing ability for interpersonal dialogue.

A Note on the Oedipal Phase and the Neurotic

The oedipal phase is qualitatively different from the separation-individuation phase, just as the neurotic presents a qualitatively different state of being apart from the problematic personality. A development of mind distinguishes the two from each other. Freud defined the basic distinction. The oedipal psyche is structurally relatively complete – it recognizes the autonomous intactness of self and other; consciousness is primary and communicates via the spoken word. The preoedipal mind, involved with its own structuring, has not fully learned to distinguish the other as apart from the self, to determine gradations of feeling, nor to subject the inner world of wishes and fears to outer experience, observation, and planning. Intuition is relied upon as much, or more than, further definition through verbal specificity and dialectic.

The successful progress toward definition and structure leads to more than yet another of the "qualitative shifts" described from Abraham to Daniel Stern – there is a transformative change. Although so much remains to be understood, it would seem that the preoedipal mind is preoccupied with basic patterns for survival – including those for social relationship – that can be stored for automatic assumption without the need for constant reiteration. Basic behavioral responses, such as fight, flight, and freeze, are stored along with patterns for territorial dominance and courting. The preoedipal world is governed by either/or thinking that resolves problems by dismissing one extreme, or by oscillating between choices. This is right-hemisphere, this-or-that thinking, meeting the demands of here-and-now necessity. Conflictual thinking, with its need for measured consideration of opposites within a simultaneous field, is initially unthinkable, for it requires hesitation, even delay, that may prove fatal in circumstances calling for immediate action.

The human mind, however, is preparing for more than basic survival. In a second, but overlapping development, the left hemisphere – essentially the left prefrontal cortex – is readying the individual for conscious, considered assessments of nonemergent situations. There is now the ability to delay impulse in safe situations, to analyze perceptions and plan actions based on overall judgment of even contradictory particulars. Conflict is managed by logic that need not rapidly choose between absolutes, but can examine, weigh, and compromise parts in terms of a larger contextual whole that includes past memory and future planning. Quiet passages of time can now be used to improve the quality of existence. In addition, spoken language is now available and can prioritize over – or work in conjunction with – intuition. Unlike intuition, which requires mental synchronicity for shared communication, spoken language can define, interchange, and refine different perspectives for common consideration. The use of words requires time, but given that advantage, words provide a bridge of dialogue between differing points of view that facilitates growth of both the individual and the communal self.

This transformation – simplistically described, from "right" to "left" brain dominance – is actually a process requiring more than the first three years or so of human growth. Indeed, the prevalence of "either/or" thinking in adult individuals ("you" or "me") and communities ("us" or "them") and their ideologies ("right" or "wrong") suggests that this stage in human thinking is still finding its way toward successful evolution. The symptom of the neurotic possibly represents a signal calling attention to an outstanding need for further brain integration; of the need for realigning fundamental assumptions or aligning insufficiently processed memories and concepts with current reality.

The Masterson Continuum

Masterson's endeavor, like Freud's, tends to be an excavation as much as a construction. In a way, the whole extension (and specialization) of psychotherapeutic knowledge inclines toward uncovering parts of a still poorly defined whole. The emphasis, of necessity, is based on the pieces that are observed and catalogued, while the totality is left to often fanciful hypothesizing until enough is gathered to reveal the completed whole. Each newly found fragment assumes special importance that may take on undue dominance as it affects our changing and sometimes competitive views of the finished picture.

Masterson, following Freud before him, realized that an open mind to new discovery leads to growing comprehension of the whole. He subsequently continually widened his field of theoretical exploration and clinical application with emphasis on synthesizing rather than replacing insights. Throughout his books, he describes patients with personality disorder – and the major theories regarding them – as dynamically interrelated. The three "major dimensions," though characteristically distinct, share a commonality: taken as a sequence, they shadow the stages of a flowing period of human growth, representing inadequately met points of developmental progression. Masterson's original attempt to reconcile personality disorder with Mahler's relationally oriented stages of developmental growth – which he returned to after a period of skepticism – shows his persistent aim toward an inclusive, rather than compartmentalized, view of the mind.

Relatedly, I believe it illuminates Masterson's synthesis to reverse his order of "discovery," and follow the sequential disturbance of personality formation in relation to Mahler's order of psychic development. If we consider the schizoid at the outset, we comprehend the psyche's beginning need for a containing, constant, personal environment to support new exploration of every momentary particular. Next, the narcissist shows us the need of the psyche to reassuringly find a differentiated world pleasurable and agreeable in order to prepare for less pleasurable and agreeable discoveries ahead. Then, in a bewildering transitional step, the borderline's confusion requires steadying from a more integrated mind in order to consider contradictory and emotionally felt discoveries within a single rational field – not just to facilitate this shift, but to support the impact of a major reorientation in psychic perception and perspective as well. In addition, just as communication evolves between the child and the adult over time (from nonverbal to increasing degrees of verbal complexity), so therapeutic language – technique – changes with diagnosis. The intervention provided by the therapeutic relationship itself is consistent, however – acknowledging and provision of the missing interpersonal experience to grow on.

For personality disorder, the building of the confidently based, adaptively related self is the task at hand. For the neurotic patient, this working relationship is the foundation, rather than the goal, of therapy. For the neurotic, with rational mind and collaborative dialogue more available, communication centers on the conscious decoding of messages of unfinished business presented by the unconscious.

However, understanding of neurosis gains in resonance when it is not defined as a diagnostic category opposed in an either/or way to that of personality disorder. Although distinguished by a boundary indicating change of qualitative significance, the stage of development marked by neurotic distortion is still part of the extraordinary process of human psychic birth. Although the oedipal child benefits from the primacy of rational consciousness, the transition of command between "old" and "new" mentation is still unfolding. Problems not sufficiently resolved by earlier dissociation must now be managed by repression, with its ability to warehouse outmoded issues. Unfinished business must be identified and stored separately from definition and management of the now front-and-center matters of sexual identity and relationship (for instance, the complications of the Oedipus complex must be disentangled from any residual inclination to divide the parents into "good" and "bad" polarities – desired vs. feared). One wonders whether analysis of neurosis may not, to a degree, be a way of aiding this transition; of facilitating communication between newly relating parts of the mind in order to clear up "old business." Is not interpretation a means of "translating" a message between the unconscious and conscious parts of the mind while these are still learning to collaborate? To extend this speculation a step further, cannot neurosis be understood in part as the last arrest in a process of unique mental development that involves coordination of unconscious and conscious mental capacities on the way to further self-realization?

It should be reiterated that the linear, categorized model presented here is a guideline for exploration of a networked problem capable of disregarding sequence and labels. A wonderful, although often bewildering, aspect of human nature is its plasticity. Most of us have traversed all the developmental stages well enough to keep going, though it is likely we all could use room to grow in some areas. The person with a disorder of the self may have a deficit in more than one area, and in varying degrees. However, the therapy begins with a presenting disorder of sufficient prominence and intensity as to characteristically trouble the person at work or at play – especially in relationship with others – and handicap functioning in either or both realms. Layers of borderline acting out may eventually prove a shield for schizoid vulnerability, and issues of neurotic conflict may later emerge as personality structure strengthens. Human nature is as adroit at hiding as it is at disclosure, and requires time and continued time to be known and to trust.

The Masterson Approach is a synthesis based on respect for patients' needs combined with respect for the ideas of others who have devoted themselves to the same concern. It is an approach continually open to concepts that inform us, but must be contributory to a living, collaborative process of healing. Philosophy tempts us, but life is demanding and short on time. Masterson's Approach is essentially a clinical one, and his therapeutic identity always, in his words, is to be "a servant of a process."

CHAPTER 2

The Borderline Personality

Because I believe this category includes a gradation from personality style to pathology, I have left the word "disorder" out of the title above. Personality inclinations such as occasional overreliance on others, arguing for argument's sake, a certain impulsivity, and unpredictability of mood do not necessarily place someone outside the norm, and may even lend some individuals a quirky appeal. I have followed this usage in subsequent chapter titles, as well.

> *Twenty-five years ago, I reported that the mother's difficulty in supporting the child's emerging self in the rapprochement stage was one of the key etiological agents in the borderline personality disorder. The child internalized this interpersonal interaction to form the intrapsychic structure. This led to a specific model of psycho-analytic psychotherapy to deal with that structure that was researched and found to be effective.*

(Masterson 2000, p. 56)

James Masterson founded his psychotherapeutic approach on a challenge encountered in real life – coming to grips with an inpatient unit of acting-out adolescents. This was in the 1960s, when the term "borderline" described a *terra incognita* between neurotic and psychotic conditions (Knight 1954), and troubled adolescents with disruptive behavior were expected "to grow out of it" (Masterson , 2005, p. l). Masterson, however, seeing that the passage of time left his patients unchanged, was determined to understand the stubbornness that kept his patients protesting, demanding, and repeatedly behaving in self-defeating ways without learning from experience. In addition, he was set on finding a way to work therapeutically with these young, misdiagnosed (actually undiagnosed) patients.

A fellow Masterson associate, William Griffith, has mentioned to me that when he remembers Masterson he thinks of the bronze statuette of Remington's Bronco Buster in Dr. Masterson's office. There was a frontier energy in Masterson that matched his professional discipline and, I expect, found a resonance in the adolescents he treated.

In 1967, *The Psychiatric Dilemma of Adolescence* initiated the steady publication of Masterson's books that continued well beyond 2000. In his writing, he continually synthesized new psychodynamic perspectives to strengthen a clinically effective definition of personality disorder in general. He extended his research and practice to include the borderline adult and then the personality disorders as a whole, which he defined as subject to maturational challenges gone awry. Although borderline personality disorder became a circumscribed part of his overview of personality disorder, it always remained critical to the entire Masterson Approach: the theoretical key to unlock the larger dynamic structure. Applicable first to the borderline, and then to the personality disorders overall, was *a combined self and object relations developmental approach directed at healing a developmental arrest sustained by defense against profound separation anxiety and abandonment depression.*

Defining the Masterson Borderline

In 1975, Masterson collaborated with Donald Rinsley to present an article, "The Borderline Syndrome: The Role of the Mother in the Genesis and Psychic Structure of the Borderline Personality." Published in *The International Journal of Psycho-Analysis*, this piece offers Masterson's most psychodynamically detailed description of borderline personality, and marks the inclusion of this perspective into psychoanalytic discourse. The article is focused on "the contribution of maternal libidinal availability and withdrawal in the aetiology of the borderline syndrome" (Masterson and Rinsley 1975, p. 176), and draws upon Otto Kernberg's (1967) application of Kleinian object relations theory to the borderline personality, together with Margaret Mahler's developmental observations and conclusions. Although in time Masterson extended the scope of the article (notably by the inclusion of self theory and neuropsychology), the main thesis prevailed: mother–infant loving interaction governs the child's healthy internalization of relationship, and the distortion of that mutual give and take during the first fifteen to twenty-four months of the infant's life may result in a borderline disorder. Specifically, maternal emotional inconsistency combines with the ambivalence natural to this developmental phase to ingrain what would otherwise be a temporary confusion of the growing child's needs both to be taken care of and to act independently.

The Masterson Borderline: Object Relations Theory

The Masterson/Rinsley article first introduces the object relations component – the Kleinian point of view adapted by Kernberg to describe the borderline syndrome (Masterson and Rinsley 1975, pp. 163–165). Following the Kleinian model of internalized object relations, Kernberg sees borderline difficulties originating within the first four to twelve months of childhood development. (This time frame is now understood – by Kernberg as well – to be premature, but the preoedipal location of the dynamic is of lasting significance. It also might be noted that Klein's child patients were two and a half years old and up [Brandchaft 1989, p. 233], which corresponds with the end of Mahler's rapprochement subphase of development and Masterson's concept of borderline disorder.) During that time, self and object images have been internalized, but they are split into "good" and "bad" representations that are perceived as separate and unrelated. Fixation at this stage of development later results in clinical manifestations typical of the borderline, notably "contradictory character traits ... resulting in chaotic interpersonal relationships" (Masterson and Rinsley 1975, p. 164).

Masterson and Rinsley observe that Kernberg "places predominant emphasis upon constitutional factors" especially "a constitutionally determined intensity of aggressive drive derivatives" (1975, pp. 164–165). This will remain a point of disagreement between Kernberg's theorizing and Masterson's conviction that it is dynamically based aggression that is resolved in the working through of the "abandonment depression" – a major resistance characteristic of the borderline condition (Masterson 2000, p. 40). Masterson's point of view is in keeping with the independent object relationist's argument that aggression has its origin in libidinal frustration.

Although Kleinian "good" and "bad" split object relations representations are central to Mastersonian conceptualization, curiously, Masterson and Rinsley do not extend their study more to the work of the "independent" object relations group of analysts. Kleinian thinking minimizes the importance of the actual mother's role. (Winnicott wrote that talking to Klein "about the part the mother plays" is like "talking about color to the color-blind" [Rodman 2003]). Furthermore, Klein retains Freud's (post seduction theory) assertion that mental disturbance is primarily the creation of the patient's inner "phantasy" world. Kleinian theory (over her protestation) was extended by her followers to include the child's incontrovertible psychic need for the actual parent. Fairbairn's conviction that the desire for a real parent is greater even than the (Freudian) wish for pleasure, and Winnicott's dictum that "there is no such thing as a baby" without the holding presence of the mother, directly support Masterson's consistent belief that "the interactions with the mother are deeply internalized to produce the object relations unit of intrapsychic structure" (2000, p. 34).

(A moment should be taken here to note Masterson and Rinsley's definition of "unit" and "part-unit." The psychic unit is composed of three elements – an "immediate sense of other," feeling, and "immediate sense of self" – that constitute the internalized representation of the mother–child relationship. Two basic components split the unit: the Withdrawing/Aggressive part-unit [WORU] and Rewarding/Libidinal part-unit [RORU]. These are distorted part-representations that, in the arrested development of the borderline, continue to alternate rather than support psychic integration.)

The introduction of Mahler's developmental theory complements Kleinian object relations. It allows the Masterson/Rinsley article to consider the mother's role in the building of the child's psychic structure. It also exemplifies the characteristic Mastersonian synthesis of apparently disparate theories to illuminate his concepts.

The Masterson Borderline: Developmental Theory

After reviewing Kernberg's work, the article by Masterson and Rinsley next considers "Mahler and the Role of the Libidinal Availability of the Mother in the Development of Normal Object Relations" (1975, p. 166).

Mahler's position is clear:

My view places special emphasis, however, on … the circular pro-
cesses between infant and mother, in which the mother serves as a
beacon of orientation and living buffer for the infant, in reference to
both external reality and his internal milieu.

(Masterson and Rinsley 1975, p. 166)

Mahler's child researches, in collaboration with Pine and Bergman, establish the "psychological birth of the human infant" as a process of separation-individuation taking place in the period approximately from the fourth to the twenty-fifth months of life – and she adds that, "like any intrapsychic process, this one reverberates throughout the life cycle" (Mahler et al. 1975, p. 3).

(Here it is useful to review Mahler et al.'s [1975, pp. 52–120] subphases of the separation-individuation phase of childhood, which form the developmental basis for the Masterson/Rinsley concept of the borderline:

a. Hatching/Differentiation – 4–5 months to 9 months
b. Practicing – 9 to about 16 months
c. Rapprochement – 15 to about 24 months
d. Object Constancy – 24 months and ongoing.)

The Masterson/Rinsley article continues, quoting Mahler's conclusion that the emotional availability of the mother is essential to counterbalance the anxiety evoked by the normal process of separation-individuation. In particular, "It is the mother's love of the toddler and her acceptance of his ambivalence" that enables the toddler to form and internalize self and object representations (1975, p. 166).

From the reference to "the toddler," it is evident that the mother's acceptance of her child's "ambivalence" is critical to a specific subphase of early development: the period from about fifteen to twenty-four months that Mahler refers to as the "rapprochement subphase" (Mahler, Pine, and Bergman 1975, pp. 76–108):

In the third subphase of the separation-individuation process, the
rapprochement period, while individuation proceeds rapidly and the
child exercises it to the limit, he becomes more and more aware of

his separateness, and begins to employ all kinds of partly internalized and partly still acted-out coping mechanisms in order to deny the separateness. One of the frequently observed coping behaviors is the toddler's insistent claim for the mother's attention and participation.

(Mahler et al. 1975, p. 228)

Mahler herself hypothesizes a connection between difficulties in traversing this subphase and later borderline issues: "In some children, however, the rapprochement crisis leads to great ambivalence and even to splitting of the object world into 'good' and 'bad' ... In still other children, islands of developmental failures might lead to borderline symptomatology in latency and adolescence" (Mahler et al. 1975, p. 229).

It should be added here that Mahler's work depicts early child development in a vivid way that brings theory to life. Her description of the height of rapprochement ambivalence (the "rapprochement crisis") is readily identifiable as what is commonly referred to as "the terrible twos": "If the observer in the mother's absence became the 'bad mother,' she could not do anything right, and a mood of general crankiness prevailed. The 'good mother' was longed for, yet she seemed to exist in fantasy only" (Mahler et al. 1975, p. 99).

If the reader is a clinician struggling with a borderline patient, this parallel glimpse evokes a perhaps unexpected understanding of the patient's seemingly chaotic states – let alone of the clinician's own sense of frustration. The mother–child picture brings the therapist–patient's experience into a normalizing perspective. I suspect that this and other descriptions of Mahler's may have reverberated with Masterson's strong clinical sense of his borderline patients. Clinically, even the most aggravating of borderline activity can be made more comprehensible (and countertransference more manageable) when one pictures Mahler's two-year-old caught inside the patient's psyche, protesting the contradictory nature of human relationship.

The Defensive Sub-units and Technique

In the Masterson/Rinsley article, the Kleinian "good" and "bad" introjects also assume a more clinical immediacy as Mahler's separation-individuation perspective is incorporated. The article proposes a corresponding parallel in the pathology of the borderline – the "rewarding" and "withdrawing" sub-units:

> *the borderline child has a mother with whom there is a unique and uninterrupted interaction with a specific relational focus, i.e. reward for regression, withdrawal for separation-individuation …* the unique push–pull quality of this sort of mother–infant interaction becomes powerfully introjected and forms the basis for the progressive development of the borderline syndrome.
>
> (1975, p. 167)

They describe how this developmentally arrested split in the borderline's self and object representations can be clinically mended by the steady containment of the patient's divided ego within "the therapist's healthy ego." Through "interpretive confrontation" within the strengthening therapeutic alliance, the patient's conscious awareness of the sub-units grows and, through introjection, a new, unified self and object relations unit is created. With this integration "the patient is now able to complete the work of mourning for these 'lost' images, which characterizes the final work of separation from the mother" (Masterson and Rinsley 1975, p. 172).

The clinical challenge (and where the patient's changeability tends to be matched by reactivity on the therapist's part) is described. "Confrontive clarification" of one part-unit leads to activation of the other part-unit which, during the working-through, leads to a "circular process" of defense (1975, p. 171). In the case material presented, this fluctuation is articulated by an observant patient: "When my work on one side went well, one side of me was pleased … the other side said why did I do that and I wanted to drink" (1975, p. 173).

Mahler's "toddler" is at a developmentally normal time of indecisiveness, whereas the borderline is notoriously stuck in an unchanging back-and-forth between opposite states: *"it is as if the patient has but two alternatives, i.e. either to feel bad and abandoned (withdrawing part-unit) or to feel good (rewarding part-unit) at the cost of denial of reality and self-destructive acting-out"* (Masterson and Rinsley 1975, p. 171).

Masterson differs from Kernberg in using confrontation rather than interpretation in this first, alternatingly defensive phase of treatment. Unlike interpretation, which addresses repression, confrontation is

directed toward the splitting defense: the dissociative, preoedipal forerunner of repression. For example, a Mastersonian confrontation juxta-
poses the patient's conscious verbalization with the patient's acted-out
expression, thereby bringing the patient's potentially conflicting feelings
into awareness: "You say you are eager to be here, but you also arrived
late, and now you tell me you want to cancel the next session." It should
be emphasized that it is the maladaptive defenses that are confronted,
and not the patient's self.

It is here that one might question a point in theory/technique put forward by the article. The article, in an attempt to integrate drive theory, likens
the withdrawing object relations sub-unit (the WORU to use Masterson's
acronym) to the pleasure ego that must be modified, while suggesting that
the rewarding unit (the RORU) provides the basis for building the reality ego. The abandonment depression, which must be faced beneath the
layer of defense, is seen to be evoked by confrontation of the withdrawing
sub-unit only (Masterson and Rinsley 1975, pp. 169–172). It would seem,
however, that both WORU and RORU represent a distortion of the normal
developmental opposition of alternative inclinations toward dependence
and independence. Would not some degree of perception of pleasure and
reality be intrinsic to both positions?

Are not both part-units defensive, and in equal need of confrontation
before the abandonment depression can be reached? As the article says,
"*Both part-units are pathological*" (1975, p. 171), and it would seem that the
evasive alternation of the part-units is itself an overall defensive maneuver
that needs to be acknowledged as resistance to the deeper, depressive phase
of treatment. (It might also be considered that this repetitious alternation is,
in fact, a developmentally frozen form of the psychic oscillation that typically
precedes stages of psychic unification.) Both the patient's acted-out rebellion
and acted-out clinging must equally be brought into conscious awareness,
and themselves be confrontationally juxtaposed and integrated within a
steady therapeutic alliance. The patient then would have the strength and
assurance to face the transformative but devastating feeling that has been
warded off: the sense of loss of early (and insufficient) maternal support that
must be exchanged for growing (but insecure) independence.

In the parallel of Mahler's healthy model, the mother must be
consistently emotionally available and stable despite the toddler's
conflicting desires to be independent and dependent. She describes the
maternal reaction that may be the potential origin for future borderline

difficulties: "During this subphase," she notes, some mothers cannot manage "the child's demandingness" any more than others "are unable to face the child's gradual separateness" (Mahler et al. 1975, p. 78). It would follow that the overdependent clinging of the borderline may be as much a conditioned response to maternal overprotectiveness as borderline rebelliousness is formed by a reaction to maternal disapproval for self-assertion. Maternal possessiveness may be as problematic as maternal restrictiveness, and maternal failure to contain the general ambivalence of this time in a consistent-enough way may be the most pathology-making situation of all. In this way, the child's natural drive toward independence becomes rebellion, and the need for reassurance, clinging, with no prospect of reconciling the two states.

In the therapeutic parallel, the clinician is challenged not only to confront the sub-units in turn, but also to remain objectively all-encompassing (and "a beacon of orientation") as the patient shifts back and forth between defensive polarities. Clinging acting out is identified without being overindulged, while rebellious activity is brought into words within protective boundaries rather than arbitrary (or punitive) restrictions. And, through consistent confrontation, as the patient shifts defensive position, the clinician exemplifies the capacity to hold opposites within an inclusive context. Initially, the acting out of the predominating sub-unit – often the withdrawing sub-unit – is confronted: "If you want your point of view understood, how come you present it in a way that's so hard for people to hear?" When confrontation holds steady despite reactive storms, insight and its attendant painful feeling is avoided by the patient's shifting to the alternative defense – in this case, the rewarding sub-unit. Once again, it is the clinician's job to steadily confront: "If I give you all the answers, how can you learn to figure things out for yourself?" And again, when persistent confrontation modifies the defense to the point of revealing insight and feeling, the patient once more shifts to the alternating defense. In time, and within the growing reassurance of the therapeutic relationship, both defensive alternatives begin to give way to the patient's natural integrative capacity that was blocked by the developmental arrest. Essentially, the therapist's inclusive consistency has begun to reshape the patient's pathological determination to force the therapeutic interaction into a recreation of the original dysfunctional relational pattern. This transformation depends in part on the ability of the therapist to show the patient how one person can contain conflicting perceptions. This contributes to the patient's perception of a new maternal figure which can be internalized in the building of a new inner model of self and relationship, as well.

At this stage, confrontation is shifting to focus on the integration of both sub-units. For instance, the therapist can begin to make such observations as: "Seems like I can say something you hate without your having to hate me."

Abandonment Depression and the Triad

And it is here, with the taking in of the new, integrated maternal image, that the "abandonment depression" is evoked. In healthy development, this would probably be equivalent to the major psychic shift described by Klein as the "depressive position," with its maturing capacity for conflict, guilt, and reparation (and, in Freud's terms, the ability to mourn). For the borderline, however, the old pattern of relating – to the split mother-figure – has been so entrenched as to have become a kind of belief system. The loss of the inner representation of the rapprochement mother is not met with a transitional sadness, but with a devastating sense of loss (supported by memory of the actual mother's discouragement of the individuating attempts of the "real self"). It will take a stressful time in psychotherapy to reduce abandonment depression to developmental mourning (Kavaler-Adler 2014, p. 2), and the patient will revert to defense repeatedly in the attempt to disavow it.

Technically, with the emergence of the abandonment depression, repression begins to replace splitting/dissociation, and interpretation starts to replace confrontation as the effective intervention. However, confrontation will still be needed when the patient at times regresses into the old defenses.

These predictable times of defensive regression were observed by Masterson, and later formulated into a pattern he initially called "the borderline triad." Later he extended the concept to personality disorder generally, renaming it "the disorders of the self triad." He wrote that, predictably, "self-activation leads to separation anxiety and abandonment depression, which leads to defense" (Masterson 2000, p. 40). In other words, getting better seems paradoxically to lead to feeling worse. This invariably occurs to some degree with effective treatment of personality disorder, and is perhaps related to the analysands "destroyed by success" who baffled Freud. If the triad is not anticipated and then managed as part of the treatment process, it can sabotage progress, making success seem like failure. Successful termination, especially, combines a separation from the therapist (including the "loss" of the therapy itself) with a decisive step toward individuation, and so may occasion the borderline's regression to defense when the patient had seemed least vulnerable. Masterson's identification of the triad allows this regression to be a foreseen possibility in the order of things, and consequently a powerful resistance to be worked through.

Masterson's special strength, I believe, is in the effectiveness of his clinical insights. Maternal availability, the persistence of the real self, interventions that acknowledge rather than interpret inner states, fear of individuation, abandonment depression, the triad, are concepts that apply readily to the clinical setting. In the case of the borderline, confrontation of the split object relations sub-units illuminates how to work with a type of patient often considered frustrating, even incorrigible, because of apparently chaotic disruptive and seductive behaviors. The shift in emphasis I have suggested – uncovering the abandonment depression beneath the alternating defense of the sub-units rather than within the withdrawing sub-unit alone – would seem to be supported not only by a second look at psychic structure, but mainly by the clinical experience myself and colleagues have noted and questioned.

Further Consideration of the Defensive Sub-units

Masterson's elaboration of Klein's "good" and "bad" introjects by way of Mahler's rapprochement polarities is especially clinically relevant. Mahler's description of the ambivalent two-year-old shows us the healthy model of development underlying the pathological distortion, and so provides the clinician with an understanding that makes sense of the work and gives it direction. One can literally picture the healthy model of relationship that the therapist and patient are locating and reinforcing in place of the pathological model.

The withdrawing sub-unit is bad-feeling because it reflects a time of profound, bewildering change that has been intensified and distorted by a tug-of-war between mother and child. This distortion is repeated in the patient's argumentative and oppositional behavior with the therapist. Here, it is easy for the therapist to fall into the countertransference error of replicating the early mother's misdirected reaction and therefore treating the patient's behavior as "bad" – something to be disapproved of and eliminated. Of course, a limit must be set for harmful behavior, just as "healthy" maternal concern sets protective boundaries for the independently exploring child (and the limit should be presented in these terms – as a matter of concern rather than disapproval). Confrontation is intended not to eliminate disruptive behavior, but to begin to transform it into adaptive self-assertion. With effective confrontation, the interchange between therapist and patient changes from a tug-of-war to a give-and-take that supports individuation. Eventually this becomes a dialogue that will facilitate the subsuming of self-assertion within the whole-self-representation. "Badness" – preoccupation with disagreement and loss of approval – becomes containable within the interpersonal situation, and can even be handled playfully.

The rewarding sub-unit is good-feeling because it offers a relief from trying to deal with the growing sense of conflict stirred up by individuation, as well as confirmation of the mother's continued presence, but it has been pathologically distorted into a way of discouraging further attempts at trying. This situation can be tempting to replicate in the therapy: the trials of the withdrawing sub-unit can be exhausting, and therapist as well as patient may be reluctant to resume the struggle. The therapist may adopt a so-called "empathic" approach that acknowledges the patient's wish for a less demanding situation (not a bad initial move), but with a lack of confrontation to point out how independence includes taking initiative and responsibility, the treatment is stalemated. Nothing happens until, perhaps, separation anxiety is evoked by the therapist's absence in some form. Mahler describes the healthy parallel of the rewarding unit as a comforting moment of reassurance that supports the child's return to independent activity. She mentions that the truly supportive mother even gently encourages the resumption of assertiveness, just as a mother bird will sometimes give a nudge to the fledgling on the edge of the nest (Mahler et al. 1975, p. 79). The transformation of the rewarding sub-unit from a place of regression to a place for reassurance and reactivation is probably crucial to the eventual unification of the sub-units – a sense of whole being. A deeply ingrained belief in the mother's consistent ongoing support, throughout fluctuations in the child's feelings and perceptions, must be confirmed by the child if the "bad" is eventually to be redefined and integrated with the "good" within the whole unit. This realistic consistency provides a "beacon" for the child's inner sense of the indestructability of the mother's love.

From Borderline to Personality Disorder

It has been over half a century since the field began the debate (still perhaps a never-ending process) over how to define "borderline" and "personality disorder." Following Knight's diagnostic mapping of "borderline" psychic territory, Klein's extension of psychoanalysis to children, and the growing interest in the preoedipal psyche elaborated by developmental research, an important shift took place in the diagnosis and treatment of a major number of patients. In addition, Knight's "borderline" region of pathology – a location between neurosis and psychosis – began to be divided into subtypes: a clinically critical endeavor complicated by a confusion of terms.

This complication is vividly demonstrated in one of Masterson's early books. *New Perspectives on Psychotherapy of the Borderline Adult* (1978) preserves a landmark conference organized by Masterson, where leaders in "borderline" theory and treatment presented their respective orientations.

Peter Giovacchini, Otto Kernberg, Harold Searles, and Masterson himself, described and interchanged points of view, noting similarities (Kernberg and Masterson) and dissimilarities (Masterson and Searles). The discussion led Giovacchini to comment: "We have to acknowledge, at the beginning, that we don't really know what we are talking about when we speak of borderline." And he perceptively added: "I believe the spectrum from early schizoid states to the patients Searles has been talking about up to the more structured patients Kernberg and Masterson are discussing can be considered borderline from the phenomenological viewpoint … It's going to take years before we come to some kind of consensus" (1978, p. 108).

Since the time of that discussion, the term "borderline" has given way to the inclusive term "personality disorder," which contains discrete subcategories (among them, the "more structured" borderline of Masterson and Kernberg). The definition and arrangement of these subcategories is still under debate, but the borderline – as suggested by Giovacchini, and supported by Mahler's development model – would seem to belong closer to the neurotic "border" than the psychotic "border," as other types of personality disorder do. It would also seem likely that Searles' patients in the discussion, who appear nearer the schizophrenic "border," most likely represent the subcategory of schizoid personality disorder.

An additional observation only suggested by the discussion is that the subcategories of personality disorder may fall into a pattern related to maturational phases. Masterson first adopted this linear model in his work with the borderline, and then extended his hypothesis to work with the narcissistic personality disorder (which he saw as analogous to Mahler's "practicing" subphase of child development). I believe this developmental model is implicit as well in Masterson's inclusion of the schizoid personality disorder as a third major subdivision of personality disorder, although he did not pursue this possibility. If only Kohut could have been included in this conference (*The Analysis of the Self* [Kohut 1971] was just beginning to find adherents)! Perhaps a possible "spectrum" from schizoid to narcissist to borderline personality might have been explored, but, more likely, an even livelier discussion would have taken place. (And incidentally, Kohut apparently defined "borderline" as a near-psychotic condition, and unanalyzable.)

In the years to come, Masterson continues to expand his definition of borderline personality, synthesizing important new concepts in the field. As Masterson incorporates self theory (an inclination brought into focus with the independent object relationists who tend to interchange "ego" and "self"), he draws upon the developmental theory of Daniel Stern (1985), as well as Mahler. Stern places an emphasis on the child's evolving self, which seems to counteract Mahler's emphasis on the importance of the mother's libidinal availability. However, if one resists a tendency to polarize rather than to integrate, one can consider how these two perspectives complement as well as differ from each other. Eventually, Masterson retains Mahler's work in his synthesis, satisfied to see her work supported by the neuropsychological findings of Allan Schore and the "mentalization" concept of Peter Fonagy, both of which emphasize the subtle and vital influence of mother–child interrelationship on the formation of self.

The theory and therapeutic treatment of the borderline personality disorder remains the cornerstone of James Masterson's contribution to psychoanalytic psychotherapy. Its originality and clinical effectiveness establish its relevance, and it has creative influence. Like all sound ideas, it calls forth more ideas – both in Masterson's own work and in the work of others he taught and encouraged.

In the evolving understanding of personality disorder, I believe, it will remain indispensable.

CASE STUDY

Confrontation of Hysterical [Borderline] Transference Acting Out

This case study describes the first two years of my work with Annie (a pseudonym), a hysterical borderline personality of the most chaotic and colorful sort. She was tyrannical, frantic, quick-minded, seductive, alarming, and always changing. Annie had been the picture of the clinically baffling hysterical patient who drove therapists to despair and recurrently maneuvered herself into the limbo of chronic hospitalization.

However, with the appropriate therapeutic support, Annie is now getting better. Her capacity to change is as dramatic as her personality. Recently, she told me: "I could have been 'Sick Annie' all my life if I hadn't found the right therapy. I could be locked up somewhere. My God, there must be a lot of people like me who are still in hospitals, who are letting their lives go down the drain because they don't know any better – and their therapists are letting them get away with it!"

I had been working with Annie for over two years in twice-a-week confrontive psychotherapy, but her treatment really began six years ago, when she first applied to the Masterson Group and was seen by Dr. Jacinta Lu Costello. Dr. Costello made the diagnostic assessment and set the boundaries for treatment that established the foundation of all subsequent psychotherapy for Annie. This is Dr. Costello's description of Annie, of her history and the nature of beginning treatment:

> Annie, age twenty-nine, was referred to the Masterson Group immediately prior to her release from the psychiatric inpatient service. This hospitalization was her fifth in six years and had been precipitated by severe regression following the separation from her husband. The previous hospitalizations were precipitated by suicidal gestures following the break-ups of other relationships.

Although a complete history was not available at the time of the referral, it was known that Annie had had functional difficulties from the onset of puberty. Although she had completed high school and a one-year business school program, her performance and attendance throughout were erratic. From puberty on, her weight vacillated by as much as fifty to seventy-five pounds, she was picked up repeatedly for shoplifting, and she made multiple aborted efforts at outpatient treatment. In almost every therapeutic effort, Annie would improve functionally within the first month and then deteriorate. Her subsequent demands upon the therapist would then escalate, and, when they were not complied with, she would either threaten to take, or actually would take, an overdose of pills. In two cases, her therapists refused to see her again after discharge.

The most recent hospitalization followed the break-up of her four-year marriage. Although the first years were described as idyllic, the relationship deteriorated as Annie became more dependent and demanding. Her husband finally left. Annie remained out of the hospital for four months following the break-up by moving home, entering treatment, and gradually demanding more and more from her parents and therapist. She insisted one parent remain with her at all times. Her parents finally requested hospitalization for Annie when she insisted on sleeping with them.

This time, Annie had been hospitalized for fifteen months. During her stay, she was described by staff as "bright, articulate, demanding, pushy, and manipulative." She was diagnosed as having a borderline personality disorder with hysterical features. At the time of her discharge, staff was angry and frustrated with her. They felt that, while Annie expressed a desire to be more self-sufficient and responsible, she thwarted every effort to realize it.

Before I met Annie, I knew the following: her track record since puberty, and perhaps before, was poor; separations precipitated all hospitalizations; she had frustrated her husband, parents, therapists, and hospital staff to the point where they had fled. And, finally, she was impulsive.

From a positive point of view, I knew she was articulate and bright, seemed to have been successful in engaging people, and on occasion demonstrated the capacity to take initiative and responsibility on her own.

I began seeing Annie four times a week. The primary aim of the treatment was to foster more behavioral control and to alter Annie's self-destructive pattern of managing her life and feelings. Although Annie articulated her agreement with these goals, her behavior suggested that she viewed therapy as a place where you come to feel better. Each time Annie actually considered behaving responsibly, she became extremely anxious, and in order to dissipate the painful affects associated with autonomy, she would avoid, act out, or look to me to take over her life.

While the dynamics were clear from the outset, Annie's potential for control was not. Annie was not convinced she was capable, was scared to death to even try, and used every available opportunity to demonstrate to me that I was asking for something she couldn't deliver. I wasn't sure that Annie had the wherewithal to control her behavior. But I also knew that, if I varied my stance by giving in to her regressive demands, I would lose all therapeutic leverage.

Dr. Costello held the line while Annie threatened and maneuvered to be taken care of; when thwarted, she called Dr. Costello a "cold bitch," phoned endlessly, traveled repeatedly to emergency rooms, twice was hospitalized, and frequently persuaded doctors and family members to contact Dr. Costello and question the competency of her treatment approach. But, in time, Dr. Costello's professional stamina brought results:

Luckily, Annie demonstrated increasing strength. Instead of throwing them, Annie began to describe how she would have temper tantrums to get her own way. She felt that often therapists had complied with her demands when they should not have. She warned me that this demandingness would probably continue, and she hoped I was strong enough to take it.

Through confrontation and clinical consistency, Dr. Costello established a therapeutic frame or "holding environment" for Annie, and Annie began to use her energies for (instead of against) herself.

Unfortunately, circumstances intervened when Dr. Costello left the Masterson Group. Annie resumed with another practitioner who was familiar with the Masterson Approach, helped Annie through the separation from Dr. Costello, and then determined that Annie could benefit from a maintenance dosage of phenelzine sulfate (Nardil); however, under the impact of Annie's behavior, the new clinician began to slip from the therapeutic stance.

I began to work with Annie when her current therapy had reached a crisis point.

Annie had her therapist on the run, along with an entire day care center. Her therapist had cut Annie's sessions to once a week and had referred her to day care for the balance of treatment. Probably reacting to the growing tenuousness of treatment (and, of course, testing as usual), Annie began to act out with a vengeance: stealing, getting drunk, running around in public semi-dressed, telephoning her therapists with frantic persistence (at their home phones when she could), and generally carrying on in such a way as to expose the vulnerability and fray the patience of all those involved in trying to help her.

Individual and day care therapists met with Annie and her family and said that Annie would have to go into residential treatment. Annie, to her credit, said she would be damned if she would give up the gains she had made: her own apartment and her household of four cats. She returned to the Masterson Group with the blessings of the individual therapist and the day care center.

In her initial session with me, Annie presented herself as aggressive, incisively intelligent, emotionally sensitive and labile, and a slob. A veteran of psychotherapy, she had come to look me over, and told me she needed a therapist she couldn't con, who would hold the line. She said that she tended to trip herself up, especially when she started to feel better, and thought that her sickness somehow held her family together. Over the next few weeks, she repeated that I hadn't seen her at her worst and was worried whether I could tolerate her. Over the next few weeks, as she had done with Dr. Costello, she gave us both a chance to find out just how much the traffic would bear.

Annie came into my office licking an ice-cream cone and attired in something like a mini negligee. She faced me through impenetrable sunglasses, and petulantly dumped responsibility for the session on me. This was testing elevated to the level of a challenge and I had my colleague's experience to build on. I began my verbal confrontation on the same level as Annie's nonverbal communication: "Is this your idea of how to build your self-respect here? What's the ice cream? You tell me you're here to stop kidding yourself, but you act like you're at a party! And that dress – if that's what you're wearing – are you telling me you expect to be taken seriously when you come out in public as if you're sleepwalking?"

In response to this confrontation, which had matched the level of her challenge, she pulled herself together in a dignified, introspective way, and I had my first impression of Annie as she could be. That weekend she controlled her drinking and told me later that modifying her behavior had brought her in touch with fundamental feelings of rebelliousness (feelings she could not be aware of while she was channeling them into behavior).

These first sessions were to set the tone for the first year of therapy. Essentially, this year was devoted to the re-establishment of the therapeutic frame or holding environment. Annie strove to maintain her gains – to keep her apartment and hold her new job. Persistently, she sidetracked these priorities with momentary crises, but confrontation held her to the presenting problem: she wanted to keep her apartment, her autonomy, and to do so she would have to observe and alter how she stood in the way of her own goals.

Only by contrasting her maladaptive behavior with her chosen goals could I begin to provide a frame of reference within which she could start to perceive the borderline triad in operation. Otherwise, the emotional and behavioral chaos swamped reason and observing distance.

Repeatedly, I returned to her initial statement that she undermines her own progress – for instance, makes a statement of positive intent, then almost at once does something self-destructive – and so avoids the feelings attached to a responsible attitude toward herself. Unfortunately, I would point out, avoidance of the feeling means avoidance of change, as well.

By the end of the year, as Annie began to curtail her acting out and increasingly tolerated her emerging feelings, she began to allow her real self freer expression.

During this first year, Annie began to be aware of, and let go of, a false self she named "Sick Annie." Whenever she began to get her life in order, she would complain of feeling "empty" or "bored" – the beginning of feelings of abandonment depression – and would start to act out. She claimed that shoplifting provided her with a sense of excitement, and that she was uncomfortable feeling "normal."

I asked why she seemed to prefer setting herself up as a mental case and a victim. She replied that it was the only identity she knew. This insight was reinforced by a dream (curtailing of acting out leads to internalizing phenomena, such as insight and dreaming). In her dream, all her relatives surrounded her and called her schizophrenic. The dream expressed not a criticism, but a command.

Annie began to realize that her family had needed her to act crazy to create a diversion from problems not of her making. She then expressed profound sadness over the years wasted in acting crazy. She said that she knew Dr. Costello had understood that the craziness was an act (a manifestation of the false self), and she expressed bitterness over the time lost with therapists who had bought into it.

Annie became increasingly able to experience abandonment depression – to give up the frenetic, "crazy" self that satisfied the needs of her family (and herself) to pass the buck, and so avoid individual responsibility. Part of the time she struggled with an "empty feeling" that marked this psychic transition, and felt bewildered, as though she found herself in an unfamiliar place. Then she would maladaptively ward off growing depression and ambivalence by creating another diversionary crisis; by jeopardizing her lease and her job with on-stage battles with her boyfriend; and by acting out in her treatment with repeated phone calls between sessions.

Annie would call me from a bar, between sessions or during the time of her sessions, drunk, enraged, and despairing. I, in turn, would point out that she was diluting the effect of her sessions by calling instead of coming in on schedule to talk, as was her agreement. I pointed out that these calls were often followed by silent sessions. I said she was avoiding or sabotaging her sessions in order to avoid direct expression of her feelings to me, and ultimately to herself (this type of here-and-now interpretation adds effectiveness to confrontations that have become familiar to the patient and are partially integrated).

By the end of the year, she had built enough confidence in her sessions to try out her feelings on me directly (once the initial line of confrontation has been absorbed by the patient, the resistance shifts increasingly from the external world to the therapeutic sphere of the sessions and the transference). She first practiced on her boss, creating such a scene at work that he called the police, and she was taken to the emergency room of a nearby hospital. Once there, she realized she had outgrown that particular game, and used her manipulative skills to get herself discharged. She returned to work to face the music and was moved that her co-workers stood up for her, and that her boss took her back. She then focused her feelings on me.

Annie came in smoking, eating, yelling, slamming the door. She cut off my attempts to intervene and drowned out my voice. I escalated my confrontations to verbally match her actions – that is, to a point where I could be heard. I shouted her full name and inquired whether she was interested at all in hearing any feedback from me, whom she was paying. I reminded her (at full volume) that she was throwing away her therapy as she had lamented throwing away her life. Finally, I asserted that therapy could not be conducted at a shouting level, that this was another way of avoiding the work, and I refused to be a part of it. Once again, I was only speaking in a tone of voice she could hear – I think, from her point of view, I was not shouting at all, but using the tone of voice the family used (only, for once, using it to set limits).

She began to compose herself and speak more quietly, and the depression began to come through. She said she fought me because I made her face her feelings of hopelessness and craziness. It was easier to go on the warpath than to become aware of deep anxiety and loneliness.

As long as she continued to report her feelings, I simply listened. Once she began to attack herself (instead of me) and tried to manipulate me into scapegoating her, I confronted her attempt to recreate her family role as "Sick Annie." ("You tell me you regret the time wasted conforming to your family's need to blame someone for their problems, but now you want me to treat you as they do!")

When she began to build a panic around the notion her mind was playing tricks on her, I commented: "You are escalating your anxiety. You are not psychotic, but you would rather drive yourself crazy than be yourself and face your own feelings." She pulled together and told me the source of her anxiety: everyone lately was telling her how much better she seemed, and it was difficult to relinquish her sick, family identity. She was still trying to trip herself up, to distract herself from knowing she was better and did not need to remain a dependent child.

This first year of treatment re-established the therapeutic frame in two essential ways. First, I helped Annie set firm limits for herself, much as one would contain a child in a temper tantrum until the child can take hold of his/herself again. Second, I systematically confronted the contradictory goals of Annie's reality ego and pleasure ego, questioning her maladaptive splitting defense – for instance, how she expected to keep a job if she did what she pleased and not what she was hired to do, or how she thought she could get the benefits of therapy, while missing sessions when the feelings got difficult. In effect, I refused to be the rewarding unit: the overly permissive mother who let her run wild and run the show. She subsequently saw me as the withdrawing unit – as someone who refused to let her have her cake and eat it, too – and she flew into a rage. When I confronted her rage, pointing out that it was serving to defeat her own goals, she began to allow depression to come through. With some toleration of depression came insight into her crazy act – "Sick Annie" – a false self that she used to evade responsibility and to defend against a deeper feeling of real depression and craziness.

Annie realized after her first year of work that her chaotic behavior, promiscuity, rages, drinking, and shoplifting were all ways to avoid the responsibility of growing up, because growing up was associated with feelings of hopelessness, emptiness, loneliness, self-loathing, and craziness. As she began to catch on, she internalized my limit-setting, and confronted her own maneuverings. A pattern of shifting behavior began, in which she would activate herself positively, then plunge into chaos, then pull out again.

This pattern still continues but is approaching a more realistic level. She seems to have satisfactorily tested her ability (like a child) to run, fall, pick herself up and run again, while depending on my continuous presence for support in a rapprochement-like way. As her own ego strengthens, she provides her own sense of continuity. This sense of continuity derives from the knowledge of my being there and the discovery that life is not a choice between running free and falling down but, rather, is mastery over a process that includes both.

Then and now, Annie continues her maintenance dosage of Nardil. Annie firmly believes that the Nardil helps her to keep her anxiety level under control, so that she is less likely to work herself into a panic. She has allowed herself an experience of mourning in relation to the medication, as well, for it represents a delimitation of herself – a point at which her conscious will has to give way to biological processes.

The second year of therapy saw two significant advances in Annie's treatment: within the sessions, she began to show more insight and experience more feelings and memories; outside the sessions, she functioned on a consistently higher level, and tolerated both success and separation in a way she never had before.

Margaret Mahler stresses that the phase of development critical to the psychic maturation of patients like Annie runs on a double track: separation and individuation. For the patient like Annie, whose defenses (acting out, splitting, projection) operate on the more primitive level, I believe the issue of separation, laden with feelings of panic and persecution, represents the most challenging aspect of the abandonment depression. Annie, as she individuates, has been able to anticipate the resurgence of depression, and no longer catastrophizes over it for more than a day or so at a time – her recoveries are quicker, and the depressive descent is shallower. The separation issue – terror of non-being, of reprisal and eradication from some omnipotent source – is gradually becoming an issue she is willing to face. This not only relates to the interpersonal experience of gaining confidence from healthy emotional support; it also depends on the building of an inner sense of encouragement, or self-worth.

After Annie was able to be angry at me directly (and no longer needed to apologize at the end of the session or call back after the session to say she was sorry), she then began to express positive feelings for me and for her therapy. She said: "I don't know what to call this relationship we have. You aren't my friend, but you're more than a friend. This is like a kind of love." And, as she found me both hateful and lovable, she began to see how both qualities could exist and coexist in herself, as well. She began to dress consistently well, with enthusiasm and with flair. She lost thirty pounds. She completed two years at her job and told me with satisfaction about her raise: "$25,000 a year! How's that for an ex-loony?"

As she experienced herself as more competent and whole, she was able to face deeper, more symbiotic anxieties, and to then experience the consolidation of a strong and good inner sense, a positive introject. Annie noticed that when she was aware of feelings, she didn't need to steal. So, she reasoned, she stole as a substitute for feeling. She decided to experiment by not stealing, and subsequently reported a strange event. Alone in her apartment, she had sensed "evil forces in the room, trying to suck me up." It was "like a nightmare." She impulsively telephoned her mother (it was three o'clock in the morning), and then "felt something I had never felt before." The feeling was that her mother was "*really there.*" She associated this experience to similar (but unresolved) terrible feelings she had endured in the course of her acute hospitalizations. I asked her if she had had nightmares as a child (I was remembering her insistence on sleeping with her parents prior to the last hospitalization). She said yes, and that, after the nightmares, she would cry for her mother. So, this strange experience simply became a child's cry in the night that had waited thirty years to be answered, as Annie at last learned to believe in the reliability of her own existence.

So, Annie was making progress on the individuative track, and was building inner structure that would support her progress in healthy separation. This was confirmed by a "first" (as she said): Annie threw out her boyfriend, and felt stronger for the separation, for which she took full responsibility.

Annie had clung to George the entire time she had been in treatment with me. In many ways George's personality paralleled Annie's, and, like a typical borderline couple, they alternately rescued and undermined each other. When one was up, the other was down, they always kept a crisis going, and, in short, neither took consistent responsibility for their individual selves. But, finally, Annie had had enough. The separation was not easy, and Annie regressed. I received drunken phone calls from bars, there were missed sessions, and Annie brought George along on one occasion (this was not altogether impulsive, as we had discussed the possibility; Annie seemed to need to bring George in as a transitional device to help her to anchor better in reality). For a while, Annie could not clearly differentiate her feelings from George's. She could not decide whether he was a victim or a user and was afraid of misjudging him until she was able to get beyond her guilt and see *herself* as *both* victim and user. Then it was easier to deal with him realistically: as a con artist she had to protect herself from, but also as a confused human being deserving of her forgiveness.

In the process, the break-up took epic proportions. Annie was alternately strong and devastated and appeared for her sessions acting accordingly. And then it was over. For the first time, Annie had set a limit in an intense personal relationship and felt as though the ground was still solid under her feet.

Delighted with her accomplishment, Annie decided to try another "first," and went on vacation, out of the country, and without her parents. She came through with flying colors and brought me photographs so that I could share her pleasure. The rapprochement-like quality of such moments is unmistakable, and they provide an additional source of satisfaction for the therapist, who always hoped such a turning point was attainable but knew that only the patient could take the decisive step.

Candace Orcutt (1989a). In: J. F. Masterson and R. Klein (Eds.)
Psychotherapy of the Disorders of the Self: The Masterson Approach (pp.
231–240). New York: Brunner/Mazel. Copyright 1989 by Brunner/Mazel, Inc.
Reprinted by permission of the publisher.

CHAPTER 3

The Narcissistic Personality

*My own point of view is that the narcissistic personality
disorder is a developmental arrest, since in treatment the
patient's abandonment depression or fragmentation of the self
can be precipitated either by narcissistic disappointment at the
hands of the object or by his own efforts toward self-expression
or self-individuation. It is this latter that suggests a true
developmental arrest of individuation has occurred.*

(Masterson 1981, p. 26)

The narcissistic personality, in its more evident self-important appearance, is perhaps the most commonly recognized of the personality disorders. The self-preoccupied assurance of the type, combined with a notable reactiveness to criticism or even difference of opinion, is part of the public caricature – especially attributed to artists and politicians.

Psychoanalysts themselves have at times been seen to fit the picture. As Ellenberger (1970, pp. 888ff.), and Atwood and Stolorow (1979/1993, pp. 6–7) have observed, the most profound insights into psychic states can often be credited to those who sought to understand them in themselves. Heinz Kohut, undeniably a master of the narcissistic dynamic, exemplified it as well. As his biographer, Strozier, reflects: "He had a way of imposing himself on others. He was brilliant, lively, outgoing, truly charismatic, and at the center of any conversation or meeting … at the same time, he could be impossibly self-centered, at times almost with a certain innocence, and grandiose to a fault" (Strozier 2001, p. x).

This perceptive description, taken within Masterson's developmental context, gives us a glimpse of the early child caught in time, as well as the present-day adult who commands the scene, but who is flawed by the need for others to reinforce this stance. Regarding personality disorder, Masterson is specifically referring to the pathological counterpart of

Margaret Mahler's "practicing subphase" child: "Mahler noted that the chief characteristic of the practicing period is the child's great narcissistic involvement in his or her own functions and his/her own body, as well as in the objects and objectives of his/her expanding 'reality'" (Masterson 1981, p. 12). This is an exuberant time which, reinforced by the child's sense of oneness with an admiring mother, prepares for the turmoil of the rapprochement subphase. For the practicing child will need to incorporate an underlying sense of assurance in order to sustain the self through the next developmental transformation, which will be challenging. Masterson writes: "toward the end of the practicing period, there is increasingly clear differentiation between the self-representation and the object-representation … It begins to dawn on [the junior toddler] that the world is not his oyster, and that he must cope with it on his own" (1981, p. 12). In the therapeutic setting, one observes that the narcissistic patient is not yet ready for this developmental transition and – to some degree – has paused at the time of blissful but illusory importance. Masterson continues: "clinically the patient behaves as if the object representation were an integral part of the self-representation – an omnipotent, dual unity. The possibility of a rapprochement crisis doesn't seem to dawn on this patient. The fantasy persists that the world is his oyster and revolves about him" (1981, p. 13).

The narcissist, like the eight- to fifteen-month infant, can be impressively self-confident, even charming, when surrounded by admiring others. But, without this reassurance, the narcissist can become dismissive or even attacking (especially when criticized). The difference, of course, is that the practicing child is experiencing a normal, expectable stage of development which involves delighted, encouraging parenting, while the narcissist, psychically caught in that time, assumes that the adult world will continue to respond in the manner of proud parents. The narcissist has not been able to complete the developmental task of establishing enough healthy narcissism to sustain the self through realization of separateness and negative feelings, and so resists this awareness. By dismissal or anger, the narcissist rejects what Masterson describes as a disillusioned sense of being "humiliated, attacked, empty" – a state analogous to Kohut's "fragmented self" – and rapidly reinstates the defensive self-representation of being grandiose, "superior, elite, exhibitionistic" (1981, p. 15).

Masterson, in 1981 and onward, owes much of his definition of narcissistic personality disorder to Kohut's pioneering work, which found its culmination and increasing influence throughout the 1970s. It is characteristic of Masterson to synthesize major current concepts into his growing Approach when he has found them to be clinically effective. It is noteworthy that both Masterson and Kohut are substantially in debt to Margaret Mahler's developmental studies, and find commonality there as well as in "clinical manifestations" (Masterson 1981, p. 16).

The Myth and the Mind Doctors

The term "narcissist" comes from the Greek myth that acknowledges the compelling nature of great aesthetic beauty while cautioning against the destructiveness of valuing it for itself to the exclusion of all else. In "On Narcissism: An Introduction" (1914), Freud credits first P. Nacke and later Havelock Ellis for initiating the term to describe a perverse state of sexual self-pleasure (1914, pp. 30–59).

In *Metamorphoses*, the Roman poet Ovid's retelling of classical myths, the beautiful young man Narcissus falls in love with his own reflection. As reality fades around his timeless and exclusive rapture, his physical presence is transformed to no more than a beautiful flower, and his spirit, ferried down to the underworld, still bends over the boatside to gaze at its reflection in the River Styx (Ovid 2004, pp. 106–111).

As Freud again reminds us, pathology is not some unique, superimposed condition, but the distortion of a normal state. Freud's intention is to define the workings of the healthy mind through an understanding of what goes wrong with it: "Once more, to arrive at what is normal and apparently so simple, we shall have to study the pathological with its distortions and exaggerations" (1914, p. 39). As Freud continues, "we postulate a primary narcissism in everyone" (1914, p. 45) – it is the basis of a healthy self-esteem.

That Narcissus is aware and confident of his own attractiveness is not the issue – it is the regressive, unchanging self-absorption to the exclusion of others that is problematic.

Freud posits a normal early time of primary narcissism, "a blissful state of mind" (1914, p. 46) that is regretfully outgrown. Secondary narcissism – in varying degrees unrealistic – longingly draws us back when "so relentlessly assailed by reality, security is achieved by fleeing to the child" (p. 49). Primary narcissism simply characterizes "the charm of a child"

(p. 46). Secondary narcissism may take a normal-enough object-related form as parents cherish their infant child: "he is really to be the centre and heart of creation, 'His Majesty the Baby', as once we fancied ourselves to be" (p. 48). Secondary narcissism, however, can take on an increasingly regressive nature in idealization of the other: "whoever possesses an excellence which the ego lacks for the attainment of the ideal, becomes loved. This expedient is of special importance for the neurotic ... This is the cure by love, which he generally prefers to cure by analysis" (pp. 58–59). Still deeper in pathology, the schizophrenic (Freud's "paraphrenic") "seems really to have withdrawn his libido from persons and things in the outer world, without replacing them by others in his phantasy" (p. 31). This exclusive directing of libido into the ego (according to the hydraulic metaphor reflecting the science of the time) drains libido from the object, and with this the ability to form a transference is prevented. Consequently, schizophrenics would seem to be untreatable, and what will be later referred to as "personality disorder," as well.

As opposed to the later concept of developmental arrest, Freud's libido theory describes "narcissistic neurosis" as an extreme regression to a point of fixation in the early psyche. In addition, given the concept of the libido as a kind of fluid force that can be drained from a part of the psyche, the capacity for transference is emptied out, and cure is unattainable. With more recent investigation of preoedipal psychic structure, both Masterson and Kohut redefined the nature of transference in the newly conceptualized area of personality disorder, and therefore were able to show that treatment was accessible. Both Masterson (as he describes "transference acting out") and Kohut (as he shows in the patient's need for mirroring) posit a form of the transference that tries to induce an interpersonal replication of the early child–mother attachment, not a distortion in the fairly evolved oedipal relationship: the elusive narcissistic transference.

In "On Narcissism," however, Freud does begin to define the region of "narcissistic neurosis," sometimes seeming to puzzle out loud over its nature and place in human mental development. Although it is complex and sometimes unclear, this "introduction" is an astonishing look into Freud's thinking, especially his valuation of unfolding hypotheses over stubborn adherence to static theory. His definition of narcissistic neurosis as a categorization of schizophrenia and certain profound depressive states is tentative, but it opens a territory for psychic exploration that prepares the way for the mapping of preoedipal disorders.

Freud's narcissistic neurosis roughly includes the schizophrenic and the patients we would describe today as personality disorders. Although "On Narcissism" and other studies such as "Some Character Types Met with in Psycho-analytic Work" (1915) begin to prepare the way for a developmental model based on preoedipal states and personality style, this will not be carried forward in Freud's own work. Freud's regression/fixation formula does not make room for the dissociation/developmental arrest hypothesis. Indeed, Freud resisted the ambitions of Rank and Ferenczi to proceed in that direction, apprehensive that it could undermine the scientific authority of the Oedipus complex (Gay 1998, pp. 470–484).

Then Heinz Kohut decisively shifted the analytic perspective on the narcissistic neuroses. Kohut, in 1971, put forward the new dynamic and treatment of narcissistic personality disorder in *The Analysis of the Self*. Here, Kohut introduced "a new structure within the mind" – the self (pp. xiv–xv). Kohut had his predecessors: Hartmann (whom he credits) for "the conceptual separation of the self from the ego" (p. xiii), and Fairbairn and Winnicott (whom he does not acknowledge), but the ascendency of self-psychology over "narcissistic neurosis" is Kohut's achievement. This shift in metapsychology is supported as well – as cited by Kohut – by Erikson's study of identity and by Margaret Mahler's revelation of "a gradual crystallization of a separate biological existence out of the matrix of the union of mother and child" (Kohut 1971, p. xiv). Kohut believes that Mahler's contributions – "derived from the psychoanalytically sophisticated observation of small children" – are "most useful and influential," and demonstrate the uniquely defined presence of object relations earlier in life than does the Freudian view. He makes the historical statement that it is

> the frequently made assumption that the existence of object relations excludes narcissism. On the contrary, ... some of the most intense narcissistic experiences relate to objects; objects, that is, which are either used in the service of the self and of the maintenance of its instinctual investment, or objects which are themselves experienced as part of the self. I shall refer to the latter as self-objects.

> (Kohut 1971, p. xiv)

Kohut does not relate narcissistic disorder to a particular subphase in Mahler's developmental model, however, but locates it more generally in Mahler's "developmental phases which probably correspond predominantly to the transitional period between a late part of the stage of symbiosis and an early part of the stages of individuation." His theoretical view is "in harmony" with the findings of Mahler and her colleagues: "Mahler observes the behavior of small children; I reconstruct their inner life on the basis of transference reactivations" (1971, pp. 218–220).

Kohut's overall conceptualization of narcissism is complex and parts remain open to debate. However, his definition of the self-object (later referred to in a verbal ideogram as "selfobject") is a compelling translation of Mahler's practicing subphase, as it is developmentally arrested within the narcissistic personality disorder. Masterson's clinical instinct, especially, will later realize the value of incorporating this view into his Approach.

Kohut seems to elide late symbiosis with the differentiating and practicing subphases, but it would seem that the self-object is located well into the transition to the practicing subphase. Kohut's narcissist, like the eight- to fifteen-month-old child, has achieved the differentiation between inner and outer worlds, is welcoming feeling – although only in its positive form – and has become more perceptive of the other – although mainly as the other reflects back the positive feeling. Self and object representations are beginning to take on definition, but are little more than polarities of a merged sense of gratified being. Kohut's "cohesive" self (1971, p. 137) at this time still involves the child's sense of wellbeing and oneness with the other, and this delicate merger relies on the mother's willingness to sustain the perception. For a time, the mother reflects back the junior toddler's discovery of exclusive good feeling and personal congruence in order to prepare a stable base for her child's growing awareness. A premature imposition of the mother's personal "reality" – either by misattuned response or unresponsiveness, or by an equally problematic excessive merger – may lead to the child's perceived loss of the "object" component of the still combined selfobject. This leads to a sense of "fragmentation of the self" (pp. 94, 102–103). However, if the mother's attunement consistently supports the child's cohesive sense of being, a secure perception of an individuating self begins to evolve, and becomes "the reliable initiator and performer of joyfully undertaken activities" (p. 134). An emerging self, retaining the positive qualities of the self-object, is becoming defined apart from the other through the natural growth process, and the fragmenting effect of premature division has been avoided.

Mahler's description of the practicing child at the height of the sub-phase presents a vivid developmental parallel with Kohut's self-object. At this stage, the infant "walks freely with upright posture," but still re-quires the mother's presence as "a stable point, a 'home base.'" Without this maternal "refueling," the child experiences a depressive-like state of "low-keyedness," from which Mahler and her team of observers conclude "that there was a dawning awareness that the symbiotic mothering half of the self was missed" (Mahler, Pine, and Bergman 1975, pp. 65–75).

Kohut's Narcissistic Personality Disorder in the Consult Room

How does Kohut (1971) describe the transferential presence of the nar-cissistic patient in the consulting room? What follows is a brief summary of an extensive formulation, oversimplified where Kohut is definitive.

According to Kohut, the narcissistic personality disorder manifests itself in three varied expressions of the self-object. Transferentially, these embody the three ways in which the narcissistic patient perceives the an-alyst as an extension of his or her psychic being: as a mirror, as an ideal, and as a psychic duplicate. The analysis is founded on the analyst's initial acceptance of this perception, which clinically protects the patient's im-mature sense of self from fragmentation.

The Mirror Transference (Kohut 1971, pp. 105–114)

In this manifestation, the exuberant feelings of the self-object are weight-ed toward the rudimentary sense of self, with the potential sense of other (like Narcissus' reflection in the water) perceived as a mirror of the self's grandiosity. The other is "expected" to serve the mirroring function lest (as though the reflective surface had been disturbed) the image of the self be disrupted. The failure of the psychotherapist to sustain this reciprocal oneness evokes an existential anxiety that manifests itself in the abrupt devaluation, or often the anger that the grandiose narcissist is known to demonstrate. As Kohut observes, this is why, when traditional interpretation is used instead of mirroring, the narcissist feels rebuffed and unprotected from an underlying sense of depletion and may withdraw or lash out. The defensive transferential position of positive merger is reinstated when the analyst is "accepted as a silent presence or … as an echo of what the patient had expressed" (Kohut 1971, p. 251).

The Idealizing Transference (Kohut 1971, pp. 37–56)

In this instance, the more other-directed polarity of the selfobject is favored. The analyst is placed in the somewhat uncomfortable (it is hoped) position of being seen as a marvelously knowing, impeccable authority. A sense of oneness is again evoked by the therapist's "empathic resonance" (Kohut 1971, p. 211n.).

Curiously, an alternative telling of the myth of Narcissus suggests this perspective: the powerful draw toward great beauty that may result in being possessed rather than possessing. In the Homeric Hymn, Persephone is irresistibly lured by a beautiful purple flower, the narcissus – the enticement created by Hades to seduce her into his kingdom. As she claims the flower, the earth opens beneath her, and she falls into the underworld and her lover's rule. Like the first tale of Narcissus, this account warns of the danger in the exclusive preoccupation with great aesthetic beauty, with its consequence a descent into the possession of another in the world of shadows (Hamilton 1942, pp. 112–113).

The idealizing narcissist, unlike his or her counterpart, often appears subdued and self-effacing, molding to whom or to what is idealized. In my own clinical experience, I have come to suspect that this patient is more to be found in our caseloads than has been realized. I expect this patient may often be the conscientious member of a conservative community who leads a responsible, lackluster life of self-deprecation compensated for by dedication to the rules, morals, and institutions that govern his or her predictable daily existence, but that offer little individual confirmation. In some way, disillusionment has set in – perhaps resulting from the fall from grace of someone in a leadership position, but more likely because of a steady wearing-away of unquestioning devotion to the community, or a part of it, that had substantially defined the patient's self in terms of social role.

The patient is beset by a dim feeling that is not so much depression as a troublesome sense of incompleteness. The loss of that which was idealized diminishes the patient's sense of coherent being. The therapist, experiencing the patient's transferential need for an idealized other, may be mistakenly gratified by rapid appearance of an apparent therapeutic alliance. But, as sessions continue, it is increasingly clear that, although the patient seems impressed by the therapist's wisdom, the patient nevertheless adheres to the familiar way of dealing with problems with a tenacity, almost stubbornness, that resists change. The therapist begins to realize that, to the patient, he or she is an idealized transference figure whose presence feels reassuring to the patient, but holds little promise for change beyond that. If the therapist remains caught in countertransference, the illusion of therapeutic effectiveness remains, and the enactment continues ad infinitum – the ouroboros (that legendary serpent that eats its own tail) has settled in place.

In a related manifestation, the idealizing transference may take a dramatic form in the popular scene in the emotional dedication of fans toward artists, politicians, and religious leaders who are idolized by their followers. Especially when the grandiosity of the idealized figured complements this narcissistic enmeshment, the summoning up of positive feeling can be ecstatic, and, when demonstrated in a group, can reach extremes of intensity.

The Alter Ego or Twinship Transference (Kohut 1971, p. 115)

This transference manifestation is described as a variant of the mirror transference, where the other "is experienced as being like the grandiose self or as being very similar to it" (Kohut 1971, p. 115). In this instance, "the patient assumes that the analyst is either like him or similar to him, or that the analyst's psychological makeup is like, or is similar to, that of the patient."

In my own clinical experience, I have noticed that this transferential state, accompanied by the predictable welling up of positive feeling, can present a subtle countertransference challenge, as it can be confused with the therapeutic alliance. It may have been one reason why Ferenczi's "mutual analysis" proved unproductive. (An indication of the presence of such a countertransference tendency is the analyst's foregoing of the "parental" stance: the responsibility for the objective structure and continuity of the treatment process itself.)

In all three transference situations, although treatment cannot directly replicate childhood, there is a "therapeutic restatement of a normal
phase of development" that offers a basis for new psychic growth. As
Kohut (1971) summarizes:

*(1) In all three forms the analyst becomes the figure around whom
a significant degree of object constancy in the narcissistic realm can
be established, however primitive the object may be; and (2) with
the aid of the more or less stable narcissistically invested object, the
transference contributes … to the maintenance of the cohesiveness
of the self of the analysand.*

(p. 125)

A stable psychic ground has been established to support a growing sense
of self that can "in a fractionated way" (p. 50) take in qualities of the
object without seeming to threaten it. Through the analyst's continued
empathy, "transmuting internalization" of the maternal representation
facilitates a strengthening of self and a beginning of separation from the
other without fragmentation. The self-object is becoming restructured as
related self and object.

Empathy

In 1959, in his groundbreaking and controversial Chicago presentation,
Kohut begins to define his terms: "the trained introspective skill which
the analyst uses in the extension of introspection (vicarious introspection)
… is called empathy" (1971, p. 463). In 1971, as he starts to consolidate
his following, Kohut writes: "the listening, perceiving, and echoing-
mirroring presence of the analyst now reinforces the psychological forces
which maintain the cohesiveness of [the] self image – archaic and (by
adult standards) unrealistic though it may be" (1971, p. 125). The analyst's
empathic understanding participates in a narcissistic state that largely
precedes the verbal (p. 124), and therefore requires a level of intuitively
based communication. Since the selfobject is a merged representation,
therapeutic experiencing of the narcissistic transference requires that the
analyst enter a somewhat fluid state of mind ("vicarious introspection,"

p. 119n.). The analyst must, to a degree, enter the patient's psyche, while simultaneously remaining anchored in objective interpersonal reality. This merged condition replicates the mindset of the early mother–child relationship, where the practicing subphase infant is in process of internalizing more evolved aspects of the attuned mother. As the child matures, the mother is able to be more reliant on words, as over time, in the parallel process, the analyst can become more explicit, carefully shaping the process by "optimal frustration" (pp. 49–50), and eventually traditional interpretation (p. 292).

The necessity for the analyst to merge with the patient's narcissistic state has led to concern that Kohutian treatment of narcissistic personality disorder verges on loss of objectivity (Kernberg). This may be an example of the ambivalence in the field over the nature and use of intuitive analytic processes (for example, when countertransference is seen as an elaboration of therapeutic communication). But it would seem that the less differentiated the patient's psyche, the more the intuitive capacity of the therapist is called into operation. For instance (as Searles amply illustrates), the schizophrenic often is only comprehended through the play of his or her projections on the analyst's psyche, and is engaged as the analyst verbalizes this phenomenon. In the psychotherapy of personality disorder, the use of the therapist's intuition as an instrument increases as the developmental level of the patient's psyche is increasingly early. Developmentally, the practicing subphase child is only on the edge of verbal interchange, and intervention with the narcissistic patient must be modified accordingly. The establishing of "optimal trust" in this instance requires that the therapist psychically merge on that predominantly preverbal level through empathic communication – through attitude and interventions that reflect a sense of positive-feeling unity beyond the use of words.

Kohut's definition of empathy arises from the therapeutic necessity, in the case of the narcissistic patient, to first establish a primarily nonverbal sense of trust. In *Restoration of the Self*, Kohut is specific: "first the analysand must realize that he has been understood ... Some of the most persistent resistances encountered in analysis ... are mobilized in response to the fact that the stage of understanding – the stage of the analyst's empathic echo of or merger with the patient – had been skipped over." He continues: "the analyst will even have to realize that a patient whose childhood selfobject has failed traumatically in this area will require long periods of 'only' understanding before the second step – interpretation … – can be usefully and acceptably taken" (Kohut 1977, p. 88).

Additionally, Kohut (with his capacity for explicit verbalization of the preverbal) defines empathy not as something vague and impressionistic, but as a specific use of a "sector" of the analyst's total thought capability. He writes:

During the analytic process the analyst's psyche is engaged in depth. The essence of his evenly hovering attention is not to be defined in the negative, as a suspension of his conscious, goal-directed, logical thought processes, but positively, as the counterpart of the analysand's free associations, i.e., as the emergence and use of the analyst's prelogical modes of perceiving and thinking.

(1977, p. 251)

The analyst who treats forms of personality disorder derived from the earliest developmental phases is called upon to paradoxically maintain a simultaneously logical and prelogical attitude. Although this is an everyday occurrence for the good-enough mother, who instinctively balances intuition and common sense in caring for her infant, it would seem that this presents more of a challenge when the mature-enough analyst must relate to the developmentally arrested, but in many ways adult patient. As Kohut implies, the provision of therapeutic empathy enables the therapist as well as the patient to attain the mindset of the healthy mother and the practicing subphase infant. As described by Kohut, this is a creative (or, more accurately, re-creative) therapeutic relationship guided by therapeutically informed awareness.

Masterson and Kohut: Convergence

In 1981, Masterson includes a theoretical and clinical formulation of the dynamic treatment of narcissistic personality disorder in his Approach. In *The Narcissistic and Borderline Disorders*, he assesses narcissistic personality disorder – to a considerable degree synthesizing Kohut's self psychology into his Approach – within the context of a definition of personality disorder drawn in part from Mahler's developmental model.

First, Masterson describes the generally agreed-upon clinical picture of the narcissistic personality:

> *The patient … seems to be endlessly motivated to seek perfection in all he or she does, to pursue wealth, power and beauty and to find others who will mirror and admire his/her grandiosity. Underneath this defensive façade is a feeling state of emptiness and rage with a predominance of intense envy.*

> (Masterson 1981, p. 7)

Masterson names this type of patient the "manifest narcissist," analogous to Kohut's mirror narcissist.

Masterson also describes a complementary type, the "closet narcissist," who is similar to Kohut's idealizing narcissist: "I am referring to the patient who presents him/herself as timid, shy, inhibited and ineffective – only to reveal later in therapy the most elaborate fantasies of the grandiose self" (1981, p. 8).

In reviewing Kohut's work, Masterson lists other points of agreement between himself and Kohut: "The differences in developmental level between therapeutic psychopathology of the [narcissistic] self and the psychopathology of oedipal conflict; the origin of excess aggression is not inborn, but [more often] comes from early trauma; the need to pursue and recall serious and latent, but denied parental pathology" (pp. 18–19).

Both Masterson and Kohut relate narcissistic pathology to a preoedipal level of development observed by Mahler and her associates. Masterson, though, is more specific, placing the origin of pathological narcissism in Mahler's practicing subphase "because clinically the patient behaves as if the object representation were an integral part of the self representation – an omnipotent, dual unity" (pp. 12–13).

Here Masterson pauses, puzzling over the apparent inconsistency between the fused self and other of the narcissist and a higher-seeming ego state "that is believed to come about only as a result of separation from that fusion" (p. 12). The answer might be found in the narcissist's readiness to display a false assurance based on his or her assumption of capability. Like the practicing child's sense of oneness with the encouraging adult, the narcissist can maintain a deceptive appearance of autonomy as long as the illusion is "borrowed" from admiring others or adherence to an idealized figure. In this way, the narcissist is often able to present a social façade that deceptively appears more high functioning than the self-contradictory borderline. It also should be kept in mind that the intelligence level and the emotional level in personality disorder may be significantly out of balance (that the intellect may overcompensate for emotional immaturity is a hallmark of the schizoid), and may pass for ego strength in select circumstances, especially when relationship is not the primary issue. In addition, more recent self-state theory would support this possibility, as parts of the self may mature unevenly. Ultimately, however, the charismatic persuasiveness of the manifest narcissist is not to be underestimated, and can even sway the critical senses of masses into accepting unquestioned leadership strength from a fundamentally insecure individual.

Masterson and Kohut: Divergence

When it comes to the intrapsychic structure of the narcissistic personality disorder, Kohut and Masterson are in partial agreement. Both describe a fused sense of self and other, sharing "an affect of feeling perfect, special, unique" (Masterson 1981, p. 15). But, for Kohut, this is the presentation of the entire self-object, whereas, for Masterson, this is only half of the picture. This grandiose presentation is only one side of the split object relations unit, and is matched by an opposite feeling of being "humiliated, attacked, empty" – a fused partial unit that is held at bay by "the continuous, global projection of [the] defensive unit" (p. 16).

It would seem that Masterson and Kohut have diverged in following different applications of object relations theory.

There is a theoretical dilemma potential in Melanie Klein's timeline for the child's psychic growth. The chronology for Freud's libidinal stages was probably based to some degree on his observation of his own children, which was deeply interesting to him. Klein's developmental progression, for all its brilliance, seems drawn more from the realm of her own ideas than from studying her own infants. In addition, her child patients began at about two and three-quarters years of age – a time far different in development from the first year, the time to which her conclusions were applied. As Winnicott wrote to Joan Riviere: "My trouble when I start to speak to Melanie about her statement of early infancy is that I feel as if I were talking about colour to the colour-blind" (Rodman 2003, p. 127). Klein's transposition of early psychic development from the first three years (Freud) to the first year in its entirety potentially raises an issue about the evolving of the splitting defense – in theory, and consequently in clinical practice. After Klein's conceptualization (even beginning with Klein's own followers), analytical theory has been steadily reinstating Freud's developmental pacing, with conclusive support from observers of childhood. The period of preoedipal psychic development would appear to have been definitively placed within the first three years of life. This raises a question about splitting: with the self and object now considered so rudimentary within the first year or so, when is there enough object to split? To the point, Winnicott distinguishes the "environment mother" of the earliest months from the "object mother," who is increasingly perceived as the recipient of both good and bad feelings (Rodman 2003, p. 398, n. 20). From the differentiation subphase, where the primary developmental task is distinguishing inner from outer reality, somewhere into the practicing subphase, the mother is more a "holding" presence than an object, with "good" and "bad" being more generalized sensations rather than defined feelings connected to personhood. A Kleinian sense of specific good (loving) and bad (aggressive) feelings attributed to specific mental representations of self and other would not seem to be in operation much before the rapprochement subphase (leading to the typical turmoil of that time in childhood).

Kohut's definition of the narcissistic personality, somewhat like the schizoid personality described by Winnicott and the independent object relationists, would seem to linger in a psychic world shaped by the "environment mother," although, with the narcissist, a more defined sense of object relations is forming in a benignly polarized mental representation of being. It is an inner world sustained by a sense of unity with a good-feeling other, and which still holds back recognition of negative influence.

Masterson (similar to Kernberg in his concept of borderline personality organization) applies the concept of Kleinian splitting throughout the personality disorders. Although Kleinian splitting is critical in understanding the intrapsychic structure of the borderline, I believe an important question is raised when it comes to applying the concept of good/bad splitting to disorders based on developmental stages preceding rapprochement. Kohut (who does not appear to distinguish between the differentiation and practicing subphases) makes it clear that he believes any psychic experience that questions the integrity of the self-object is destructive for the narcissist.

For Kohut, the psychic world of the narcissist is not split. The internal representation of being is still the self-object – a polarized but still merged sense of self and other joined by the beginning of relationally experienced affect that favors the positive. The introduction of more specifically de-fined relationship, experienced in the context of negative emotion, is experienced as an attack on the very nature of the self-object: an assault on the newly achieved, cohesive sense of being. Such a perceived assault results in a sense of fragmentation of the self. This disastrous feeling of incoherence is immediately fended off in any way that works. According to Kohut, premature use of interpretation with the narcissist evokes such an existential experience that it threatens the treatment.

In his teaching, Masterson accepts the necessity for mirroring with the narcissistic patient, but modifies Kohut's intervention with a touch of interpretation. This "mirroring interpretation" would perhaps seem more suited to a late stage of narcissistic development – a transitional time of readying for the rapprochement subphase, with its distinctive part-self and part-object representations and bad as well as good feelings. Here, the good-feeling part-unit defends "with a seemingly invulnerable" continuity against the emerging bad-feeling part-unit (the part-units of the borderline can alternately be used for defense against perception of reality). In this more advanced stage of psychic change, introduction of a less synchronized point of view between patient and therapist does not threaten the cohesiveness of the patient's sense of self. Masterson's nar-cissist has moved past the degree of self-fragmentation more potential for Kohut's narcissist, and may experience, instead, a beginning sense of abandonment depression – a feeling of loss of the other as much as the self. In a more defined, although split, stage of self and other develop-ment, an increasingly realistic view of self and other can be entertained, although at the expense of a utopian perception of relationship.

Kohut's mirroring harmoniously reflects the patient's feeling state, such as: "It causes you distress when I fail to understand you."

Masterson's mirroring interpretation ("pain – self – defense") in-troduces observing distance as it feelingly acknowledges the patient's resistance against the pain of disillusionment: "You feel hurt to realize

I sometimes have a different point of view from yours, so you protect yourself by angrily pushing me away."

Masterson's mirroring interpretation would seem analogous to the "optimal frustration" and "fractionating" of mirroring that Kohut advocates for the working-through stage of analysis with the narcissistic personality.

In my own clinical experience, I have found it initially advisable to begin psychotherapy with the narcissist by limiting intervention to purely empathic statements and attitude. Later, a tentative trial of mirroring interpretation can be introduced – in fact, this can only be a second step, since it is based on reliable tracking of defensive patterns – with a readiness, on the therapist's part, to deferentially retreat if necessary. The ability of the narcissistic patient to tolerate mirroring interpretation is an indication of the level of self-cohesiveness the patient has been able to achieve and maintain.

Abandonment Depression versus Fragmentation

Masterson originally defined the dynamic disorders-of-the-self triad ("self-activation leads to anxiety and depression, which leads to defense") in relation to the borderline, and eventually widened it to relate to all personality disorders (2005, p. 3). This describes the necessity to replicate clinically the decisive "moment" in early growth where the mother withdrew her libidinal availability in consistent response to her child's expression of self, and to move through and past it in the therapeutic relationship. The negative maternal response was once enough to motivate a more compliant activity (or inactivity) on the infant's behalf to insure loving care (actually to insure survival) with the mother. This feeling of imminent loss and profound alarm is repeatedly evoked with each therapeutic challenge to the dysfunctional defensive structure that holds back the natural emergence of the self. Increasing self-activation becomes problematic, as the patient must rely on a new, relatively untried personality pattern, and fears loss of the old pattern that once sustained the sense of self, however precariously. Masterson sees the resulting "abandonment depression" – the fear that self-assertion has evoked retributive maternal loss – as the reason for a predictable regression at times when patients move closer to healing, especially near termination. This is the phenomenon (first noted as a therapeutic enigma by Freud) that has tended to sabotage the gains of some patients in response to apparent therapeutic "success." Masterson identifies this as a technically workable resistance to psychic change. He therefore continues the course of psychotherapy despite this powerful transference/countertransference resistance (both patient and therapist are being psychically induced to withdraw), and continues the treatment.

For Masterson, the ability to work through the abandonment depression resolves the developmental arrest that, in the narcissistic patient, inhibits constructive psychic growth beyond the practicing to the rapprochement subphase of separation-individuation. For Kohut, however, there is no psychic process to be undone and redone. In fact, he seems to caution against such a "fragmentation" of the increasingly "cohesive" self as anti-therapeutic (1971, p. 12). Ralph Klein, in a consideration of this critical theoretical difference, succinctly states that, for Kohut, "development essentially proceeds from immature selfobjects to mature selfobjects" (1989, p. 319). Apparently, the Kohutian narcissist gradually learns to be a more adaptive narcissist. (Kavaler-Adler also refers to this Kohutian creation of "better narcissists," 2014, p. xxvi.)

It is interesting to note that, in 1993 (*The Emerging Self*), Masterson draws an analogy between his concept of abandonment depression and Kohut's concern with self-fragmentation in the narcissistic personality. He writes: "What differentiates the closet narcissist from the other personality disorders is … the experiencing of the abandonment depression as the self 'falling apart' rather than as 'losing the object'" (p. x). Masterson sees "fragmentation anxiety" as a variation of abandonment depression specific to the narcissistic personality disorder. Both Masterson and Kohut understand this crucial reaction is potential whenever the narcissist's fundamental defensiveness is challenged. However, they radically differ as to how it is to be technically managed.

Kohut would proceed indirectly: by an empathic stance that increasingly strengthens the patient's sense of psychic cohesiveness, thereby minimizing concerns of falling apart psychically. In contrast, Masterson would see a therapeutic necessity to work through fragmentation anxiety in order to progress developmentally once the self has gained the strength to do so. Masterson's Approach foreshadows the trauma model of personality disorder. Initial terror of maternal/self loss, that had overwhelmed and defensively frozen developmental initiative, must be faced within the support of a "safe" therapeutic relationship in order to restore psychic growth. Analogous to the challenge of Masterson's abandonment depression in the borderline and Winnicott's annihilation anxiety in the schizoid (which will require "regression to dependence" for healing), Masterson sees the working through of the traumatic resistance of Kohut's dreaded "fragmentation anxiety" as central to resolution of narcissistic personality delay. The preparation for eventual readiness to accept separation of self from other is perceived as transformational, rather than as a destructive fracturing of the "whole" self (the self-object). Perhaps an added distinction here is that Masterson is referring to a traumatic fear of fragmentation, whereas Kohut is concerned with actual loss of self-cohesiveness.

Right Brain/Left Brain

Masterson became more receptive to the value of the purely empathic response in 2005, when he applied recent neurobiological findings to psychotherapy based on early infant development and attachment (*The Personality Disorders Through the Lens of Attachment Theory and the Neurobiologic Development of the Self*). Masterson cites Allan Schore's integration of neurobiological brain research with psychodynamic theory (there seems to be an affinity between two synthesizing minds here). Summarizing the aspect of Schore's work applicable to his own, Masterson describes neurobiological support for the critical role of the mother in the infant's mental development in the first years of life. The right brain, "the container and regulator of emotion," is "dominant for the first three years of life," while the left brain, which is cognitive and verbal, will not begin to assert its influence until the second year. Therefore "the core of the self is thus nonverbal and unconscious, and it lies within patterns of affect regulation." While this "neurobiologic center of the self" is emerging, "the child is unable to regulate his or her own affect, and thus the primary caretaker's interaction with the child becomes the principal regulator of emotion." This "affect synchronicity" (essentially, the mother's emotional mirroring of her child) is fundamental to the growth of the child's self (pp. 9–11).

Neurobiology, then, explains the importance of emotionally attuned interventions, essentially preverbal in nature, in the therapy of the patient whose personality problems originate in mother–infant misattunement in early development. In the case of the narcissist, there has been damage done during Mahler's practicing subphase specifically – at the time of the cohesion of the self described by Kohut.

It is both provocative and exciting to find that Masterson and Kohut, as divergent as they sometimes are, are also much in agreement. If one follows Masterson's example of synthesizing rather than opposing, one sees two original thinkers, traditionally trained but open to new perspectives, significantly reinforcing each other in finding ways to treat the "untreatable" patient. They are further supported by the emerging understanding of personality disorder, and thus are shaped by the times while shaping them in turn. Both as well are inspired by Mahler's developmental model, and so strengthen the analytic belief that the normal and the pathological are keys to the understanding of each other. But perhaps the deepest kinship between these two traditionally based innovators is their receptiveness to ideas that ring true in the clinical setting, and the determination to pursue these ideas in the service of the patient.

CASE STUDY

A Patient with Manifest Narcissist Personality Disorder and Developmental Trauma

Harry H., fifty-nine years old, was the owner of a small real-estate company. The success of the company fluctuated, as did his relationship with his partner. His marriage of thirty years was also in a changeable state and was headed for divorce. His three grown children all seemed to have acted strongly on their parents' emphasis on material acquisitions, and their father's driving ambition. The oldest, a son, pushing himself to accomplish, gained marginal success, an ulcer, and a constant need for his father's approval.

The middle child, a girl, was an aggressive achiever on her way up the corporate ladder. The youngest, a girl, reigned over a following of attentive boyfriends, while wearing only the latest fashions and running up her assortment of credit cards. Mr. H presented with a sense of frustration, depression, and loss – his problem was situational and characterological, but not traumatic. The traumatic elements would emerge as his personality disorder modified.

Mr. H had put on a little too much weight. His hair was graying and slightly balding above regular features that could turn contemptuous or unexpectedly boyish. Although he wore expensive clothing, he maintained a mildly disheveled look: his tie would be loosened and off center, or his shirt partly pulled out. He spoke quickly, articulately, and used hand gestures for emphasis. He wore a heavy gold ring with his initials engraved on it.

Presenting Problem

Mr. H described a personal crisis that had traumatic overtones. He believed his world had fallen apart overnight. Inexplicably, he thought, his wife had declared she was "fed up," and was suing for divorce. His partner was tampering with the books and would have to be confronted. Business was failing. His son lacked push and was too dependent on him. His oldest daughter, by contrast, contacted him rarely and ignored his advice. His youngest, his little princess, was surely going to bankrupt him. To ice the cake, he was almost sixty years old, and his father had died at sixty-one. Was his health poor? He had to be careful of his high blood pressure, but his father had keeled over entirely unexpectedly, and in apparent top physical condition.

Mr. H kept up an almost jaunty manner while presenting his situation. He seemed to want to give the impression of a man able to carry a heavy burden lightly, and with humor. He also seemed to be maneuvering me into becoming his responsive audience. I felt a double reaction – to argue or admire – so noted it as probably a diagnostic clue and settled for a neutral stance with a touch of mirroring.

History

Mr. H was the youngest of two brothers, the sons of immigrant parents. The father worked long hours establishing a dry-cleaning business – he made a college education possible for his sons and was determined to see them become professionals. The mother worked with her husband, making clothing alterations. She supported his ambition for their sons, but also protected them from his demands and domineering temper. She favored her youngest, Harry (the patient), and made him her confidant.

Isolated by barriers of culture, class, and family ambition, Mr. H had a lonely childhood and adolescence. He had difficulty concentrating and spent extra hours over his books. A good report card meant approval from his father and praise from his mother, while bad grades brought disgust and grief, respectively.

Unable to gain acceptance to medical school, or to succeed in passing the bar examination, he finally began to build a real-estate business with the help of a wife as ambitious as his parents. His wife also provided the social life he had rarely experienced. His family grew, his business prospered, and he took on a partner.

However, his early middle years were darkened by losses. His brother suffered a mental breakdown while starting a second career at dental school and committed suicide. His father died suddenly, probably of a stroke, and his mother passed away soon after, following a harrowing series of heart attacks.

Bereft of his family of origin, Mr. H, in his late middle years, focused all his concerns on his immediate household and real-estate business. The partial collapse of this core of his reality brought him to psychotherapy.

Psychotherapy

Mr. H adjusted his chair to a more commanding spot and scrutinized me.

"You could do better than this stuff" – he indicated my furniture – "I can give you the name of a good wholesale place. Just mention my name."

"Thanks, but these things have been with me a long time."

"They look it. This is just some friendly advice. You want to impress people when they walk in."

I felt devalued by way of my furniture and realized that my patient was assuming authority. The diagnostic signs of the manifest narcissist appear quickly. I tried to reclaim my position.

"Tell me, what brings you here?"

"No 'thank you'?" He was half-joking.

"For what?"

"For the advice, of course. Are you usually this slow on the uptake?"

I decided he had a point and began to mirror him: "Sorry, I should have appreciated your concern; thanks for the offer and for your good humor about it." [Acknowledging my "rebuff" and his attempt to joke it off.]

He settled back in his chair, apparently mollified.

"Let's get on with it, doc. I don't mind telling you this isn't usually how I spend my lunch hour."

The easy part came next, as I asked him to tell me his background. He told me his story seriously, especially becoming solemn at describing his relationship with his parents. He wiped his eyes (with the back of his hand, like a little boy) while speaking of his mother. He spoke briefly about when his brother "croaked," detaching himself quickly from the topic.

The hard part for him was addressing the complex of events that made up his presenting problem:

"Doc, how can I deserve this now, when I should be successful and happy with my family around me? I earned it; I created it; it's part of me. I worked; I gave; I deserve gratitude. My wife, my partner, my kids, they'd be nowhere without me.

"But I tell you, the worst is this feeling I've been left alone to die. I think – why are they leaving me when I have only one year to go?"

"This is painful to think about. What does your doctor say?"

"Doctors! My dad had a clean bill of health – then wham! He took my mother with him, and now I figure he's going to take me."

I decided that Mr. H's separation anxiety had focused powerfully on the idea of death, and that probably it was a defense that would have to stay intact for now to protect against his intolerable sense of loss. I would try to help him contain this anxiety by focusing on the more concrete problems of the here and now. These present issues in themselves threatened his functioning both at home and at work, and approached traumatic proportions (this was the third time the structure of his life had been threatened – once when he failed to achieve a profession; twice when his immediate family had died; and now when his entire sum of success was being demolished, leaving him with fears of death).

Since the patient was in a crisis situation, I thought I should place the therapeutic emphasis on strengthening of Mr. H's self-esteem. I planned to be an empathic listener who understood his point of view, and thus lowered his need for unrealistic and grandiose defense. He might then have better access to his healthy intellectual and assertive capacities.

Introductory Phase

During the first few months of treatment, the pacing of the work went ahead carefully. It was necessary to mirror Mr. H's sense of vulnerability so that he would feel understood – and would begin to idealize me in return. The transference acting out shifted from his need to maintain his grandiosity by putting me (or my furniture) down, to a sense of our being merged in a self-satisfied emotional entity.

Pt.:   I get all the lousy luck.

Th.:   Do you think you might play some part in this?

Pt.:   You trying to tell me I brought this on myself?

Th.:   Just trying to say you can have some control over what starts with you. You can be less helpless.

Pt.:   Now it's all my fault, plus I'm just a helpless wimp.

Th.:   Sorry. I guess that sounded like an attack. There's no question you've had more than your share of tough times.

Pt.:   You bet your tail. What's with you today?

Th.:   I didn't show understanding. You had to protect yourself by challenging me.

Pt.:   I thought you knew me.

Th.:   I disappointed you.

Pt.:   That's what I like about you, doc. You admit when you're off base. You keep an open mind, like me.

As time passed, it was possible to increase interpretation of defenses, as mirroring established a sense of idealized unity. We could begin to tackle his problems more directly.

Patients who enter therapy in crisis tend to be relatively open to change. The more narcissistic the patient, however, the more the openness approaches break down. Narcissistic defenses are brittle and inflexible and need to be reinforced in order to meet a crisis – it may then be possible for the self to feel protected enough to face facts.

Mr. H. was least defended about his work life. He was able to express a range of feelings about the partner who had once been a close friend, and had now betrayed him. But he began to lose objectivity when talking about betrayal and was more extreme when considering his wife.

Pt.:   (Furiously.) I have been screwed by my best and closest! These are people I put my trust in.

Th.:   You've been betrayed by people who should have supported you. [Mirroring to moderate]

Pt.:   I've been stabbed in the back!

Th.:   People who you depended on attacked you, so you
        protect yourself by going on the attack yourself. [Mirroring
        interpretation of defensive, externalizing rage]

Pt.:   (Mollified) You said it.

My hope was to acknowledge Mr. H.'s rage to the point where the
actions he must take would not be impetuous and self-destructive.
With so much at stake, and the patient so incendiary, it was necessary
to "frame" interventions consistently from the patient's point of view:

Pt.:   That sonofabitch partner of mine thinks he's going to get
        away with stealing my business. I'll kill him.

Th.:   I know how serious this betrayal is. But don't you think he'll
        be expecting just this – for you to be so hurt and angry
        you'll strike back without concern for yourself?

Pt.:   Meaning?

Th.:   Meaning maybe he's counting on your acting before you think.

Pt.:   Meaning?

Th.:   Meaning he's counting on your idealism getting in the way
        of your reason, so you'll make a mistake and he'll take
        advantage of you.

Pt.:   You're right. I should get off my white horse and think.

At this stage, I simply empathized with his complaints about his
children, as I did with his fears of dying. These issues did not take
critical priority in the here and now.

Short-term Treatment

As I continued to mirror Mr. H.'s grandiosity, he included me in his
halo of idealization, and I was able to intensify the interpretive side of
my interventions. If I went too far and he attacked, I then emphasized

the mirroring of his narcissistic vulnerability. This mended the narcissistic rift and restored our imagined oneness.

Pt.: I'm going to counter-sue this so-called wife until she appreciates what she had with me.

Th.: I know she's hurt you, but are you really defending yourself by turning this into World War III?

Pt.: What are you saying? I count on you for understanding, and you tell me I'm Saddam Hussein!

Th.: So now you feel attacked by me, too.

Pt.: What do you mean "feel" – you attacked me!

Th.: I hurt you with my lack of understanding. [Mirroring]

Pt.: (Mollified) Damn right.

Th.: It pains you when someone you want to value lets you down. You fight back to maintain your rights. [Return to mirroring interpretation]

Pt.: I'll do it for sure.

Th.: Maybe it's important to remember sometimes that that reaction plays into the other person's hands.

Pt.: I have to remember ... slow down and remember. I know you're thinking about what's good for me.

The divorce hearing began, and Mr. H. found himself constantly humiliated. He responded with anger in court and in his sessions.

Pt.: Her and that shyster! They're taking me for a fortune, plus my house.

Th.: This is a painful situation. What does your attorney say?

Pt.: The sonofabitch tells me I'm lucky she doesn't get a piece of the business.

Th.: Husbands can have a rough time in divorce court. Maybe you should play it cool before her demands escalate.

Pt.:   I know you want the best for me, but are you saying I should give in to this bitch?

Th.:   You're right. I hope this can work out for you as well as it can. I know it hurts you, but do you think it's in your best interest to challenge the proceedings? Your wife might end up with even more.

Pt.:   But I hate it! I'll hate myself if I don't fight.

Th.:   Look – you've already put up a good fight. You want to change the courts, but even your attorney tells you you've reached the limit. You can't keep your money, but you can keep your pride. You can show her she can't get to you.

Pt.:   That's a lot to ask. Off I go with my tail between my legs.

Th.:   No. You stand your ground with dignity, whatever insults they hand you. You show your kids that at least one parent has dignity.

Pt.:   Thank God the kids are on their own.

Th.:   And they'll appreciate it if their father has the courage not to drag this out, despite the pain.

Pt.:   It really hurts. I don't know. I don't hear a word from the kids, but maybe this will bring them around.

The divorce proceedings ended as soon as such matters can, primarily because Mr. H. decided to hold his temper and keep his dignity. However, he was humiliated by having to move into his own apartment, and worried by the instability of his business. He rapidly transposed his anger from his wife to his partner.

He threatened to take the latter to court, although he himself could ill afford it, and the partner was offering to make a reasonable arrangement. Beneath the anger, Mr. H. was suffering from loneliness. It became clear that he needed to set up a fight, not only to ease his humiliation at the divorce, but also to ward off a sense of abandonment. Eventually, he extended the projection of his anger into transference acting out when I slipped and tried to reason with him instead of using mirroring interpretation.

Th.:   Wouldn't it be easier just to stop fighting and accept his offer?

Pt.:   Are you kidding? I put all my life into this, and I'm going to let this little jerk, this shit, take it all away from me? I thought you were on my side.

Th.:   [Resuming mirroring] I let you down – You don't feel I'm supporting you when you're in a spot.

Pt.:   Supporting me? God damn it. You and your two-bit degree. What do you know? You're not going through it.

Th.:   [Persisting] I left you alone when you expected me to be there.

Pt.:   [Calming down somewhat] So up yours, doc, with all due respect.

Increasingly mollified by mirroring and mirroring interpretations of his narcissistic vulnerability, the patient settled into a more thoughtful mode.

Pt.:   At least if my business was going well, I could have some consolation.

Th.:   It's really tough to tend to the business when you have to deal with your partner, too.

Pt.:   I feel so lousy – he's betrayed me, and now he wants to settle. I want to see his hide on the wall of my apartment. That's what I'll settle for.

Th.:   That's a lot of grief for you – to have only the business for your morale, and your partner is ruining it. No wonder you have to stay angry to keep your courage up.

Pt.:   [Weary and coming around at last] To tell you the truth, the guy can go to hell, but I don't have what it takes to send him there. [Letting go the projection]

Th.:   Look: you've been fighting hard to defend yourself on all sides, but even the best fighter is going to get disgusted. Nobody else is going to give you a break. You're stuck with your own pain, and all you can do is take it out on yourself.

Pt.:   I'm coming to a decision. It makes me sick just to hear this guy's voice. I'll compromise for the sake of peace with the bastard.

Th.:   A tough decision.

Pt.:   [Very serious] To tell you the truth, sitting in my apartment staring at the TV and trying to figure out where I'm going is not for me. But even making a decision feels lousy. Work stinks. My kids don't call. I don't sleep much; I keep thinking about all this crap that has come down – over and over – and then it's morning.

Th.:   Tell me some more about that.

Pt.:   All this – it takes me back, you know – life never was so great.

Th.:   [Unexpectedly choking up, and realizing it is projective identification] You know, I think there's a lot of sadness here. Do you think you're being tough and covering over your feelings more than you have to?

Pt.:   [Close to tears] I haven't felt this crummy since I was a kid. Just a snotty little kid alone in my room. Doc, I don't want to go back to that place again.

Mr. H. left in a dejected state of mind, and next session reported that he wanted to "get out of this; I think we should call it quits." I replied: "The feelings coming up here are difficult for you. Because the feelings are coming up in the session, you figure you can make them go away by stopping the therapy." [Countering his acting out] He answered: "Okay, okay. But I don't like where this is going. I'm trusting you to make this come out right." [Re-establishment of idealization].

With the completion of the divorce and settling of matters with his former partner, Mr. H. grew increasingly depressed. He still searched for a place to project his anger, and so to ward off the depression. Consequently, he focused it on the relationships with his grown children.

Pt.:   There's no empathy, doc, they're all staying away. All I get is the credit card bills from the little one.

Th.:   This is hard for you.

Pt.:   How could they forget everything they got from me – advice, money – they always had the best.

Th.:   They stay so far away from you; you reassure yourself by recalling all you gave them.

Pt.:   Someone should remember. Any advice, doc?

Th.:   It's hard to believe you've run out of ideas.

Pt.:   Well, I thought about calling – reaching out, you know. But those kids, I spoiled them. How do they know how to give?

Th.:   You're so disappointed, you shield yourself from possible increased disappointment by assuming their reaction. [Addressing devaluing defense]

Pt.:   Maybe I should put in a call to my son. He sometimes listens to me.

Mr. H. reached out to his children and was gratified to find them responsive. They had been cautiously waiting for him to make the first move.

Mr. H. was not gratified, however, by the increase in his depression after his temporary elation. His anger again turned to me – a risky happening with the narcissist who requires harmony with the idealized therapist. But, uncomfortable as this was for both of us, it seemed to show that our relationship was becoming more realistic: transference acting out might be shifting toward a real relationship where transference was not so much the entire interaction as a distortion in it.

Pt.:   What is this? The more I follow your advice, the worse I feel! I think you better go back to shrink school.

Th.:   You've got a point. The more progress you make, the more the feelings come out. You've become strong enough to handle what was too painful before.

Pt.:   Yeah. It's "too painful," and now I'm going to "protect myself" by getting out of here before it gets worse. [Sarcastic demonstration that he is integrating mirroring interpretation]

Th.:   So, I use jargon. Could you ever run your real-estate business
          without talking the talk? The main thing is, since you've been
          here, you've gone through one crisis after another, and you
          still have your business and your kids and your pride. You're
          managing.

Pt.:   Big gold star! And I sit in this hole of an apartment with my
          blank walls and my nightmares. My recreation is thinking up
          ways to kill you slowly.

Th.:   This is hard work. You've met your practical problems, and now
          this thing with feelings comes up. Easier to blame me than say
          this is what you didn't want to experience. [Taking a chance
          with patient's increased strength to try a mild confrontation]

Pt.:   You're what I don't want to experience. Like all the others,
          you have my money, and I have my grief.

Th.:   It's easier to experience me than experience that grief.

Once again, I felt an unexpected wave of sorrow flood me, and
realized I was identifying with his projected sadness. I tried to remain
still and neutral, but my nose started to run. As I sniffed and reached in
my pocket for a tissue, I said:

"It's really tough when you work so hard and it comes up crap anyway."

My patient put his head in his hands and was silent for many seconds.

Then he said: "It's too much like her. You make me think of my mother.
You tell me to spit it out, and then you rub it all over my face."

I waited.

"My mom. She told me all her troubles, but she couldn't listen to mine.
'Tell me one of your jokes,' she'd say. That's how I got to be the God
damn life of the party."

We sat together in silence gain.

"Doc, there's things I never talked about to anyone, I don't want to
here, either. What's the point?"

"Maybe this will be the toughest decision you make here."

"I don't know. I have to think this one out, maybe next time."

But he did not return to the subject for the next two sessions. Here-and-now sessions took center stage and I did not press him. Narcissists tend to be under the pressure of an unacknowledged obligation, and encouragement, however well meant, is perceived as an excess obligation. Mr. H. had been in therapy for two and a half years and was shifting from acting out his issues defensively to examining them realistically despite transference distortion. This transference distortion had led him to trace anger at me to anger at his mother, and now he hesitated on the brink of needed but unwelcome insight.

He said: "After all these years, I have nothing to say to her: so why should I have anything to say to you?"

"Just tell me what you choose to."

He shifted uncomfortably. then looked me in the eye.

"My dad was pretty mean, you know. I didn't tell you, but he slapped me and my brother around some. He slapped my mom around, too. My brother ran and hid, but I always took it, and I stood between him and my mom, too, 'til he knocked me down.

"When he slammed out of the house, my mom would put her arms around me. She said: 'Harry, you're my guardian angel.' Then she'd kiss me."

He looked down. "This is the part I don't talk about. She'd kiss me on the mouth and take me to her bed. She used to snuggle me, and we'd stay there a long time."

A silence passed.

"It felt good, but it felt all mixed up."

A quick gesture of dismissal.

"What's the point of this? Let the dead rest."

Long-term Treatment

Mr. H. had reached an important juncture in his therapy. He had achieved some observing distance with his defenses and was less inclined to impulsively act out. He had dealt with his critical presenting problems and had begun to look within himself. And he had established a rapport with me primarily as a real person, rather than an idealized protector or adversary.

For the next several weeks he talked about his childhood – especially about his father's abusive sternness and his devotion to his mother. He also grew increasingly depressed and dropped the joking façade that had marked the first years of treatment.

Pt.:   I feel lousy.

Th.:   Allowing for the unhappiness you feel, it's almost like meeting you for the first time. You know how you said you had to be "the life of the party" to please your mother? Well, it's like I've had to be your straight man to keep things going. We've had to keep the one-liners going, you know?

Pt.:   Yeah. Keep the sunny side up. Never cry in front of mom – she's been through enough.

During his first two years of therapy, Mr. H. passed his sixty-first birthday, the age at which his father had died. The safe navigation of that year, plus the completion of his divorce and settlement with his partner, gave him a sense of relief, but left him with fewer hiding places for his anxiety and depression. He refused medication, although he reported insomnia, angry outbursts, and persistent recollections of his mother's death.

Pt.:   I keep thinking how she was at the end; she was so pale. Her nose and chin were so sharp, and she didn't recognize me. I can't get rid of this picture. I see myself kissing her goodbye and I feel sick. I get this ringing in my head. I feel like I'm a little lost kid.

I said very little, not wishing to interrupt the deepening and flow of his feelings. I also had an uneasy sense that something was surfacing that had been held down as his feelings had been held down. One session he took and deep breath and looked at me earnestly.

He said: "There's more I haven't talked about, doc. Maybe now is the time to tell someone and get it said." He hesitated, then continued, "When I was a little kid – when my dad hit her – she did more than take me to bed. She used to stroke me, if you get what I'm saying, and she took it pretty far."

He shook his head slowly: "It was too much like she needed me even if it wasn't good for me. I think that's why I always feel like a phony – this important phony who's someone's favorite toy."

He was silent for a long time, staring ahead of him.

"This is too much, doc, I'm leaving early today."

I did not attempt to confront the pain that seemed appropriate, and not a characterological bluff.

I said: "Are you sure you want to call it quits for today? You're talking about some important stuff."

"I really want out. I'll pick it up next time."

I believed he was calling for a necessary pacing, and we ended the session.

The next several sessions were marked by long silences interspersed with painful memories that became more graphic as they came into focus through dreams and verbal descriptions. He said: "I dreamed I was lying next to Mom. It felt like the most wonderful thing in the world. Then this is really tough to say – I came in my sleep. I woke up and hated myself, but you know, even more I hated that I couldn't go back into that dream. Why did she do this to me?"

"I can't tell you that. But don't you think this is a reason you often feel so betrayed by life?"

"Yeah, I do. I feel bad and keep on putting on a show to get the magic back. I'm a phony. It's all false."

Mr. H. had always been partly aware of his mother's sexual abuse of him. With his increasing ability to face his feelings, he was also able to face his traumatic memories more clearly. He saw how the sense of sexual longing, being used and needing to please, intertwined traumatically and characterologically. He began to understand why he expected to be the center of attention yet felt undervalued at the same time.

Termination

Mr. H. had been in therapy over three years. The sessions slowly became reports of daily events, anecdotes, and jokes. I questioned him about this.

Th.:   Your sessions have changed. It has been painful for you to talk about your past and your mother, but it has helped you to know yourself better.

Pt.:   It's true. But it's too much. The dreams keep coming, and the sexual feelings, and the nausea. I want to remember my mom differently. I want this to stop.

Th.:   If you let yourself fully acknowledge the past, it will stop. And you'll be in a better place than before. The bad feelings that have blocked some of the good feelings about your mother will be gone. You'll remember her realistically but mixed with the love you always had.

Pt.:   And honestly, how long is this supposed to take?

Th.:   I can't say. And honestly, it may get worse before it gets better, although it will be better in the end.

Pt.:   I don't know. I'm not sure I'm looking for this better reality.

Mr. H. did not pursue his early trauma. I made certain his choice was a deliberate, conscious one, but he was aware of the path he was taking.

Then one day he came in with his spirits raised.

Pt.:   Doc, you know I've signed up with this dating service. Would you believe I've struck it rich?

Th.:   You found someone you like?

Pt.:   For real! You know how you always said "real" is best? She's no pin-up, but nice. She cooks, she likes the same movies, she helps me talk to my kids!

Th.:   Sounds like this may be something solid.

Pt.:   Believe it! And no more bad dreams.

Th.:   You're truly affectionate?

Pt.:   Oh, yes. This is love-making. Makes me happy to wake up in the morning, you know?

The weeks passed, and Mr. H. began to talk about the possibility of marriage. He was aware that he had made his choice in part to close over the early trauma.

He said: "That was a bad trip. I needed to get it off my chest. But there's no point going back there anymore. What's done is done, and it's time to move on.

"Look – my business is okay, my kids even visit me, and I'm marrying a good woman. I know I used to rub people the wrong way, but I'm more mellow now. And I got good people to set me straight when I stray.

"You got to know I was never made to go it alone. Now I'm complete. Why should I go back there somewhere in a bad past when it's okay in the present?"

He stayed a few more sessions but, as he had pointed out, he had resolved his presenting problems, modified his character issues, and found a satisfactory life for himself. The early traumatic issue that had emerged as a result of the strengthening of his personality had been partially dealt with; but it was no longer a secret and was woven into the conscious narrative of his life. His new relationship had offered him a short-cut to resolution but seemed substantial. Fundamentally, patients know their own limits and tolerances – it is the therapist's job to bring this knowledge as much into awareness as possible. The patient then makes his own choices.

Candace Orcutt (2012b). "A Patient with Manifest Narcissist Personality Disorder and Developmental Trauma." Excerpted from: Candace Orcutt (2012a) Trauma in Personality Disorder: A Clinician's Handbook – The Masterson Approach (pp. 78–98). Bloomington, IN: AuthorHouse. Copyright 2012 by Candace Orcutt, Ph.D.

CHAPTER 4

The Schizoid Personality

The clinical importance of the schizoid disorder of the self was only hinted at in my previous work. The development of the understanding and treatment of this disorder in a developmental, self and object relations perspective has now advanced rapidly through the efforts of Ralph Klein, Clinical Director of the Masterson Institute. With the publication of this volume, the schizoid disorder of the self takes its place alongside the narcissistic and borderline disorders of the self as a third major dimension of psychopathology.

(Masterson and Klein 1995, p. ix)

Although the schizoid disorder of the self is late in joining the Masterson Approach, it is actually mentioned in Masterson's first book (1967, *The Psychiatric Dilemma of Adolescence*), where even the borderline has not yet been introduced. This is worth noting, because the schizoid seems to have been reluctantly incorporated into analysis and dynamic psychotherapy generally, although the work of Fairbairn, a major proponent, began to appear in the 1940s. Guntrip's *Schizoid Phenomena, Object Relations, and the Self*, probably the primary reference for therapists seeking guidance in understanding and treating the schizoid – and cited as Ralph Klein's primary reference – appeared as far back as 1969. Because the writings of Winnicott, also central to the subject, have recently gained full recognition, it may be hard to believe that some of his articles pertinent to the schizoid date as far back as the 1940s ("Transitional Objects and Transitional Phenomena" was published in 1951). The work of Masud Khan (dating back to the 1960s) extensively promoted the importance of this disorder, but has been disregarded despite the excellence of its content.

Stephen Silberstein, in the 1995 volume *Disorders of the Self: New Therapeutic Horizons*, in which Masterson and Klein as co-editors introduce the schizoid, observes: "until recently relatively little attention has been paid to the schizoid disorder of the self. It was almost as if mental health professionals were resonating with schizoid patients' fears of the dire consequences of their being seen or heard" (1995, p. 143). Masud Khan, Winnicott's editor and to a degree his collaborator, noted: "Winnicott was to run into a special sort of difficulty with his analytic colleagues, from the start – that of being politely disregarded" (Winnicott 1975, p. xiv). To an extent, Winnicott absent-mindedly contributed to the situation himself, as Khan was astonished to come across the typescript of "The Manic Defense," set aside unpublished for over twenty years (Winnicott 1975, p. xiv). A somewhat similar situation occurred with Fairbairn, whose evolving ideas owe much of their systematization and accessibility to Guntrip.

The characteristic reticence of some of the major thinkers on the subject, and the tendency in the field to give them a proportionate underacknowledgment, almost seems related to the nature of the schizoid disorder itself – it is tempting to wonder about a reciprocal dynamic that exceeds coincidence.

Be that as it may, Masterson's inclusion of the schizoid as the "third major dimension" of the disorders of the self takes place some twenty-seven years after the publication of Masterson's first book, and is the contribution of Ralph Klein, the clinical director of the Institute. This eventual inclusion is undoubtedly an outcome of Masterson's shift in focus from borderline patients exclusively to a wider definition of personality disorder generally, especially in terms of the growth of the self. The schizoid is introduced as the contribution of Ralph Klein – Masterson's right-hand man from Payne Whitney days – first as a short summary in *The Emerging Self* (Masterson 1993, pp. 39–50), and then as the substantial opening section of *Disorders of the Self: New Therapeutic Horizons* (Masterson and Klein 1995, pp. 3–178). After that, the schizoid was incorporated systematically into the Masterson Approach.

The Masterson Approach and the Schizoid

Ralph Klein's contribution to the understanding and treatment of the schizoid, a small volume in itself, is a dedicated exploration – descriptively and clinically strong and sensitive to the nature of the schizoid patient.

His presentation is indispensable to the wholeness of Masterson's model. The following review and critique is directed, in good part, to Klein's 1995 book-within-a-book.

Klein's case studies, guided primarily by Guntrip, but also clearly by Klein's own extensive experience and empathy, make this a meaningful contribution to the literature on the schizoid and to the work of the therapist, as well as an integral part of the Masterson Approach. However, three meaningful considerations I believe extend Klein's clinical presentation: (1) Fairbairn's assertion (taken up by Guntrip and others) that the fundamental schizoid split is between the patient's inner and outer worlds, and is the pre-ambivalent predecessor of the Melanie Kleinian good/bad split; (2) the consensus among the Independent object relationists that schizoid issues have their origin in the mother-infant relationship in the first year of life, which suggests that a closer look at Mahler's mother–infant observations of that ("differentiation") period of child psychic development could inform the clinical relationship with the schizoid as it does the borderline and the narcissist; (3) the work of Winnicott – especially in regard to transitional phenomena, play, and regression to dependence – would seem to add a significant dimension to technique in treating the schizoid self.

In regard to theory, I believe Ralph Klein's presentation would also benefit from some additions. I suggest this could be focused in four areas of consideration: (1) the place in the evolution of analytic thinking of the independent object relationists, and closely allied colleagues, who strove to establish the schizoid disorder as a psychic condition stemming from mother-infant relational and developmental issues in the early "oral" stage; (2) the paradigm-changing accomplishments of Fairbairn that facilitated the shift in analytic thinking from an emphasis on inner phantasy to relationship, and from the ego to the self; (3) the monumental work of Winnicott which, combining pediatric observation and analytic thought, offers a living picture of the mother–infant relationship in the early months of life, in turn illuminating how the sense of self may become divided by early misattunement, and how that schizoid condition may be treated in both children and adults; and (4) how Mahler's developmental studies of separation and individuation may once again be incorporated (especially in conjunction with writings of Winnicott, Schore, and Fonagy) to support the relevance of the original object relations/developmental model to the Masterson Approach to the schizoid.

My intention here is to both acknowledge and sometimes question

Ralph Klein's contribution to Masterson's unfolding work with disorders of the self – as part of that growing process of ideas and their clinical application that Masterson envisioned his Approach to be.

Theoretical Background

Klein's review of theory on the schizoid takes a somewhat cursory look at an already underacknowledged field of literature. He notes traditional descriptive psychiatry as represented by Bleuler and Kretschmer. Classical analytic positions are represented by Melanie Klein and two of the independent object relations theorists, Fairbairn and Guntrip. Notably absent are Winnicott, Khan, Little, Sutherland, and Deutsch, and also Balint, Bion, Laing, and Searles, whose writing on schizoid pathology significantly contributes to the literature.

Melanie Klein (1882–1960)

Ralph Klein's exploration of traditional dynamic therapists begins with a brief consideration of the contribution of Melanie Klein. He points out what may be her major shortcoming: her failure to relate theoretical abstraction to a human picture of "schizoid experience" (Klein 1995, p. 6). (Melanie Klein's work seems to demonstrate a striking split in itself, in which an inner world operates with a near-apocalyptic intensity that lacks substantial correspondence to outer interpersonal reality. Her adherence to inner "phantasy" as the near-exclusive cause of pathology is a related issue.) But, as Ralph Klein continues, Melanie Klein brilliantly contributed "to the understanding of character pathology and early intrapsychic structures" (1995, p. 6). He mentions her concept of introjective and projective mechanisms, and the splitting of the pre-oedipal inner reality into "good" and "bad" perceptions (Klein 1946) – phenomena crucial to the understanding of character pathology generally and, it might be added, central to the Mastersonian concept of transference acting out, especially in regard to the borderline. He does not note, however, that she worked with children two and a half years of age and older (Brandchaft 1989, p. 233; Gay 1998, p. 467), which led her to prematurely attribute this good/bad split to the psychic level of the one-year-old. The good/bad split is developmentally related to the two-year-old level of the psyche, or Mahler's rapprochement child, and Masterson's borderline patient.

Melanie Klein widened the study of character pathology to the point where she not only extended it to the earliest time of childhood, but initiated a new school of analytic thought in doing so: object relations. Her picturing of an inner psychic world inhabited by changing representations and part-representations of important figures in the outer world began to shift analytic perspective from the ego and the drives to the ego and the object, and eventually to self and other. Her inner-object approach would lead to a new concept of transference – based on what was described by her once-follower, Bowlby, as psychic internal "working models" of relationship (1969). As it is now understood, these inner models strive to actualize themselves in the therapeutic situation: this is defined by Masterson as transference acting out, and constitutes what is now described by the relational analysts as the rigid unconscious "enactment" of past dysfunctional interchange in the present treatment situation. Melanie Klein, a loyal drive theorist who would vehemently disown much of her legacy (and important followers along with it), nevertheless was unwillingly instrumental in inspiring followers such as Fairbairn and Winnicott to transform the drive-theory-based concept of character disorder to the relationally directed concept of personality disorder, shaped from the human need for relationship and fulfillment of the self.

Yet another contribution of Melanie Klein, which should be added here, was the introduction of play therapy. This method not only opened the way to dynamic treatment with children, but was adapted by Winnicott for the use of the transitional capacity for play with patients of all ages, especially the nonverbal and the schizoid.

W. R. D. Fairbairn (1889–1964)

If Ralph Klein omits identifying Melanie Klein as the originator of object relations theory – a foundation-block of the Masterson Approach – it is also perplexing that he does not allow Fairbairn credit for transforming object relations – actually psychoanalysis itself – into a relational endeavor focused on the self as "object-seeking" (the transitional nature of Fairbairn's work is reflected in his tendency to use "ego" and "self" interchangeably). Without the creative, humanizing influence of Fairbairn on analytic thought and practice, the Masterson Approach might have taken on a very different shape, or possibly not exist.

Fairbairn and Melanie Klein were contemporaries, and their work was inter-influential. Fairbairn was successful in convincing Klein to modify the "paranoid position" of her schema of preoedipal development to the "schizoid-paranoid position," in which the ego/self learns to split itself in the process of defense.

Fairbairn's further elaborations on Freudian/Kleinian theory were not incorporated by Melanie Klein, but became touchstones for the "Independent" group of analysts, whose concept of object relations concerned itself with the outer as well as the inner world, and the interdependency of the two. Among other concepts, this group adopted Fairbairn's emphasis on: the external "object" as well as the internal "object representation"; the need for the "other" predominant over the pleasure-seeking drive in dependent early infancy and beyond; separation anxiety as the earliest form of anxiety; the "pre-ambivalent" differentiation of inner and outer worlds; the splitting of the ego/self into subselves; and the eventual coalescing of subselves into split "good" and "bad" inner representations of the ego/self and object/other. The listing here can be only partial.

Fairbairn's heritage is extensive and still developing; as Mitchell says of both Fairbairn and M. Klein, their theories are "complex, incomplete, and often internally inconsistent," but "traces of their influence are discernable in almost every area of contemporary psychoanalytic theory and practice" (Grotstein and Rinsley 1994, p. 67). Perhaps Fairbairn's influence, and his greatest contribution to the Masterson Approach, can be summed up by Sutherland:

> Clearly Fairbairn has left much that needs to be expanded, and what he ended with points to tasks for a more complete theory of the self as fashioned from relationships. His primary text, so to speak, is that the individual from the very start has to be loved for himself by the unconditional loving care of (at first) the mother.
>
> (Grotstein and Rinsley 1994, p. 20)

The schizoid disorder of the self results from a failure in that "unconditional loving care" in the first months of the infant's life. Fairbairn describes the schizoid disorder as related to a psychic "position" to be traveled through in the maturational process, and probably to be maintained throughout life at the core of the individual's being: a capacity and vulnerability to split the ego/self in the process of defense. He describes the schizoid disorder as a specific type of character pathology originating from maternal devaluing of the self at the earliest time of its development: the socially withdrawn, emotionally detached schizoid personality – a "closed system" protected from outside encroachment, but constantly subject to a painful inner sense of futility.

Ralph Klein demonstrates Fairbairn's "significant developmental understanding [of] the genesis of the schizoid disorder" through the following quotation from Fairbairn: "In early life they [schizoid patients] gained a conviction whether through apparent indifference or through apparent possessiveness on the part of their mother that the mother did not really love them as persons in their own right" (Fairbairn 1984, p. 113; Klein 1995, p. 9). Continuing in Fairbairn's terms, Klein describes how a subsequent sense of starvation for validation of being leads to the characterological impasse of the schizoid: "The great problem of the schizoid individual is how to love without destroying by love ... He becomes afraid to love and therefore he erects barriers between his objects and himself" (1995, pp. 8–9). Emotional deprivation in the early oral phase of development, according to Fairbairn and later stressed by Guntrip, creates fantasies of ravenous devouring and therefore destruction of the very source of sustenance – aggressive fantasies that, in turn, are projected onto the representation of the object itself. Such fantasies lead to the tension between need and fear characteristic of the schizoid's approaching-and-distancing maneuvers with others.

Ralph Klein outlines the major elements in the nature of the schizoid's endopsychic structure. In addition to the schizoid's "need to regulate interpersonal distance" and the accompanying "dynamic, pervasive tension between the need for attachment ... and the defensive need for distancing," the schizoid typically demonstrates "the ability to mobilize self-reliant and self-preservative defenses," and "a general overevaluation of the internal world at the expense of the external world" (1995, p. 8).

As Klein points out, Fairbairn's work "foreshadowed the important focus on maternal emotional availability that became a central theme in the understanding of the borderline disorders of the self (Masterson

1976), and the narcissistic disorders of the self (Kohut 1971; Masterson 1981)" (Klein 1995, p. 10). He adds a poignant and impactful observation:

> *The critical difference between the schizoid patient developmentally and those with other self disorders is that the awareness of maternal emotional unavailability is an actual, explicit experience and not a potential, implicit possibility. There is a world of difference developmentally between these two positions. The former leaves little room for hope and little reason to turn to external reality to consummate the yearning for attachment.*

(Klein 1995, p. 10)

Harry Guntrip (1901–1995)

Guntrip, a somewhat younger contemporary of Fairbairn and Winnicott, sought out both, in sequence, for analysis, and patterned much of his theory and clinical practice on this intense personal experience. He is most remembered for his exposition and systematization of Fairbairn's work, and, through publications and untiring presentations, for making the thought of that reticent innovator known to practitioners in Britain and the United States. Throughout the 1960s, Guntrip continued to bring to the fore Fairbairn's concern with the schizoid personality and the wholeness of the ego/self: the "fundamental" schizoid problem as "uncertainty about the basic reality and viability of the central core of selfhood in the person" (Guntrip 1971, pp. 150–151).

Guntrip's books and travels brought Fairbairn's achievements to a wider audience with a near-evangelical dedication that reflected his calling as a Congregational minister as well as his analytical knowledge and philosophical discipline. One suspects his identity as a preacher–therapist contributes to the human immediacy and persuasiveness of his style, as well as his perseverance toward an edifying resolution of things.

Ralph Klein acknowledges Guntrip's skill in "developing Fairbairn's observations into a more precise and exacting description of the schizoid patient" (1995, p. 10). He identifies two character patterns extrapolated by Guntrip that dynamically identify the schizoid patient. The first Guntrip refers to as "the schizoid dilemma" (also as "the in-and-out programme"), which explains the seemingly self-contradictory nature of schizoid relationship. The isolated schizoid longs for relationship, and approaches it in various guarded ways, but drawing close he experiences the fear of the old pain of failure and hurt and pulls away again into the security of his private world. However, the pain of loneliness and the fear of getting lost in it forever are also unwanted, and the outward search begins again. Second, "the schizoid compromise" is Guntrip's term for the halfway solution to this "dilemma." The schizoid may find a degree of social participation through some mutual interest or, by taking on the protective coloring of a socially designated role, or by expressing the self indirectly through creative endeavors (acting would be a notable example). In regard to this last point, Klein offers an especially valuable insight: "Guntrip was also clear in describing the importance of fantasy life for the schizoid individual. However, he focused on the defensive, regressive use of fantasy, while generally neglecting the aspect of fantasy that makes it an excellent example of schizoid compromise" (1995 pp. 10–11).

Klein reviews the nine characteristics Guntrip lists in categorizing the schizoid personality (Guntrip 1969, pp. 41–44). The specificity and diagnostic usefulness of these criteria earn them the better part of Klein's next chapter. They are: introversion; withdrawnness; narcissism; self-sufficiency; a sense of superiority; loss of affect; loneliness; depersonalization; regression (Klein, pp. 15–23).

Omitting an important clinical approach used by Guntrip, Klein does not mention the process of "regression to dependence" developed by Winnicott and hesitantly considered by Fairbairn. This intervention will be described in the section of this chapter entitled "Annihilation Anxiety and Abandonment Depression."

D. W. Winnicott (1896–1970)

Although Klein does not include Winnicott's name in his listing, the work of the distinguished pediatrician/analyst Winnicott completes the entwined introduction of schizoid personality disorder by the foursome of Fairbairn, Guntrip, Winnicott, and Khan. Fairbairn introduces the description, essential dynamic, and relational origin of the schizoid, and transforms analytic thought in so doing. Guntrip systematizes Fairbairn's work, makes it more clinically useful and accessible to clinicians, and places it within an exhaustive overview of a rapidly evolving psychoanalytic field (1971).

Winnicott, intensively working with actual infants and their mothers, anticipates the growing dimension of developmental study (including the concept of developmental arrest) and integrates it with analytic object relations theory. He brings unique experience and insight to the understanding of the schizoid, continuing the humanizing of the condition as he meets with it in its progression through childhood to maturity. He is extraordinary in his ability to clinically address the schizoid personality – from play with child patients (and adults), to the therapeutic "holding" of deep regressive states with adult analysands.

Winnicott's writings (reminiscent of Fairbairn) do not progress in a scrupulously evolving fashion. Winnicott seems to have set down his ideas somewhat as they came to him. We owe the organization of his work to Masud Khan, his analysand, editor, and to some degree co-author. Khan (reminiscent of Guntrip) was significantly responsible for making his mentor conceptually clear, well-referenced, and well-known. There is no better review of Winnicott's work than Khan's introduction, as editor, to *Through Paediatrics to Psycho-Analysis* (1975) – a labor of love and exacting research.

Winnicott's thinking on the schizoid focuses not so much on clinical description (he was insistent on the privacy of his patients, and therefore avoided casebook examples) as on the developmental and dynamic conditions that promote the disorder. His pediatrician–analyst's observations, over a span of forty years or so, of infants and their mothers, are at the core of his contribution. As early as 1952, he writes: "it is necessary to explore the possibility that mental health in terms of lessened liability to schizoid states … is laid down in the very earliest stages, when the infant is being introduced gradually to external reality" (Winnicott 1952, p. 221). He continues: "Environmental failure … shows clinically so early and so clearly that one can forgive those who (not knowing about infant psychology) explain it in terms of heredity" (p. 226).

Winnicott is speaking of the early months of the infant's life (basically within the first year), when the infant does not yet experience the mother in terms of an object, but rather as a "maternal environment" surrounding, supporting, nourishing, but not yet altogether defined apart from the infant's self (1965, p. 75). Developmentally, at first, "the individual is not the unit," and therefore "The intimate study of a schizoid individual of whatever age becomes an intimate study of that individual's very early development, development within and emerging from the stage of the environment-individual set-up" (1952, p. 222).

This is Winnicott's description of the potential origin of the schizoid personality disorder. The mother, as a nurturing environment, devotedly offers "a sensitive and active adaptation to her infant's needs." In this harmonious situation, the infant "makes a spontaneous movement and the environment is discovered without loss of a sense of self." However, "Faulty adaptation to the child" results in "impingement of the environment, so that the individual must become a reactor to this impingement. The sense of self is lost in this impingement and is only regained by a return to isolation" (1952, pp. 220–222). At this time of development, the self is learning to make a healthy distinction between the inner "reality" of the self, and the outer "reality" of his environment. However, consistent "impingement" creates a defensive split in the self (the meaning of "schizoid"): the "True Self" – the origin of that first spontaneous impulse – goes into hiding, and a "False Self" is formed in compliance with the influence from the maternal environment. This process is frozen into the schizoid style of relating, where a tentative authentic move toward the other produces "loss of the sense of self" (1952, p. 222).

Here, Winnicott not only reinforces Guntrip's description of the schizoid dilemma, but also contributes to the crystallization of the concept of developmental arrest (he refers to this as a "frozen" state). Margaret Mahler's developmental studies, well underway at the time and appreciated by Winnicott, delineate the childhood phase of psychic "separation/individuation," placing this early division of the child's inner and outer worlds in the approximately six- to ten-month "differentiation subphase" (Mahler, Pine, and Bergman 1975).

Winnicott is known for other concepts pertinent to the subject of schizoid personality: the "True" and "False" selves (1965, pp. 140–152); transitional space with its occupant transitional object (1975, pp. 229–242); the importance of creative play (1965, p. 185), and the clinically challenging "regression to dependence" that strives to reinstate the "True Self." These concepts relate importantly to the mother–infant relationship in the first year of the infant's life, and are based on literally thousands of mother–infant observations within Winnicott's practice as a pediatrician and medical director at Paddington Green Hospital.

The "True Self," Winnicott writes, is essentially unknowable, but is the source of aliveness and creativity in the individual. It first reveals its presence in the infant's "spontaneous gesture" that becomes "a living reality" when met with the mother's "facilitating" response. In this maternal "holding," the mother joins the infant's perception of the world as his own magical creation, something to be discovered with delight and confidence. Winnicott writes that the true self "does no more than collect together the details of the experience of aliveness," and "it cannot become a reality without the mother's specialized relationship." The acknowledging mother's "holding" in effect provides a shaping presence that does not enforce a definition of things, but meets with the infant's curiosity and excitement as he discovers reality in his own terms (1965, pp. 140–152).

When there is "good enough," "devoted" mothering, the infant's true self emerges in the individual's distinctively alive and creative approach to life, rather than hiding behind an accommodating false self – the individual's reactive response to unattuned maternal care.

In *The Real Self* (1985), Masterson compares his concept of the real self with Winnicott's true self, and provides an insight that suggests a useful distinction between the two terms. Quoting Winnicott, "Only the True Self can be creative and feel real," Masterson comments, "I would emphasize that the true or real self has a function in reality as well as feeling real" (p. 22). Masterson makes a good point – there is not a clear description by Winnicott of how a good-enough adaptation of the true self would appear in daily life – that would be both individual and yet in harmony with the environment without becoming false. As even Khan reflects, Winnicott's true self is too idealized (Kahn 1974, p. 303), and Winnicott himself tends to picture the true self as ultimately isolated (more the way it might be described in personality disorder). Winnicott's concept of true self and Masterson's concept of real self seem somewhat complementary, though, as more existential and more relational aspects of the same phenomenon.

In 2000, in a less accommodating mood, Masterson questionably associates the true self with the id, considering Winnicott's "pioneering effort" as based on Freudian drive theory as it predated "modern developmental studies" (p. 61). There is a historical inexactness here, as Winnicott was a significant contributor to the analytic move away from drive theory, at least insofar as it has limited use in the understanding of preoedipal conditions. Winnicott writes: "the instincts are not clearly defined as internal to the infant … Id-excitements can be traumatic when the ego is not yet able to include them" (1965, p. 141). It should also be noted that – far from being unaware of "modern developmental studies" – Winnicott was a contemporary of Spitz, Mahler, and Bowlby, and his minute pediatric observations are a comfortable companion to their more formal studies. (It has also been brought to my attention by my colleague, William Griffith, that Bowlby and Winnicott collaborated on a government-commissioned study of British war orphans.)

In the matter of the "false self," though, Masterson seems to adopt Winnicott's concept into his own nosology. They are in agreement that the false self is a defensive construct originally formed to minimize the psychic pain of having to adjust to maternal misattunement. As the true/real self represents the essence of personality, the false self is the embodiment of the disorder in personality disorder. The false self may even achieve a fairly convincing social accommodation, but will lack the "aliveness" of the true self.

Winnicott's theory of transitional space, and his belief in the importance of play, are additional concepts I find vital in clinical work with the schizoid patient. These ideas, together with his technique of "regression to dependence" – similar to Masterson's working-through of the abandonment depression – will be discussed in the "Annihilation Anxiety and Abandonment Depression" section of this chapter.

In another instance of the baffling "polite disregard" of Winnicott until present time, Ralph Klein does not include Winnicott in his overview of pertinent figures. This is puzzling, given the extensive range of Klein's presentation, and the importance of Winnicott to the subject. Klein does make brief reference to Winnicott, describing the false self concept as adopted by Masterson (1995, p. 124), and referring twice to Winnicott's depiction of annihilation anxiety in the schizoid as: "an inherently terrifying experience similar to the primal agony of falling forever" (1995, pp. 46, 48).

Masud Khan (1924–1989)

As previously mentioned, the accessibility of Winnicott's work is in large part owed to Khan. Additionally, Khan made his own contribution, primarily in *The Privacy of the Self*, where his opening essay (originally published in 1960) is specifically devoted to "Clinical Aspects of the Schizoid

Personality: Affects and Technique" (1974/1996, pp. 13–26). Further, Khan introduces the concept of "cumulative trauma" (pp. 42–58) to explain how subtle maternal misattunement can gain in pathological effect over years beyond the earliest childhood development, foreshadowing Schore's more recent concept of "relational trauma."

Developmental Theory

Margaret Mahler (1897–1985)

Masterson's original developmental, object relations theory of personality disorder relies substantially on Margaret Mahler's studies (researched together with Fred Pine and Anni Bergman) of early mother–child relationship. His highlighting of borderline pathology, by showing its basis in the distortion of the healthy dynamic of the rapprochement subphase of the separation-individuation process, makes sense out of sometimes chaotic patient behavior and provides a rationale for constructive therapeutic intervention. In dealing with narcissistic personality disorder, Masterson initially (like Kohut) incorporates Mahler's work, but then hesitates to follow through as comprehensively as he did with the borderline. In the integration of the schizoid personality disorder to the Masterson Approach, Mahler's model is set aside almost altogether. I believe the omission of Mahler's developmental view is a loss to the understanding of the schizoid and to the fulfillment of Masterson's model of personality disorder. The opportunity is missed for the integration of a truly useful paradigm once integral to the Masterson Approach: the matching of stages of healthy infant development with distortions of personality that arise from the failure to master those same early states. Such matching is highly useful, because it reflects a developmental progression that is clinically informative: technical "language" is matched to the developmental "language" needed to be "heard" in order to communicate with a specific arrest.

One of the saddest, but also most potentially liberating of Freud's discoveries was the realization that mental illness has its origin in the deformation of normal conditions. Seeing the potential to reclaim the normal state – Mahler's growing child – within a disordered personality, not only guides the therapeutic process, but humanizes pathology.

Before going further, it should be stressed that seeing the potentially healthy "inner child" within the adult suffering from developmental arrest is not the same as finding a literal child encapsulated within a grown-up presence. It has more to do with witnessing signs of a potential for liveliness and relatedness that have not been able to find expression in the forming personality at the time of a significant step forward in psychic growth. Developmental arrest, in addition, does not describe an inability to grow past a certain stage of maturation: it refers to varying amounts of success in meeting developmental tasks typical of that stage, with the result that there is some characterological delimitation of personality-building. In order to grow up at all, we have all passed through all the consecutive developmental stages of childhood to a greater or lesser degree of accomplishment. But those who carry with them an overriding "basic fault" (Balint) in a specific area of early development show a personality that embodies that incompleteness.

The schizoid personality disorder characteristically displays difficulty in negotiating interpersonal space because a sense of safe differentiation between and within himself or herself and others has not been securely established. These personalities are commonly recognized by their shyness or aloofness from others. This type nowadays is commonly caricatured as a socially withdrawn gameboard player or computer "nerd," whose detachment is a subject of perplexity and amusement. Popular mythology, I suspect, would not hesitate in agreeing with Winnicott that the asocial behavior of the schizoid indicates a serious issue with the "environment-individual set-up" (1975, p. 222).

There is a consensus among the analysts who originally concerned themselves with the schizoid, that the withdrawn nature of this personality is related to an equally detached or unattuned relationship with the mother in early infancy. Mahler's description of the differentiation subphase of separation-individuation (Mahler et al. 1975, pp. 52–64), by demonstrating what goes right, illuminates what can go wrong at that crucial time of infant–mother attachment – around six to ten months of age.

According to Mahler and her colleagues, the differentiating infant emerges from a harmonious undifferentiated state with mother – undergoing a necessary transition from the total dependency of the womb to preparation for the infant's increasing defining of a physical, together with psychic, sense of separate being. The differentiation process is reliant on the mother's provision of a consistent, secure base (Bowlby), minutely sensitive to the infant's tentative oscillation between the reassurance of closeness, and the growing curiosity, increasing perception and motility that draws him or her apart from her. The mother will navigate a similar transitional state along with her infant as she will, to some degree, throughout the subsequent formative stages. But here she must be both guide and participant in the initial birthing process of the psyche, as critical to future psychic growth as the actual physical birth is to the subsequent bodily growth of the child.

In the first three or four months of life, the infant requires a near-oneness with the mother, but as differentiation begins the mother must be sensitive to her infant's increasing need to "discover" the world while remaining confident and safely supported. This requires a fine-tuned attentiveness on the mother's part, which may be compromised by her excessive possessiveness – or, conversely, neglect – distraction, or inconsistency. (The attachment styles observed by Bowlby, Ainsworth, and Main are pertinent here, as well.)

If all goes well, though, the infant begins to bring into focus a sense of things, discernible in what Mahler calls "the hatched look" – "a certain new look of alertness, persistence and goal-directedness" (Mahler et al. 1975, p. 54). This leads to a minute exploration of the mother, and eventually of others. In time, the infant's adventuresome discovery of a differentiated, safe environment outside the self (and the establishment of its inner representation) will support the confident moving away from mother.

It seems that, in order to differentiate the sense of self from the sense of other (from not-self, or maternal environment), it is necessary for the infant to establish a feeling of security in both locations. The balance is delicate, and the mother's reception of the situation significantly affects the outcome. It is not so much a matter of a decisive event so much as a sequence of missed opportunities that begins to establish a maladaptive pattern. Mahler et al. refer to Khan's concept of "cumulative trauma" (1975, pp. 45, 87, 119), as taking part in this "developmental" effect: "These early differentiation patterns … seem to set in motion patterns of personality organization which seem to remain consistent in the further development of the separation-individuation process and possibly beyond" (1975, p. 60). In my clinical experience, these observations of Mahler's illuminate psychotherapy with the schizoid in a way that makes an often perplexing initial encounter meaningful, and provides an important guide for a therapeutic approach.

To begin with, the first contact with the schizoid patient tends to be a notably "unhatched" interpersonal standoff. The therapist's attempts to make therapeutic contact, especially of an emotional sort, encounter a discouraging lack of response: the patient replies in a flattened, detached way, or is avoidant or withdrawn. An expected level of interpersonal energy seems missing, and an apparently mutual feeling of frustration or even futility sets in (this may be a predominating transference/counter-transference situation with the schizoid patient).

However, if one keeps in mind Guntrip's "schizoid dilemma," together with Mahler's differentiating infant, one may hypothesize that the therapist is experiencing with the patient a repetition of that frozen moment in development when persistent maternal misattunement has led to an impasse in the infant – namely, when the need for self-expression, but anxious concern with the mother's response become irreconcilable. This is an impasse that neither the infant nor the patient can resolve alone. The dilemma that might have been worked out, should the mother have learned to adopt a securely attuned "holding," waits for a new opportunity in the therapeutic situation.

Because this early developmental arrest has become an established personality pattern, and because it protects the infant's core sense of being (Winnicott's "true self"), the patient retains a guarded distance from any possible "impingement" (Winnicott) by the psychotherapist. This continues until the therapist's neutrally concerned response (more non-verbal than otherwise) begins to suggest to the patient that the therapeutic environment may be a place of safe "holding." Establishing this base requires considerable patience on the therapist's part – but a special kind of patience that offsets boredom and frustration with genuine interest in understanding the individual (the difference is quickly sensed by the schizoid). This approach, important throughout the work, is essential to beginning psychotherapy with the schizoid patient, and will be further discussed.

Sooner or later, and related to the degree of the sense of safety felt by the patient (Ralph Klein's emphasis on safety cannot be overemphasized), the patient will tentatively offer some opening to the restricted area of interpersonal possibility that is the equivalent of Winnicott's "transitional space." In this place, the patient is willing to describe, with increasing detail, an area of subjective interest that can be shared with the therapist. The topic may at first seem inconsequential, but it concerns a subject of possible common interest that the patient feels confident enough to offer for mutual consideration, as long as the patient's point of view is the one maintained. This offers a potential bridge (transition) between the patient's inner world and the therapist's outer reality, but only if the therapist can "enter" this safe place on the patient's terms. Superimposition of the therapist's subjectivity closes off the attempt.

Although the psychotherapist experiences a degree of tension in maintaining exclusive other-directed attentiveness to detailed accounts of another's favorite intellectual/creative pursuits, ideas, activities, hobbies, and so on, the wait is well worth it. In this subtle collaboration, where the patient "takes charge" of the therapeutic process in his or her own way, the therapist discovers where the "hatched look" has been hiding. Able to describe his or her special interests unimpeded, but in the other's interested and acknowledging presence, the patient reveals that "certain new look of alertness, persistence and goal-directedness" that had been protectively walled off long ago: the original "spontaneous gesture" that was frustrated by a consistently "impinging" response from the mother.

This is the beginning of the therapeutic restoration of the essential mother–infant synchrony – an equivalent of the vital right-hemispheric mutuality later described by Allan Schore (2014), which is crucial to neural growth and essential to facilitating the therapeutic "rebirth" of the patient's psyche. This is the discovery of the self in the reflection in the other, and the reciprocal interchange that allows the self to continue building on the other's ongoing reception of this very continuity: Winnicott's "holding," Mahler's "mutual cueing," Lacan's "mirror stage," Bateson's "positive feedback loop," the origin of Fonagy's "mentalization." This attunement allows the encouraging and shaping of the curious, adventuresome, resourceful expression of the self into a unique sense of being in a widening world of discovery and relationship.

Daniel N. Stern (1934–2012)

In maintaining the "developmental" element of the "developmental, self, and object relations" definition of the Masterson Approach, Ralph Klein chooses to follow the model proposed by Daniel Stern over the model set forth by Mahler and her colleagues, Pine and Bergman – the study that has been basic to Masterson's theorizing and clinical formulation. It is not

altogether clear why this is necessary, as Stern himself finds commonality with Mahler's actual observations of behavior, while presenting his
different perspective on the hypothesized inner dynamic. Stern is concerned with the "organizing principle" of the "self," at work throughout
the lifespan as much as concentrated in "age specific" stages (1985, p. 12),
a shift that seems to a degree more complementary than oppositional to
Mahler's view. Klein's choice seems counter to the synthesizing nature of
the Masterson Approach and, indeed, Masterson will eventually include
both Mahler and Stern within the neurobiological/analytical framework
provided by Allan Schore (2005, pp. 4–5, 9–11).

Stern and Mahler, despite differences, represent a mutual belief
that early childhood entertains a lively and creative psychic process,
both subjective and collaborative, that supports a lifetime "on-the-
way" journey to self and object constancy (Mahler). As Stern says: "The
developmental account described in this book … is closest to the accounts
of [Melanie] Klein and Mahler in that its central concern, like theirs, is
for the infant's experience of self and other" (1985, p. 19). Although Stern
and Mahler diverge in emphasis, their fundamental difference seems
based on complementary perceptions of similar phenomena: Mahler's
work is harmonious with that of the independent object relationists and
is focused on mother–child interaction primarily in the first three years
of life; Stern's work is viewed through the lens of self psychology and
is centered on the shaping power of the ever-evolving "domains" of self
throughout all our years. Both make an affirmative presentation of our
capacity to be in charge of our own destiny, which is reassuring in a field
that tends to be dominated by the pathological view.

A few points of difference between Stern and Mahler are pertinent to
dynamic understanding of the schizoid.

The first relates to Stern's rejection of Mahler's "normal autistic" and
"symbiotic" phases of infant development (equivalent to Stern's "emer-
gent" sense of self) that occupy the initial few months of life before the
start of Stern's time of "core relatedness" and Mahler's "differentiation
subphase" (the beginning of the "separation-individuation phase"). Stern
does not accept an undifferentiated period of self preceding differentiation. However, in the exchange between them noted by Stern, Mahler
herself has second thoughts about her use of terms so absolute and suggestive of pathology: "In a recent discussion, she suggested that this initial phase might well have been called 'awakening,' which is very close to

'emergence' as it has been called here [Mahler, personal communication 1983]" (Stern 1985, p. 235).

How much is semantics, how much an arguable degree of distinction when observing the infant's barely extrauterine state? And how about the intrauterine state itself – does the unborn child already know the mother's voice? It might be simpler to not try to too closely define the beginning of a sense of self at this stage of our knowledge (possibly if ever). Is the sense of self created by the differentiation process itself, or is the sense of self already immanent and the *source* of the differentiation process? This may be one of those endless paradoxical debates favored by schizoid thinking, but it was important to Fairbairn, and to Glover before him, who proposed that the sense of self is first integrated from subselves (Fairbairn) or "ego nuclei" (Glover), an inquiry that appears to be forming again in current concepts of "self-states" (Donnel Stern, Philip Bromberg, Frank Putnam).

Be that as it may, except for the pertinence to Fairbairn's theory, the Stern/Mahler divergence concerning the first few months of infant development may be somewhat beside the point in considering a developmental base for schizoid personality disorder proper in the remaining months of the first year of life.

A second point of divergence between Stern and Mahler relates to the larger part of the infant's first year – a time critical to the origin of schizoid disorder, as defined by the British object relationists. Both Stern and Mahler seem essentially in agreement once observation of infant–mother interreactiveness becomes more distinctly visible to the observer himself or herself. The developmental period of (roughly) from about four to ten months of age is more or less equivalent to Stern's time of "core relatedness" and Mahler's "differentiation." (Both theoreticians would agree that human development is subject to individual time frames. Furthermore, even these relative time frames overlap with adjacent periods of development, as well – notably Stern's "intersubjective" domain and Mahler's "practicing" subphase). What significant maturational accomplishments are achieved during this time do not seem basic to the divergency of theory here. Mahler tends more to categorize and highlight the interplay between mother and child, while Stern maintains a focus on the infant's increasing sense of self, but they both appear to be watching the same baby and mother.

Stern acknowledges the observable psychic stages of early growing up: "Development occurs in leaps and bounds; qualitative shifts may be one of its most obvious features … At each of these major shifts, infants create a forceful impression that major changes have occurred in their subjective experience of self and other. One is suddenly dealing with an altered person" (1985, p. 8). Additionally, Stern acknowledges that human psychic growth has been understood in terms of "organizing principles" (libidinal phases, ego adaptability, evolving inner and outer object relations), but adds: "They are all right, and that is both the problem and the point." The "point" for Stern is the need to include these categories within one fundamental overview: "the sense of self as the primary organizing principle" (1985, p. 26).

With more recent neurobiological findings in hand, it would seem that the Stern/Mahler difference in emphasis is just that. During the first year of life, infant and mother are to a meaningful extent reciprocal life-systems, both physically and psychically. More than the conclusions of either Stern or Mahler, Winnicott's perceptions – based on pediatric experience, analytic training, and extraordinary intuition – come the closest to the dream of Freud, the once-neurologist. Now, with the help of continuing neurobiological findings, Freud's hope for a truly "scientific" knowledge of mental processes is taking shape. It appears that, in the first year of life, there is still a mind–body oneness between mother and infant that can be "scientifically" proposed: a right-hemisphere brain synchrony essential to the infant's neuronal increase and cortical growth. The mother is the auxiliary psyche for the infant at this time of the infant's coming-into-being (Schore).

In another point of disagreement with Mahler, Stern takes issue with the location of the origin of pathology within "age-specific sensitive periods" of childhood, and rather finds pathology as having its start in relation to "various domains of life experience" as they recur at different times over the lifespan (1985, p. 12). He writes that "Development is not a succession of events left behind in history. It is a continuing process, constantly updated." He argues that the onset of pathology may sometimes relate to a later "narrative point of origin," or result from the buildup of "cumulative interactive patterns" (p. 261). Again, this seems to be a somewhat arbitrary emphasis. Mahler's categories are not absolute; specifically, the last subphase of separation-individuation, "on-the-way-to-object-constancy," is left open-ended as a task to be pursued throughout life: "It is dependent on the context of many other developmental factors" (Mahler et al. 1975, p. 112). Additionally, Masud Khan's concept of "cumulative trauma" supports the idea of the destructiveness of the persistence of relational stress throughout early life (Khan 1974/1996, pp. 42–58, later echoed in Schore's concept of "relational trauma," 2009). Nonetheless, one wonders whether failure to sufficiently meet early developmental tasks may not establish a fundamental weakness (à la Balint and Fairbairn) that creates a special vulnerability to later psychic stress. As Mahler writes: "old conflicts [over separation and separateness] can be reactivated (or can remain peripherally or even centrally active) at any and all stages of life." But it is "the original infantile process, not the new eliciting events or situations," that is the underlying factor (1975, pp. 4–5).

Is Stern arguing that predominant personality patterns are not necessarily set down in the early "formative" years? This would seem to run counter to accepted thinking, and certainly contradict the foundation of Masterson's teaching. It seems more likely that Stern is advocating "greater freedom in therapeutic exploration" where we do not rigidly limit a set diagnosis to a single point in the patient's "narrative" (Stern 1985, p. 12). The "fate" element of Masterson's "nature, nurture and fate" assumes a greater potential the longer the patient lives and – equally relevant – it is the nature of the self to remain subject to change. This accessibility may leave us open to damage, but also gives us access to the reparative possibilities of relationship – notably the therapeutic relationship.

Ralph Klein, in favoring Stern over Mahler, addresses the "spectrum" question. He writes: "Is the concept of developmental levels a prerequisite to the concept of a spectrum or range of pathology? The answer is *No*. An equally suitable explanation is one that utilizes a multifactorial contribution to the clinical manifestation of psychopathology" (Klein 1995, p. 42, italics in original). This seems unnecessarily absolute, and perhaps even somewhat self-contradictory. A reasonable unwillingness to see one element as the total explanation of a complex situation might not necessarily eliminate that element as a useful partial contribution to understanding the whole.

The Masterson Approach began with a correlation between a degree of arrest in a specific developmental stage and a specific pathological outcome, as manifested in borderline personality disorder. Later, the Masterson Approach followed Kohut's lead in extending the explanation of narcissistic personality disorder to an earlier phase in Mahler's paradigm. The differences in the levels of developmental arrest not only clarified the difference in dynamic between the borderline and the narcissist, but dictated a crucial variation in technique, necessitating a more empathic approach to the more structurally fragile narcissist. Although this "spectrum" approach has not been explicitly applied to clinical work with the schizoid disorder of the self, it is abundantly clear in Klein's own case examples that the schizoid patient requires a delicacy of approach that finds even "empathic" interventions emotionally intrusive (1995, p. 79), and suggests a still earlier developmental orientation.

Developmental arrest – seen as part of a spectrum or otherwise – is itself an incomplete answer: it is only one clue (although an important one) to a multidimensional problem. Arrest does not stop development in its tracks, but gives coloration to a predominating coping (or non-coping) relational style that must be considered in our interventions if initial therapeutic communication is to be established. As the therapeutic work progresses, we may even discover that later developmental phases in the patient's childhood may have introduced new therapeutic issues for the treatment (or may even have eased the situation – the acquisition of language at the rapprochement subphase is probably of great help to the intellectually defended schizoid). There is no question that overall development (in the therapeutic process as well as in childhood) is more complicated than some lockstep forward.

Baby steps, however, are the basis of walking, even for long-distance runners. A spectrum approach utilizing developmental theory offers one entrance and guide to the complex treatment of personality disorder. This volume will expand on this hypothesis, leaving for now a brief restatement of this writer's conviction that Mahler's developmental paradigm, including its progressive pattern, is invaluable to the Masterson Approach, including psychotherapy of the schizoid.

Intrapsychic Structures and Clinical Considerations

Ralph Klein describes the dynamics of the schizoid personality disorder in careful detail, and with a poignancy that touches the intensity of suffering at the hidden core of the condition.

Klein sees the schizoid as uniquely different from both the narcissist and the borderline, whose issue is with the nature of relationship:

the schizoid is concerned as to whether there is hope for relationship at all (1995, p. 46). For the schizoid, he says, "the subjective experience of many, if not most … is that their efforts at relatedness were of no avail and encountered either indifference or neglect." The family experience of the schizoid "is of being a dehumanized, depersonified function that can be called upon to serve a purpose … until another service or function is required" (1995, p. 47). In this way, the schizoid learns to adopt a utilitarian existence, devoid of a sense of self-value and affect (p. 48).

Perhaps unexpectedly, Klein uses Winnicott's language in referring to the way in which this superficial persona is formed: "True connecting, interfacing, and sharing are replaced by impingements and reactions to impingements." The failure of "parental" receptiveness necessitates replacement of the child's authentic outreach with a compliant reaction devoid of spontaneity. Then, explicitly referring to Winnicott, Klein describes the "primitive agony" and "complete isolation" that, for the schizoid beyond other personality disorders, "carries with it the most profound potential experience of despair" (1995, p. 46).

Maternal Influence

Despite this significant level of agreement, there is a point of divergency that appears to divide Ralph Klein's concept of schizoid dynamics from that of the independent object relationists. Klein describes the child's inability to find receptive validation from the "parents," suggesting he may take opposition to the conviction of Fairbairn and his colleagues, that it is the lack of the mother's reciprocity in the infant's first year of life – a time when the mother is essentially indistinguishable from the source of survival – that originates the pattern for later schizoid disorder. It is not clear whether Klein intends a qualitative, either/or distinction here, questioning (as does Stern) the exclusivity of time-specific origins of pathology. Is he departing from the definitive premise of the Masterson Approach that failure of early, loving maternal availability is the foundation of personality disorder in general? There would seem to be room for various contributions to the "multifactorial" human problem of personality disorder. Cumulative contributing family relations can surely reinforce (or modify) the formative mother–child relationship. Klein's rejection of Mahler, however, including her study of the differentiation subphase (which is analogous to the infant's first year of self-definition so important to Fairbairn and Winnicott), would seem to suggest this is a point of theoretical divergence. If Klein intends this apparent theoretical shift, it is too basic to the Masterson Approach to be left so ambiguous.

To a significant degree, this developmental "debate" has become moot now that increasing neurobiological findings are available (Schore's conclusions were roughly contemporaneous with R. Klein's writings, and barely had had time for consideration – Schore's name is not in the index of the 1995 volume that contains Klein's chapters on the schizoid). In 2005, in Masterson's *The Personality Disorders Through the Lens of Attachment Theory and the Neurobiologic Development of the Self*, the work of Mahler is reinstated, along with Stern and Mahler's contemporary, Bowlby, as complementary perspectives on the crucial importance of the early mother–infant relationship sustainable within the context of brain science. Winnicott's famous (once notorious) assertion that "there is no such thing as a baby [only a baby and a mother]!" (1975, p. 99) has found support in Allan Schore's assertion that "the self-organization of the developing brain occurs in the context of a relationship with another self, another brain" – specifically within the right hemisphere to right hemisphere synchrony between the mother and infant in the first year of human life (2009, pp. 189–203). The findings of Schore and others not only support the Mastersonian contention that personality disorder arises from lack of early maternal libidinal availability, but seem to substantially confirm the contention, from Melanie Klein to the relational analysts, that mental health has its vital beginnings in the preoedipal years as well as in the oedipal phase of life.

Annihilation Anxiety and Abandonment Depression

Schizoid "annihilation anxiety" appears to qualify as a specialized form of Mastersonian "abandonment depression" – a term applicable to all types of personality disorder. In Ralph Klein's definition, abandonment depression is "an umbrella term that includes all the particular dysphoric affect states associated with the experience of nonattachment or of inter-ruptions in attachment" (1995, p. 58). In the case of the schizoid, it is the persistence of a terrifying fear of nonexistence. As Klein says, this sense of estrangement "results from the experience of having to forgo one's real self and … having to live reactively, responding to the needs, expectations and impingements of others" (1995, p. 58). This seems much in keeping with Winnicott's description of annihilation anxiety, where the mother's failure to provide "a good enough adaptation to need" creates an inadequate "holding" that interrupts the sense of "going on being" of the infant, and leads to "a *threat of annihilation* … a very real primitive anxiety, long antedating any anxiety that includes the word death in its description" (1965, p. 303, italics in original).

Klein equates this existential state either with the extreme of isolated withdrawal (1995, p. 58), or with an "annihilating" sense of "appropriation by the other" (p. 60) brought on by closeness. Attempts to seek refuge from annihilation anxiety, in either isolation or companionship, fail as defensive resorts because withdrawal into seclusion triggers fantasies/memories of loss of the source of survival, while drawing too close to another cues fantasies/memories of engulfment. Neither alternative provides safety and leads to the "schizoid dilemma" described by Guntrip. For the schizoid, there appears no safe place to *be*, or, as Klein says, "of having no choice, of being presented with no options" (1995, p. 58).

The therapeutic resolution lies in the patient's ability to face the terror underlying any attempt to *be*: the dreaded possibility that one is not even there to begin with. As Winnicott says, the patient must face that experience of the "freezing of the failure situation" (1975, p. 281), when the true self was denied and developed a false façade in order to maintain psychic survival. Winnicott devised a challenging (even controversial) technique – "regression to dependence" – to reclaim the true self. In this process, the patient releases the defensive false self and allows the spontaneous emergence of the true self. This procedure relies on the establishment of sufficient rapport with the analyst to "hold" the analysand through the devastating sense of near loss of being that was traumatically ingrained when the true self of the infant attempted its first "spontaneous gesture," and found no validation. Winnicott's description of this therapeutically managed uncovering explicitly defines a trauma mechanism: "*the fear of breakdown that has already been experienced*. It is the fear of the initial agony which caused the defense organization which the patient displays as an illness syndrome" (1975, p. xxxv). However, it remains for the patient to have gained the strength to act on the conviction of self-belief sufficiently to overcome traumatic fear and establish a new belief in the rebirth of the self.

It should be clarified that it is not dependency itself that is considered painful. It is the fear of failure to have that dependency safely met and held that is terrifying: the traumatic experience. Dependency itself, when met, is probably one of the best places to be, as observation of any well-fed, cradled, dozing infant will attest.

Fantasy

The fantasy considered here is not Melanie Klein's "phantasy" – an unconscious phenomenon that shapes the conscious in unaware ways. It is in great part the conscious, creative construction of a subjective world, of imaginary characters, scenarios, and activities that enliven the patient's personal reality. It is the partially successful attempt to offset loneliness with make-believe.

Ralph Klein offers a variety of examples of schizoid patients immersed in fantasy. He writes: "In the life of the schizoid patient, fantasy is extraordinarily important … It is a prime example of a schizoid compromise." Klein refers to schizoid fantasy as "relationship by proxy" – of connectedness, but to an object within a safe, inside world (1995, p. 64). This fantasy life is protectively hidden, a place of "substitute relationship" that serves as a defense to be relinquished as the treatment progresses (pp. 66–67).

In my clinical observation, schizoid fantasy can be more than a static place of hiding. Fantasy can act as a sort of trial run: a way of trying out varying approaches to relationship within the safety of personal imagination before venturing into a wider territory. I suspect that the schizoid's retreat into fantasy may actually represent a "frozen" arrest of the developmental phenomenon Winnicott has described as "transitional space".

Transitional space, according to Winnicott, comes into being more or less at four to twelve months of life (1975, p. 232). It is "an intermediate area of *experiencing*." It is "an intermediate state between a baby's inability and growing ability to recognise and accept reality" and exists "as a resting place for the individual engaged in the perpetual human task of keeping inner and outer reality separate and inter-related" (p. 230).

Winnicott is clear that transitional space originates with "the stage of the environment-individual set-up" (1975, p. 222), and the management of transitional space is crucial to the first major task of psychic development: the differentiation of inner and outer reality (or self from environment). The infant's "illusion" of control that is gained in transitional space (by means of play with the transitional object) will extend to a sense of confidence and curiosity in exploring the greater environment and discovering the further differentiation of things.

The mother's emotional synchrony with her infant facilitates this first great achievement of differentiation. Without the devoted attunement with the "environment mother," there is a potential for a freezing, or arrest, that compromises the very transitional nature of this state.

Although the schizoid personality disorder is a stable condition, and the person has been able to establish a sense of self separate from outer reality, there is a feeling of profound insecurity about the situation. The healthy self-confidence and worldly capability that would have formed out of spontaneous inquiry and playfulness maternally "held" has become tentative and apprehensive. There persists a degree of doubt as to whether inside and outside reality can stay reliably distinguished from each other or, conversely, whether there is much likelihood of a successful meeting of the two. Fundamentally, there is a sense of vulnerability about the self, leading to Ralph Klein's emphasis on the schizoid's need for safety and Masterson's identification of the schizoid's core feeling of danger.

Schizoid fantasy, I hypothesize, represents an arrested form of the use of transitional space as a retreat to imaginary relationship "by proxy" (Klein) in the safety of the patient's private world. When the schizoid is joined in that region, the possibility of a synchronized sense of relationship can be established. The patient's protected aliveness is acknowledged and, especially through mutual therapeutic playfulness, the transitional process is revitalized. Winnicott's concepts of transitional space and creative play offer an understanding of schizoid fantasy that may serve as an entrance to the therapeutic alliance with the schizoid patient.

As Ralph Klein points out, the schizoid is shy or reluctant to reveal his or her subjective world to the therapist. This world may be mentioned at first in a casual, even tangential-seeming way; it is up to the therapist to show the interest that will facilitate the emergence of the aliveness that has been protectively hidden. This personal world may be represented by reverie, or more realistic interests, hobbies, ideas, convictions – varied subjects, but sharing the potential commonality of interest, of elements drawn from both inner and outer reality, and invariably held under the patient's maximal jurisdiction.

The psychotherapist's ability to enter this interpsychic space is dependent on the therapist's willingness to respect the role of facilitator. This means to join the patient's psychic investment without attempting to impose a different point of view upon it, including criticism, qualification, and interpretation. This, I believe, is the therapeutic equivalent of the original transitional space, where the early self gained a beginning sense of mastery and confidence to move forward. In my experience, the schizoid patient will not see the therapist's facilitation as a collusion with pathology, but as the beginning of permission to *be* in a safe environment, and to advance to a more experimental approach to outer reality. Confirmation of this hypothesis is to be found in a quality of playfulness that develops in the alliance, and in the (very) gradual extension of the patient's confidence to a wider range of relationship. Eventually, the treatment will assume a more traditional form, although (I have noticed) the patient will retain a preference for being the one to formulate the interpretations.

Internalized Object Relations

This is a theoretical area that continues open to debate, especially since the timeline of infantile object relations development has been confused by Melanie Klein's arbitrary reduction of all preoedipal change to within the first year of life. As Kernberg reflects:

> *Both Klein and Fairbairn had important contributions to make to the understanding of the connections between preoedipal and oedipal conflicts, but, because of the strange telescoping of development into the earliest months of life, both missed the boat. Winnicott avoided the collapse of early developmental stages. He assumed an earliest stage of undifferentiation (predating self and object differentiation) and described the pathology of early differentiation as related to excessive intrusion or impingement by mother with the subsequent consolidation of a "false self."*

> (Kernberg 1994, p. 62)

According to Winnicott, in the first year of the infant's life (Mahler's differentiation subphase of separation-individuation), the ego/self consists of "motor and sensory elements" somewhat similar to Glover's "ego nuclei" (Winnicott 1975, p. 225). He continues to say that "the establishment of a unit self" is reliant on "good-enough ego-coverage by the mother … [which] enables the new human person to build up a personality on the pattern of a continuity of going-on-being." "The mother's failure to provide this consistent "holding" "sets going a pattern of fragmentation of being" (Winnicott 1965, pp. 60–61). When the baby "misses good-enough care," a unitary sense of self is lost, and "a caretaker self that is false … designed to hide and protect [the] core of the self," is split off (Ogden 1965, p. 58).

Fairbairn's concept of the early infantile origin of the schizoid personality is similar to Winnicott's. As Ogden describes it: "To the extent that the 'fit' between mother and infant is lacking, the infant experiences an intolerable feeling of disconnectedness and defends himself by means of splitting off the aspects of the ego which were felt to be unacceptable to the mother" (1994, p. 93).

Both Fairbairn and Winnicott are describing a pathological distortion in the first great differentiation in Mahler's differentiation subphase. This differentiation involves a normal division of the infant's perception of inner and outer reality. When the individual succeeds in making the division in a healthy way, a genuine sense of self is maintained as spontaneous and safe in both locations. However, when the indispensable "outside" (Winnicott's "environment mother") is perceived as unfavorable, compliant adjustment must be made for survival's sake, and the lively impulsiveness of the self must be protectively hidden in the inner world. As a result, reciprocity is lost, the self is split, fantasy is overvalued, and both inner and outer situations acquire a sense of unreality.

It is on this uncertain base that the next major differentiation is made: the distinction between self and other and associated affects. As the "environment mother" becomes the "object mother" (Winnicott), pleasant and unpleasant sensations are perceived as associated with her and her connection to the infant's self. The distinct good/bad division of the psychic world will not be fully formed and ready for resolution until Mahler's rapprochement subphase (fifteen to twenty-four months of age).

Dynamic Psychotherapy

Ralph Klein (1995, pp. 69–142) devotes three chapters to clinical work with the schizoid patient. These chapters offer a detailed examination, deeply felt and extensively illustrated. They form a hands-on study-within-the-study that amply repays a close reading by the therapist.

"Establishing a Therapeutic Alliance" (Klein 1995, pp. 69–94)

The first of these clinically focused chapters is perhaps the most critical for work with the schizoid patient, for whom the concept of alliance itself is the central issue.

Klein begins by affirming that therapeutic neutrality is both foundation and core of the Masterson Approach (1995, p. 69). He is particularly careful in defining "neutrality" in regard to the schizoid patient. Although "Therapeutic neutrality is not a dispassionate position," the feelings of the therapist must be kept in alignment with the emotional requirements of the patient. Klein's description of therapeutic neutrality with the schizoid is the therapeutic equivalent of Winnicott's "facilitating environment": "The schizoid patient has to know where the therapist stands, and the only place where the therapist can stand that feels safe to the patient before a therapeutic alliance is established is at a safe distance, one that is predictable, stable, and nonintrusive" (p. 70). Klein presents a therapeutic approach parallel to Winnicott's (and, later, Schore's) description of early maternal attunement that provides the "holding" conditions that "facilitate" the emergence of the infant's "true" (or "real" – Masterson) sense of self.

The therapeutic hazard, especially at this early phase of treatment, is that the hypervigilant schizoid patient will sense the therapist's (however well-intentioned) attempts to shape the patient's thinking/feeling, and will become falsely compliant or withdrawn, a defensive retreat to transference acting out. It is only when the therapist is calmly and consistently devoted to *understanding* the patient that the schizoid patient may begin to consider the possible *safety* of an almost nonverbal alliance.

In this chapter, Ralph Klein emphasizes the need to respect the patient's silences as an aspect of communication: the therapist needs to wait to learn where the silence may lead, rather than trying to shape it on the basis of the therapist's concern (1995, p. 76). Since even good rules are not always absolute, I might add that, during the patient's silence, when I have occasionally wondered if my own words might be useful, I have first asked, "Is it all right if I mention something that occurs to me, or would that be interrupting?" A basic guide for myself is that the patient must feel in charge of the communication that forms the relationship.

This chapter is rich in descriptive detail and clinical example of therapeutic technique, especially in regard to the heavily characterological nature of this opening phase. As Klein says, the patient's dynamic leads to a vigilant defense against "the fear of being manipulated and controlled" (1995, p. 77). He underscores the importance of avoiding "elaborate or genetically based" interpretations, which tend to be perceived as intrusive. Instead, he describes the therapist's presentations of "explanations, almost narratives, of what I imagined her experience of me to be." Further:

> *I would not make these interpretations as declarative statements but would mold the observations into the form of a question or a hypothesis to be tested. For example, I might say, "It seems to me that …" or "Could it be that …?" Or "My understanding of what you are saying is …" The emphasis was on conveying to the patient that the therapist had no specific agenda, let alone interpretation, to impose or that the patient was expected to accept.*
>
> (Klein 1995, p. 78)

Klein's clinical approach with the schizoid is respectful of the patient's need for a sense of safety based on careful pacing and an optimal sense of closeness/distance on the part of the therapist. He lists three elements that should be considered as part of an intervention: "(1) not declarative; (2) not affect defining, except in the broadest terms of anxiety and danger; and (3) referential to one part of the schizoid dilemma – being too close [or distant] for comfort" (1995, p. 79).

The chapter is concerned in detail with the addressing of Guntrip's concepts of the schizoid dilemma, the schizoid compromise, and Masterson's transference–countertransference acting out. The guidelines Klein offers and fully illustrates answer the need in the literature for more specifically described patient–therapist clinical interaction with the schizoid.

"Shorter-term Treatment" and "Intensive, Long-term Psychotherapy" (Klein 1995, pp. 95–122)

My reference to these chapters will be limited, for, as in the case of the previous chapter on the therapeutic alliance, this ground-breaking and extensively illustrated work deserves its own first-hand attention. Klein's clinical chapters provide a handbook for psychotherapy with the schizoid personality.

Briefly, shorter-term therapy focuses on character work: the therapeutic aligning of a more adaptive self based on increasing self-awareness and expression within the context of an enabling therapeutic relationship.

Intensive, long-term therapy is a dynamic, reparative process. This endeavor involves the schizoid patient's ability to face the primal anxiety of nonrelatedness – the abandonment depression (Masterson) – within a strengthened sense of self, and within a "safe" therapeutic relationship. The resolution of the traumatic block to successful mastering of an early developmental task allows the patient to accept "a fundamental, internal need for relatedness" (Klein 1995, p. 127), together with the belief that it is possible to express that need and have it met.

This is challenging work. It involves restructuring – actually rebirth (Balint) – of the self, a process that would seem to earn the designation of psychoanalytic.

Conclusion

Formal recognition of the schizoid personality disorder and its dynamic therapeutic treatment has been too long in coming. Masud Khan's declaration, in 1959, takes on a somewhat ironic coloration when one considers the span of time between then and the Masterson/Klein volume in 1995:

> *Historically speaking this type of patient has gradually articulated himself into clinical focus from the diffuse mass of syndromes that were and are designated by the term "borderline cases" … It is important, however, … to isolate this new type of case and give it the clinical status of existing in its own right.*

> (Khan 1974/1996, p. 13)

The inclusion of the schizoid disorder of the self within the Masterson Approach, brought about by Ralph Klein's essential contribution – a book in itself – rounds out Masterson's perspective on personality disorder as the dysfunctional acting out of early developmental arrest in present-time relationship. Klein's contribution, clinically strong, is theoretically weakened by the elimination, or near elimination, of the work of Winnicott, Khan, Mahler, and others, but, as I hope I have demonstrated here, the incorporation of their theorizing strengthens Klein and Masterson's claim for the schizoid disorder of the self as "a third major dimension of [personality] psychopathology."

It again should be noted that Klein's introduction of the schizoid appears in the mid-1990s, just as theories of the self and attachment are on the verge of finding new persuasiveness in neurobiology. The interpersonal subtlety of his presentation prepares the way for the next phase of the Masterson Approach, which explores the development and clinical importance of mental synchronicity between self and other.

Masterson's later inclusion of Schore's writings is a typical Mastersonian synthesizing of points of view that importantly integrates Winnicott's pediatrics with neurobiological findings, and re-includes Mahler's developmental studies. This once more opens the possibility (implied in Masterson's studies of the borderline and the narcissist) of a connection between developmental arrest in early childhood and the origin of specific types of personality disorder. Exploration of the dynamics of the schizoid, compared with the observations of Mahler, Pine, and Bergman, strongly suggest a correlation of the emergence of the true/real self (the central issue for the schizoid) with the first major developmental task of the differentiation subphase of separation-individuation. Masterson's final book, once more in collaboration with his associates (2005), is devoted to the increasingly scientific basis for understanding the development of the child's self in mental synchronicity with the mature self of the other, and includes extended consideration of attachment theory and "mentalization" by Fonagy, Gergeley, Jurist, and Target. It is my hope to further explore the correlation between unmet developmental tasks and specific types of personality disorder as fulfillment of the original intention of the Masterson Approach.

CASE STUDY

The Differentiating Schizoid – Clinical Considerations

It would seem that a return to Masterson's original developmental-object relations model is more relevant than ever. Integration of Mahler's differentiation subphase with theory regarding the schizoid as defined by the independent object relationists holds promise and is neurobiologically supported. I believe that Masterson's original model, which is so pertinent to work with the borderline and narcissist, can be equally effective in guiding understanding of the schizoid, and to the refining of clinical technique (including respect for the nonverbal) with this most exacting and hypersensitive of the personality disorders. Masterson would have found this important clinical speculation reinforced by Winnicott:

> It is interesting to examine the nature of the relationship of the infant to the mother, that which ... I have called ego-relatedness. It will be seen that I attach a great importance to this relationship, as I consider that it is the stuff out of which friendship is made. It may turn out to be the matrix of transference.
>
> (Winnicott 1965, p. 33)

I would like to briefly describe some clinical applications of therapy with the schizoid, as drawn from combined concepts from the developmental theory of Mahler, Pine, and Bergman, and that of the independent object relationists, especially Winnicott.

It should be kept in mind that these guidelines for technique are based on our understanding of how pathology can be shaped by misdirected mother-infant attunement in the first year of life. Consequently, there is an unmet need to provide what Bowlby has called "a secure base," and Erikson named "basic trust."

This is where the therapy begins with the schizoid patient. Not only must the therapeutic alliance be created, but the possibility of alliance itself must also be established. And such an alliance must be formed under the same conditions where it originally failed to be: experientially, without words.

Especially for us who have been trained to encourage the patient "to put it all into words," it may be hard to grasp that much of the work with the schizoid is nonverbal: that silence is to be valued as well as what is spoken, and that simply being with the silent patient may be one of the more demanding skills we can practice.

Silence is a hallmark of the schizoid patient. Less problematic in the higher-functioning schizoid, protracted silence may actually form the primary interpersonal link for the more profoundly disordered patient. It is important not to confront this defense in its resistive aspect. In its protective use, silence demonstrates the schizoid's need to withdraw from the pain of intimidating social interaction and the pain of stirring up inner turbulence – it approximates an attempted return to a safe, undifferentiated state. It is the therapist's task to ease the transformation of the silence from wordless impasse to the therapeutic equivalent of a mother–infant synchronous state of early dependency.

When the silence is sporadic, it may be enough to simply wait, or perhaps to say: "I think I should let you know I respect silence – it is always your choice to speak or not." But if I should decide to say something during a silence, I begin with "I may be interrupting; is it all right?" Receptive silence introduces the "holding" described by Winnicott, the "containment" of Bion, and Schore's "synchronicity." The implicit mutuality formed in this way evokes what I would like to call the "environmental transference," that begins to provide the fundamental support for further differentiation of self and other.

It is more difficult than one might expect to sit with the patient's silence, especially when one becomes aware of how much can be experienced without words. Even aside from what may be nonverbally induced by the patient, it is almost predictable that the therapist will have to contend with a sense of professional ineffectiveness and some urge to take over helpfully.

Consistently, understanding of the patient's point of view, especially the willingness to even consider it, is of basic importance to the schizoid and to the possibility of forming a therapeutic alliance.

It should be noted that, to a degree, words are not trusted as tools of communication for the schizoid patient. Perhaps words in this case might be analogous to pieces on a chessboard, useful for defense or manipulation to maintain what is perceived as an inescapable game chronically in danger of being lost. Consequently, the schizoid patient is inclined to manage verbalization not so much in terms of communication as in terms of strategy. Specifically, the schizoid often does not respond to a direct question with a direct answer. Instead, the schizoid evades or defers response, hoping to determine the questioner's position in order to strategically respond in a way that seems safe. The childhood model for this makes sense: the youngster learned to assess the mother's mood in order to respond (or not respond) in a way that would maximize the mother's positive, or at least neutral, reaction.

The intellectual aspect of the schizoid is invaluably helpful. Unlike the intellectual defense of the neurotic, which tends to be a resistant impediment, the intellectual aspect of the schizoid represents a part of the self dissociatively detached from the rule of emotion, and therefore able to objectively assess matters. As a result, within the boundaries of this self-state, the patient is able to ally with the therapist in mapping out the patient's psychic situation and can even join in logically considering and modifying ideas and behavior.

Finally, it remains to include some mention of the clinical work with self-states. Clinical application of this thinking is deserving of a presentation in itself. I can only touch upon it, with brief examples, here.

When confronted with the oppositional self-states of the schizoid, the therapist must fight the urge to label and deal with conflict. Instead, it is the therapist's job to simply acknowledge these compartmentalized, even paradoxical expressions of the patient's self, modeling the capacity of a whole self to contain differing thoughts and feelings within the same consideration. The therapist, like the mother in the differentiating subphase, "holds" the range of the patient's experience in a kind of auxiliary psychic preprocessing. This responds to the patient's unspoken developmental need, as Masud Khan says, "to hold their fragmental affective states in experiential unity over time" (1974/1996, p. 21).

An example of this is the patient who arrives late for a session, but insists he or she intended to be on time. The classic response to neurotic conflict would be to interpret the patient's resistance to the therapy. But, for the schizoid, elimination of the resistance means rejection of a part of the self. So instead, the therapist acknowledges the validity of the opposing states, saying: "It's clear that you want to be here, because here you are. But I wonder if there isn't a part of you that also wants to stay away, and deserves to be understood, as well. Perhaps you could tell me more about both sides of the argument."

The situation becomes more complex and intense, as the therapist – in brain synchrony with the patient – actually receives projections of undifferentiated, unassimilated aspects of the self from the patient. As Khan continues:

> It is the analyst whom they make to feel the anger, rage, neediness, despair, love, and tenderness, destructive violence, and panic which is inside them, for very long periods of time before their ego can build up to a unity where through identification they can experience it for themselves and in themselves.

(1974/1996, p. 21)

Recently, I unexpectedly experienced a situation of this sort with a patient who is consistently reserved while talking, and reluctant to show any facial expression. Describing his professional role as a researcher, he passingly referred to formal academic debates with colleagues. A sudden liveliness flickered in his eyes, then was gone. This seemed too significant to let go by unacknowledged, so I ventured: "I thought I might say how you seemed to light up while mentioning those professional debates – was I mistaken?" Surprisingly, he lit up again, but said cautiously that he must already have told me about those occasions. I replied that possibly he had touched upon them, but perhaps he could tell me more. To my increased surprise, he not only responded to my interest by offering more details, but also occupied the remaining session time with narratives of aggressive arguments devastating to his opponents and decidedly satisfying to himself. This was a side of this reticent patient that was very new to me, and which he clearly felt safe in expressing only in relation to a circumscribed professional situation. At the same time as he spoke, I was also becoming aware of a growing sensation in myself: an experience of intense joy, and with it a reminder that unfamiliar positive feelings also can approach the unbearable. I realized that I was helping to "hold" a feeling he was not used to expressing in close interpersonal circumstances and hung on as best I could. Then things changed again. Increasingly, I felt impelled to make some comment, some insightful observation or reflection. But now my left brain, my technical self, warned me to stay still: "Why should I interrupt him with some show of my wisdom?" The impulse persisted. I argued internally with myself. It was quite a struggle to let myself quietly enjoy his enjoyment. The session closed on a positive note.

Afterward, able to reflect, I realized how I nearly had repeated a scene too familiar to this patient, whose childhood spontaneity had been relentlessly interrupted by his commandeering mother. Somehow, I had been able to contain the persuasive enactment that had been unconsciously evoked by him, and had managed to maintain a therapeutic environment able to sustain his enthusiasm.

Such healing moments are the living center of therapeutic work with the schizoid. They offer a powerful and culminating dimension to the Masterson Approach to this most fundamental of the personality disorders.

Presented by Candace Orcutt at the Masterson Institute Turkey conference, "The Masterson Approach and Personality Disorders," Istanbul, October 5–6, 2019.

CASE STUDY

Schizoid Fantasy: Refuge or Transitional Location?

The schizoid personality, a type increasingly representative of our times, lives in a detached individual world. But this retreat sometimes can offer a place of transition, serving as a creative bridge to everyday life. An extended case illustration describes a schizoid patient who was able to use a playful form of psychotherapy to move from make-believe to real relationship.

Introduction

The ability to find some sense of security through socially detached imagination is a characteristic of the schizoid personality. It typically sets the individual apart from others, but may paradoxically offer a bridge to the larger social world. Nancy McWilliams (2011) observes that "the most exciting capacity of the schizoid person is creativity" (p. 200), and in addition, this personal creativity may even answer the needs of society: "The arts, the theoretical sciences, and the philosophical disciplines seem to contain a high proportion of such people" (McWilliams 2006, p. 4). This intersection of the schizoid's personal world and society is possibly no coincidence. The creative work of these apparently detached individuals may perhaps provide a round-about way of finding some form of social attachment. If this is so, could the schizoid's ability to play with reality become a starting point for psychotherapy with the schizoid patient? This presentation will explore this hypothesis and offer a clinical illustration to support it.

The Social Context

Popular caricature shows that the creative schizoid type has found a place – however reluctant – in human society: the eccentric and antisocial painter; the religious mystic who lives in a cave; and – the schizoid achiever of our time – the computer genius. Such figures may even advance the larger world as they seek to develop their personal space. Of course, the actual schizoid spectrum is wider than this, and varies in degrees of social withdrawal, but many representatives have gained general recognition, and even some acceptance as they have – sometimes seemingly unwillingly – served society. Consider the "enigmatic" Alan Turing, inventor of artificial intelligence, whose genius hastened the end of World War II, although his manner allowed him few friends other than his computer, Christopher (Hodges 2014).

If the time is right for it, schizoid creativity, with its ability to fantasize, may even help to articulate the forming of the collective psyche. The modern art world offers examples of this from such opposite poles as the poet, T. S. Eliot, and the rock star, David Bowie, who express the schizoid inclination of our era as hollow men in a wasteland, or as aliens who have problematically fallen to earth.

But to return to the individual situation, it is curious to think how creativity, which can facilitate the constructing and living of a solitary existence, may also provide a guarded means for presenting the self to others. Eliot (1933), typically reclusive (Ezra Pound nicknamed him "Old Possum"), once reflected: "Every poet would like, I fancy, to be able to think ... his own thoughts behind a tragic or a comic mask". Bowie, more direct, explained: "Offstage I'm a robot. Onstage I achieve emotion. It's probably why I prefer dressing up as Ziggy [his rock star alter ego] to being David" (Sandford 1997, pp. 106–107). Especially in the arts, where the fantasy world of the schizoid demonstrably intersects with society, there appears the possibility of a new sort of communication for the schizoid. In the arts especially, creativity offers a compromise expression that can ease what has come to be accepted as the schizoid predicament of being neither quite here nor quite there.

Supportive Theory

It is somewhat puzzling to note the relative scarcity of psychotherapeutic writings on the schizoid personality. Perhaps, as McWilliams (2011) notes, "much commentary on schizoid conditions is buried in writings on schizophrenia" (p. 213). It would probably be useful for the literature to make a clearer distinction between these two importantly different psychic conditions. But fortunately, the British object relationists have left us insight into the subject that is original, detailed, and profound. (Seinfeld [1991] also gives substantial attention to the object relations approach to the schizoid state.)

Guntrip (1969), familiar with the schizoid predicament because he lived it, termed it the "'In and Out' Programme," and described it as "*The chronic dilemma in which the schizoid individual is placed, namely that he can neither be in a relationship with another person nor out of it*" (1969, p. 36, italics in original).

Extensively presenting his own findings, and in basic agreement with his colleagues Fairbairn and Winnicott, Guntrip (1969) understands that the schizoid, as all human beings, longs for human relationship, but withdraws out of anxiety learned long ago because of "*the inability of the weak infantile ego to stand its ground and cope with outer reality* in the absence of adequate maternal support" (p. 102, italics in original). Withdrawal, however, is equally intolerable, and so reaching out is repeated, fearfully retracted, and so on. The use of fantasy is necessitated by the unmet need for others: "The more people cut themselves off from human relations in the outer world, the more they are driven back on emotionally charged fantasied object relations in their inner world. The real loss of all objects would be equivalent to psychic death" (Guntrip 1969, p. 20).

However, a life too detached from others again activates the need to reach out. Guntrip (1969) continues: "[the] 'alternating in and out policy' makes life extremely difficult, so that we find that *a marked schizoid tendency is to effect a compromise in a halfway-house position, neither in nor out*" (p. 61, italics in original).

Extending this thinking, might it not be hypothesized that the longing for relationship together with a developed capacity for fantasizing might combine to provide more than an escape into the inner world? That there might be a more constructive aspect to this defense that is able to establish a tentative "compromise" communication through creative pursuits? And perhaps – given its full potential and within a therapeutic setting – this use of fantasy to find a connection with others can go beyond compromise to create a "safe-enough" transition to real relationship?

Here we turn to Winnicott for his unique and deep insight into the schizoid state. Winnicott's understanding was based on extensive pediatric work, experience with "severely regressed patients," and soul-searching of his own personal condition (Rodman 2003, pp. 289–291). Like Freud, he believed that psychopathology was a manifestation of something gone awry in healthy human potential – that the abnormal could be comprehended through better understanding of the normal. Thus, Winnicott (1960) believed that the schizoid state – with its problems in relationship – has its origin in the early infant's first attempt to relate itself to the "maternal environment." He describes this as the "gesture" that, as a "spontaneous impulse" from the "True Self," needs to be met by a receptive, non-intrusive mother, thus encouraging the infant's further exploration into "Not-Me" space (pp. 144–146). (This explication of the infant's first distinction between inner and outer "worlds," self and other, is reinforced by Mahler, Pine, and Bergman's [1975] pediatric observations of what she calls the "differentiation subphase" of early human growth [pp. 52–64]).

When the infant's spontaneous gesture is not well enough received, distinction between the subjective reality of the self and objective outer reality is unsure. The schizophrenic significantly fails to master this crucial developmental task. The schizoid personality, however, has been able to make a workable differentiation, but not securely. Depending on the degree to which the early experience has been wanting, the schizoid personality will regard the separateness of inside and out, self and other as a risky business. Winnicott, it should be noted, although he tends toward an inclusive description of the origin of schizoid states, clearly distinguishes between schizophrenia and characterological forms of the schizoid condition.

Good-enough reception of the spontaneous gesture then makes possible the infant's creation of "transitional space," with its occupant, the "transitional object" (comfortably represented by the Teddy Bear). The transitional object is just that: an introduction to the real object. The transitional space it occupies is a tentative area where the first interactions, for instance via Teddy, can be experimented with on the infant's terms. Transitional space allows the creative treating of "reality" any chosen which way – a practice area that strengthens the infant's confidence to explore the environment and the growing perception of the other. We carry the transitional space with us in our mature psyche, as well, says Winnicott (1951), where it "shall exist as a resting place for the individual engaged in the perpetual human task of keeping inner and outer reality separate yet interrelated" (p. 230). In the transitional space in our minds, we maintain the ability to toss about trial concepts of reality, conforming them to our notions, and illusively reassuring ourselves that external reality will provide the same responsiveness. This touches upon Winnicott's (1952) profound concept of play. Play, he believes, defines the activity in the transitional space. It reinforces the infant's expectation that the spontaneous gesture will be met by the receptive environment, just as Teddy's reliable cooperation complements the infant's behavior. We need this ability to practice and feel reassured if we are to face bigger and less cooperative challenges, and the infant's play carries through into such adult endeavors as art, science, and religion, which give us the courage to feel we can face larger realities (p. 224). Winnicott (1967) sums up the importance of transitional space, saying: "I suggest that the time has come for psychoanalytic theory to pay tribute to this *third area*, that of cultural experience which is a derivative of play" (p. 372).

It would seem that the schizoid personality, still engaged in the uncompleted task of making a good-enough separation between inner and outer reality, takes up refuge in transitional space, rather than using it to move forward. There, the schizoid can create a personal world of intellectual invention or artistic fantasy, where he is free to play with the possibilities of a self-invented reality rather than test out his greater surroundings. How can therapy help to restore the individual's true use of transitional space: from defensive refuge to a bridge to the real world?

A Clinical Approach

First of all, what would the therapeutic situation be like? Ralph Klein (1995) has contributed substantially to the Masterson Approach to treatment of the schizoid "Self-in-Exile" (pp. 1–142). Describing the clinical work, he emphasizes that "the key word for such patients is 'safety.'" He continues: "such patients require a therapeutic alliance in which they are truly free to establish their own distance and regulate the pace of their feelings, thinking, and acting" (p. 123). McWilliams

(2006), referring to an unpublished paper by Gordon, adds that "most of what is transformative to schizoid individuals involves the experience of *elaborating the self in the presence of an accepting, nonintrusive, but powerfully responsive other*" (p. 17, italics in original).

Both these accounts suggest that therapy with the schizoid begins where the early developmental situation faltered. The therapist must be receptive to the patient's self-expression in a way (to use Winnicott's words) that is "holding" without "impinging." Other essential words used by Klein and McWilliams are "safety" and "experience." The patient must feel safe from interpersonal pressure, and understand this sense of safety comes not so much from words as from the experience of the therapist's concern, full attention, and interest.

How does this go in session? The therapist begins with showing interest in what is of interest to the patient. This may be as pertinent as the patient's intellectualized ideas about the presenting problem, or may diverge to topics of special interest to the patient such as books or computer games. This is to establish a mutual safe space with the patient, where verbal transaction can take place in an uncommitted way. This uses what Ralph Klein (1995) has called the schizoid patient's ability to form "relationships by proxy" and so defensively "act against the risks involved in connecting to, and sharing with the therapist" (p. 90). This ability can allow the patient to test out a harmless reciprocity in the sessions. Over time, the experience of this interplay may prove to feel safe enough so that the patient may begin to further test the possibility of a closer exchange. If all goes well, interchange becomes therapy as protective strategy transforms into relationship. (The extensive examples of therapeutic dialogue with a schizoid patient that I describe in my own work [Orcutt 2012b] may offer a useful guide to this technical approach [pp. 126–147].)

Those who practice play therapy will see a similar process at work here. Therapy with the schizoid individual relies on engaging the creative playfulness in the patient's inner space in order to bridge the anxiety of exploring outer reality.

And now I would like to introduce you to a patient of mine who transformed a major city hospital into a transitional space for personal change.

A Case Example

This is about a playful young patient I have always referred to as the "boy on the bicycle."

Although the experience dates to my early career, it remains vividly with me. It represents a time I had to rely on intuition more than expertise, although perhaps that was a good thing. At the time, even my training needed constantly to catch up with itself, since this was a case of personality disorder, and the importance of preoedipal states was barely taking hold, while the concept of personality disorder was just forming. In any event, this case provided part of my initiation as clinical social worker on the staff of a large psychiatric hospital in a major city.

The patient, an eighteen-year-old male, was perceptively diagnosed by the resident conducting the intake as having "a schizoid reaction to a schizophrenic mother," and was referred to the psychiatric outpatient facility for treatment.

My first view of mother and son walking toward me stays distinctly in my mind. The mother – tiny, anxious, and looking older than her age – was accompanied by her would-be-adult child, who was six feet tall, somewhat heavy, and seemed somehow larger than life. When I interviewed them together, the mother did the talking while the son appeared distracted. The problem focused essentially on the mother's feeling overwhelmed by her son's energy, unpredictable activity, and general unmanageability.

It seemed to me that the issue was less that of the mother's anxiety than the son's need for independence. And so, after a supportive session with the mother, I arranged to see the son individually. The mother, a functioning chronic schizophrenic, seemed relieved by my reassurance that her uncertain maternal instinct had rightly sent her to seek assistance in guiding her eighteen-year-old toward growing up, perhaps even to being on his own. I anticipated my meeting with the son with a good deal less confidence than I communicated to the mother.

The patient prefaced his first session by riding his bicycle down the hospital hallway. He was confronted by a clerk, who protested: "You can't ride your bicycle inside the clinic!" The patient then cheerfully replied: "Lady! You're hallucinating! This isn't a bicycle, this is a horse!"

The patient had set the stage, and it was my job to make it a setting for psychotherapy.

First, there was the matter of the horse. Making it clear that a horse must be hitched outside, I went with the patient while he cooperatively chained his bicycle to the iron railing which was fortunately located at the side entrance to the clinic.

His new experience seemed to engage the patient's attention, and he soon informed the staff and myself that his name was "Barnabas." This was not his actual (rather stodgy) name, but the name he took from Barnabas Collins, the reluctant vampire in the popular television series *Dark Shadows*.

And here we coincided. In my own teenage years, I myself escaped into a world of classic horror films such as *Dracula*. To follow this inclination, I played hooky to the extent that I still wonder how I managed to graduate high school. It was a single-minded necessity for me – impulsively followed, but with such care that I never got caught. Looking back, I imagine that the way these films dramatically presented the ambiguity of good and evil, even the elusive nature of reality, helped me find my way through some complicated feelings. Unquestionably, my personal experience helped me to create a bond with Barnabas. I could speak his language.

As the sessions began, we enthusiastically discussed *Dark Shadows*, and the dilemma of unwilling vampires such as Barnabas Collins, who was struggling to free himself from a spell. At the same time, the patient continued to entertain the staff by appearing in a cape and top hat (the bicycle remained hitched outside).

Fairly soon, the fantasy play expanded to include me. We became Steed and Peel, the sophisticated crimestoppers on the original television series of *The Avengers*. He pictured himself as the dapper John Steed, with cane and bowler hat, while I was flatteringly cast as Steed's companion, the jumpsuited karate expert, Emma Peel. Now fantasy allowed us to play with relationship in metaphor.

I should be clear that these sessions provided a context for consciously constructed fantasy. The patient had no thought disorder, and knew the difference between fantasy and reality, although he approached reality with caution and in camouflage.

Then the scope of the sessions expanded further, as Barnabas instigated an activity we came to call "scavenging" (we never verbally defined this, but it is interesting to note that the word suggests the reclaiming of something that has been considered worthless). Barnabas led me on an extensive exploration of apparently forgotten regions of the hospital. It was evident he was showing me "secret" rooms he had previously discovered, as he appeared to be confidently following a mental map. We ventured through one neglected room after another – dusty, cobwebbed places filled with stacks of papers, broken furniture, dingy test tubes and alembics. He scavenged one or two mad-scientist-looking beakers for his home use, while my white hospital coat officialized the activities.

Barnabas, with my cooperation, had transformed the hospital into an extensive playroom.

And, taking the desired direction of play therapy, our finding of hidden inanimate objects progressed to a clinic-wide game of interpersonal hide-and-seek.

On regular occasions, the hospital Department of Psychiatry conducted Professor's Rounds in a large auditorium. Over one hundred white-coated psychotherapists were there – psychiatrists, psychologists, social workers – to hear a distinguished speaker and discuss cases. I was seated toward the back, when I noticed a number of the staff turning to look at me. I also noticed that they seemed amused. My own perplexed gaze traveled toward the auditorium door, where I saw Barnabas standing and smiling at me.

I hurried to the entrance and gestured him outside. I then subjected him to a solemn boundary-setting lecture. He took it in and looked pleased.

On a later occasion, during a smaller social work meeting, Barnabas appeared at the door, singled me out, and called, "Hiya, Candy!" My boundary-setting lecture to him was repeated, to his repeated satisfaction, while I noted to myself that Barnabas bad somehow learned my nickname from the staff. I also noted that he had addressed me by my real name.

This increased my growing awareness that Barnabas had engaged the staff of the hospital, as well as their setting, in his play. The staff knew him, knew I was his therapist, was aware of who knew what about our activities, and was in good-natured collusion. Barnabas had somehow engaged them in transforming an impersonal psychiatric setting into his own supportive play world.

Looking back, now even more than then, I realize that the therapeutic work had followed a definite progression: from a solitary imaginary self to an imaginary law-enforcing couple; then next, from actual companions interacting in an inanimate location to two people engaged in a kind of rapprochement in a social surrounding. Barnabas had set the scene, I had accepted and helped shape it, yet basically all we had done was make room for the orderly nature of the self to grow.

There was consistently a more conscious part to the process, as well. Each session ended in my office, where Barnabas increasingly examined his real-life situation and made a plan for his immediate future.

He had befriended his landlady, who owned a house outside the city. Barnabas was adapting well to weekend visits, and was finding himself useful around the property. In time, he and the landlady arranged for him to work as a live-in caretaker there.

Our sessions were coming to a close, but a couple of recollections remain vividly with me.

One day Barnabas brought me a jar with a bug in it. It was some sort of fragile flying creature, all legs, that hit itself futilely against the glass container. "Isn't that the biggest damn mosquito you ever saw?" he asked. He then disappeared on some momentary task (a tendency of his) while I stared at the bug. Finally, uncertainly and guiltily, I removed the cover and let the bug fly out the window. When Barnabas returned, I apologized, and said, "I just couldn't let it stay caught in that jar." Barnabas did not object, but remained very quiet with me for a minute.

I also recall our parting. As usual, I went with him to the side entrance of the clinic, where he unchained his bicycle. We talked awhile, and then I started to say goodbye. He stopped me, saying, "I'm not ready yet." We stood together briefly in silence. Then he wished me well, jumped on his bicycle, and rode off.

Conclusion

The "boy on the bicycle" taught me, as a beginning clinician, the therapeutic importance of joining with the schizoid patient in the individual's area of personal creativity. This psychic region, so eloquently described by Winnicott as "transitional space," exists in us all as a "third" not-me, not-other mental "location." Here, we can shape our perception of outer reality in trial constructions under our imaginative control. This "illusory" activity eventually facilitates our participation in the far less manageable outer environment.

Beginning with Fairbairn (1946), the British object relationists revolutionized psychoanalysis by asserting that relationship with the other is the fundamental need of the self (pp. 30–37). As Winnicott says, the spontaneous gesture of the early infant initiates this process of object-seeking. However, the mother's capacity to hold this gesture receptively is critical for the evolution of the process, through the infant's interplay with the transitional object to the adult's capacity for relationship with others. In the schizoid individual, the early reciprocal situation has been sufficient to allow the infant's creating of transitional space, but not good enough to carry through to a confident capacity for relationship. Thus, to a greater or lesser extent – depending on the degree of accomplishment within the early situation – the schizoid adult retains the ability to use transitional space as a creative refuge, but is lacking in assurance to use it effectively for its transformative purpose.

The function of psychotherapy with the schizoid patient, consequently, first requires the therapist to meet with the patient in the safely defended area of transitional space (i.e., the patient's interests, endeavors, ideas, etc.). In this area, which is essentially under the patient's psychic control, therapist and patient engage in a trial interpersonal experience. The intent is that this interaction will prove reassuring enough to encourage the patient toward real relationship through development of the transitional ability that has always been a potential in the patient's self.

Play, as Winnicott describes, is the essential activity within transitional space. Through creative fantasy, play first forms a safe base for interpersonal exploration, and then provides a pleasurable means for entering into relationship itself. Winnicott sees play as vital not only to the individual's growth into a healthy social being, but also to the development of society itself (which is the greater collective task).

The "boy on the bicycle" introduced these concepts to me through our mutual experience which was significant for us both. He gained an increased sense of self and self-reliance through building relationship with another. I, in turn, was witness to the persistence of the spontaneous gesture of the self toward the other, and the playfulness that is inherently ready to enable this process toward relationship with creative energy and even joy.

Presented by Candace Orcutt at "The Fortress of Solitude: An Exploration of the Diagnosis, Treatment and Phenomenology of the Schizoid Disorder of the Self," a conference sponsored by the International Masterson Institute, New York City, April 23–24, 2016. Published online June 2, 2017. Clinical Social Work, 46(1): 42–47.

CHAPTER 5

Abandonment Depression, the Triad, and the Developmental Paradigm

History

In 1972, in his second book, Masterson introduces the abandonment depression: a subjective sense of identity catastrophe unique to personality disorder. This is an original concept, forged out of ten years of struggle to assure that "the Adolescent and the Borderline Syndrome are no longer used as psychiatric scapegoats" (1972, p. 5). Inpatient treatment, outpatient follow-up, controlled studies, and persistent search of the literature have led to a dynamic formulation that has proved therapeutically effective for patients who have been considered untreatable. Masterson then brings his cause to the wider therapeutic community, with his writings making "a plea for the delineation and treatment of the abandonment depression ... [that has] prevented the patient's growth to the developmental stage of autonomy" (1972, p. 15).

In this and other early works, the essential Masterson can be seen: the passionate advocate for misunderstood and underserved patients who "are actually desperate for help, although they are not able to verbalize this desperation" (Masterson and Costello 1980, p. 48). The treatment process is grounded in the need to face powerful and painful feelings understood within a developmental context. The Masterson Approach begins with the abandonment depression.

In his early writing, Masterson demonstrates the intensity of his involvement with his subject – with the "emotional sway and destructiveness" inherent in the pathology itself (1972, p. 58). He is prepared to encounter a clinical situation where "the therapy assumes the aura of a battle" (1972, p. 16). At the heart of this battle is the patient's aversion to facing the abandonment depression, and the therapist's steadfast facilitation of its healthy resolution.

To communicate the force of the abandonment depression, Masterson evokes a powerful metaphor: the implacable horsemen in the Book of Revelation, whose coming announces the end of the world. He names the "six psychiatric horsemen of the Apocalypse," saying "technical words are too abstract to convey the intensity and immediacy of these feelings … The patient's functioning in the world, his relationship with people, and even some of his physiological functions are subordinated to the defense against these feelings" (1972, p. 58).

The six "abandonment feelings" that make up this psychic onslaught are: "depression, anger and rage, fear, guilt, passivity and helplessness, emptiness and void." These are like "feelings that spring from the loss or the threat of loss either of part of the self or of supplies that the patient believes vital for survival." Such feelings must be faced if the patient is to resolve the long-ago dread of loss of the mother's nurturing, a fear that caused the developmental arrest underlying the pathological condition. Masterson describes this psychic event as central to the therapy of the borderline patient: an early crisis in the nature of mother–child attachment related to Mahler's rapprochement subphase of separation-individuation, and taking its psychic origin from then. Treatment reaches back to that early time:

As the defenses are successfully interrupted, the depression becomes more intense, repressed memories emerge, and the patient quite obviously is suffering. The patient intensifies his struggle to maintain his defenses but as the doctor interprets them the patient gradually slides to the bottom of his depression where lies, almost always, suicidal despair and belief that it will never be possible to receive the necessary supplies.

(Masterson 1972, p. 59)

The concept of the abandonment depression remains unchanged until 1981, when the Masterson model is expanded to include the narcissistic personality disorder. The same defensive maneuvering is found with both the narcissist and the borderline. But this "essential theme" – the organizing of the therapy around the persistent uncovering of the abandonment depression – extends to the treatment of the narcissist as well as the borderline with a modification. In the narcissistic personality disorder, a sense of "fragmentation of the self" is included with the abandonment depression (1981, p. 26).

Here is the suggestion that, just as types of personality disorder shift their dynamics in relation to a specific developmental subphase, so the nature of the abandonment depression may vary as well. A possible hypothesis that could perhaps lead to a more effective understanding and treatment.

In his last book, in 2005, Masterson does touch upon a variation of the abandonment depression in "the three primary cornerstones of character work." For the borderline, a sense of abandonment arises from a question of "competence"; for the narcissist, "painful vulnerability" rests on a sense of deep imperfection; and for the schizoid, there is "danger" in the possibility of not being able to make any connection at all. He points out that knowledge of this distinction "informs the therapist of what to focus on and what to listen to, as well as what the core dynamics are" (p. 149).

However, the hypothesis that the abandonment depression might have a progressive nature – evolving out of sequential distortions analogous to the progression of Mahler's developmental subphases – was never fully developed by Masterson.

This shift was in part due to the manner of Ralph Klein's introduction of the schizoid personality disorder to the Masterson Approach (1995, pp. 1–122). Klein's exposition of the schizoid is an invaluable addition and, in fact, brings a fulfilling completion to Masterson's categorization of the major self-disorders. Klein's clinical descriptions and delineation of technique are elegant and moving. His incorporation of Harry Guntrip's work provides the clinician with a reliable compass for treatment. However, I believe he throws Mastersonian theorizing off track regarding the schizoid, derailing an argument for a progressive, or spectrum, model for abandonment depression, and for personality disorder types in general.

First, this is accomplished by discarding the work of Mahler and her colleagues, Pine and Bergman, as the developmental model. This is problematic, as this research is a cornerstone of the Masterson Approach: the theoretical and treatment concept of the borderline is dependent on this model, and that of the narcissist also, though it is less stringently worked through. Second, Mahler's differentiation subphase of infant development is not only informative in understanding the healthy base underlying schizoid distortion, but the concept was evolved at the same time and in harmony with the endeavors of Winnicott and the other British analysts who put the schizoid patient on the psychic map. Dr. Klein has puzzlingly taken a separate path from the mainstream of theory, and pediatric data regarding the schizoid personality disorder.

This second point is of special import, as Klein does not acknowledge that the independent object relationists essentially represented an informal school dedicated to explicating the schizoid personality, including an agreement on its psychic origin in the first year of life: the time of the infant's dividing of the inner world of the self from outer reality. This was the existential time Fairbairn referred to as "oral," Winnicott described as the "individual-environment set-up," and Mahler was soon to call the "differentiation" subphase of separation-individuation.

Inexplicably, Klein almost entirely omits mention of Winnicott, whose concepts of true and false self, transitional phenomena, and maternal "facilitating environment," "impingement" and "holding" are related to this developmental phase.

Fairbairn, Guntrip, Winnicott, and Khan, in intercommunication, print, and lectures, established the schizoid as a personality disorder in its own right, with its unique social presence, origin, dynamics, and treatment. Winnicott's extraordinary pediatric observations were additionally reinforced by Bowlby's belief in the infant's need for "attachment," and a "secure base" (on occasion, the two men studied children as a team). On the more purely analytic side, reaffirmation came from Deutsch's "As-If Personality" (1965), R. D. Laing's "Divided Self" (1960) torn by "ontological insecurity" or an unsure sense of *being* despite an often high level of intellect and creativity, and Margaret Little's (1960) agonizing account of her own analysis.

Once the schizoid patient, as defined by the Independent object relationists, is identified with Mahler's differentiation subphase, the developmental aspect of Masterson's schizoid falls into a natural continuum with the narcissist and the borderline. This integrates the schizoid within the fundamental developmental-object relations structure of the Masterson Approach. In addition, it suggests completion of the spectrum model of personality disorder implied in early and mid-Masterson thinking.

Interestingly, Kernberg picks up this theme in Masterson's 1977 conference-cum-book that debates *New Perspectives on Psychotherapy of the Borderline Adult* (1978). Kernberg notes that "a spectrum of regressive pathology may be described," including:

*patients in whom the regression has occurred to a stage of differen-
tiation preceding the typical borderline path ... Usually, these are
patients with predominant schizoid characteristics, and one may
find such developments from early on in the treatment of some
schizoid personalities. Here, the prevailing level of regression or
fixation relates to the early differentiation subphase of separation,
where patients require "holding" (Winnicott, 1965), being empathized with and yet permitted to maintain their autonomy vis-à-vis
the therapist.*

(Kernberg 1978, pp. 86–87)

Kernberg refers to further support of this approach by Little, Balint, and,
to a degree, Bion.

Kernberg is suggesting sequential levels of distortion of the normal
progression of increasingly "structured" "overall personality organization" (1978, p. 25). This progression, within healthy development, he feels
should eventually support the psychic complexity of the oedipal phase.

The abandonment depression – if we restore and align the theoretical origins of the "three major personality disorders" – changes with the
changing structuring of internal object relations and affect management
of each phase. Then, in adapting our therapeutic approach to the varied
disorders, we must take into consideration that the less differentiated
(Kernberg would say the less structured) the psyche, the more devastating the abandonment depression and the greater the sensitivity we must
bring to the therapeutic alliance and process.

The Disorders of the Self Triad

This phenomenon, the Mastersonian "triad," has been defined as an intrinsic impediment to therapeutic healing encountered throughout the
full range of personality disorders. It is the patient's consistent undoing
of "moments" of therapeutic achievement. Freud first identified this
self-sabotage under the definition of "patients ruined by success," and
considered it insurmountable. Masterson's genius was to understand the
triad to be a predictable occurrence related to abandonment depression
evoked by the therapeutic process, and to postulate its working-through
as essential to the treatment of personality disorder.

This basic three-step formula runs as follows: self-activation leads to abandonment depression, which leads to reinstatement of defense. In the underlying dynamic, it is understood that innovative self-expression once ran counter to a favorable maternal response to the degree that attachment seemed endangered. The traumatic level of depression and/or anxiety evoked by the threat of maternal loss quickly discouraged self-activation and led to institution of a defensive personality pattern more likely to support attachment and secure the mother's presence. Therapeutic challenge of this pattern consequently evokes a primal fear and leads to reinstatement of the defensive character style. If a specific personality disorder is to be resolved, the patient's self must be strengthened therapeutically until recognition, containment, and management of this once intolerable feeling state are achieved and moved past.

The patient must be strong enough to change the dysfunctional but fundamental definition of relationship when it is modified by the therapeutic process. Based on the child's need to maximize the maternal attention required for survival, this initial adaptation takes on the tenacity of a belief system. Although the potential capacities for growth are supported and strengthened, the therapeutic attempt to reshape the self is still met with intense anxiety. This anxiety is characterized by the nature of the developmental level being addressed in the therapy. Thus, the schizoid fears annihilation – the dispersal of the self – without the assurance of maternal holding. The narcissist fears fragmentation: the loss of the new sense of cohesiveness experienced as reliant on a sense of oneness with the mother. The borderline – with a more defined concept of self and other – fears abandonment: the loss of the mother as the guide and protector still needed to find the way in unfamiliar territory. Collectively referred to by Masterson as the abandonment depression, this is anxiety that once discouraged the successful accomplishment of a developmental task, and is triggered by the good-enough completion of the task in present time. Like a traumatic flashback (which indeed it seems to be), this powerful emotional deterrent must be faced and eliminated as a threat in present time if it is no longer to enforce a dysfunctional system of belief.

In the subsequent sections, I will follow the changes in the abandonment depression as it relates to a diagnostic spectrum, or developmental paradigm. Abandonment depression shows increasing intensity as the patient's psyche shows more uncertainty about itself due to a faulty sense of authenticity acquired in the earliest years of life.

The Borderline Personality Disorder

The borderline personality disorder is the cornerstone of the Masterson Approach. Masterson's description of the borderline to a degree is based on and shared by Kernberg's concept of borderline personality organization. Like Kernberg, Masterson defines the borderline in terms of Mahler's developmental observations – as related to the maturational tasks of the rapprochement subphase. However, it is informative to keep in mind that the rapprochement subphase prepares for "on the way to object constancy," Mahler's open-ended subphase offering the potential base for the autonomous, responsible, related self – or neurosis, its pathological counterpart. Masterson's borderline is truly on the border between personality disorder and neurosis or relative mental health, and therefore may contain elements of all. As a result, the abandonment depression in the borderline is especially complex.

The borderline is the most object-oriented of the personality disorders in the Masterson model (as Kernberg would say, it is the most highly structured). It should be recalled that the early Masterson definition of the borderline is drawn in part from Kernberg's adaptation of Melanie Klein's object relations theory (Masterson and Rinsley 1975). Therefore, it can be inferred that Mahler's rapprochement subphase may be seen as somewhat analogous to Klein's depressive position: the stage brought about by the merging in the psyche of the split between the good and bad part-object representations. The abandonment depression in the borderline, based on the loss of the old, pathological representation of the mother, is consequently intensified as it combines with the normal sense of sorrow and guilt over the Kleinian inner world transformation.

In Melanie Klein's model, the depressive position fades with the mature desire for reparation (Winnicott's "capacity for concern"). In the pathological shadow of this process, Masterson describes the working-through of the depression, anger, and guilt of the abandonment depression, heightened by separation anxiety. This is a complex, combined task to be managed before the borderline is ready to accept the maturational grieving process that fosters a capacity for real relationship.

Suicidal despair takes a form unique to the borderline. The borderline's new maturational acquisition of guilt (partly an internalization of shame) may intensify the element of self-attack in the abandonment depression. Unless the patient can achieve the capacity to mourn (to "let go" idealization and accept the often-conflicted complexity of reality) the passage from personality disorder to ordinary neurosis (or even normality) is doubly hazardous for the borderline.

The borderline personality disorder draws strength from its complexity, as well. Because of the more advanced developmental level, the abandonment depression in the borderline shows more clearly defined elements than do the other personality disorders. The object, especially as the split closes, is perceived as a unique, specific person. The self, though bereft, is separate and intact. The depression, despite its intensity, is a nameable feeling attributable to a nameable cause. The maturational stress of this developmental stage – the transition from psychically dependent to autonomous – coupled with the demanding healing process of the related disorder, is now finding containment and management within the self. A more structured psyche is now supported by integration of right and left brain functions and the acquisition of language. The forming ego now has increasing ability to consciously observe, reason, communicate, and repress. Responsibility for going-on-being can now be transferred from the other to the self.

In borderline personality disorder, the abandonment depression can be described as a fearful, desolate reaction to perceived loss of a guiding, protective figure who is felt to be life-sustaining. The individual, although able to exist alone, does not feel able to continue surviving that way. This suggests a whole-object situation that can be visualized interpersonally, such as that of a terrified small child who has lost touch and sight of the mother in a huge, impersonal store. It is more focused, more comprehensible and describable than earlier forms of abandonment depression, which cannot be pictured in such a defined, two-person way.

Case Vignette: Abandonment Depression in the Borderline Patient

Ms. R., thirty-two years old, is a single woman living on her own, and precariously maintaining a job in sales. She has used psychotherapy to move apart from her family of origin (although she remains in close contact with her mother), and to initiate several brief romantic connections. Although these liaisons have been marked by alternating states of possessiveness and verbal combat, Ms. R has nevertheless maintained a degree of friendship with her past boyfriends.

As Ms. R has increasingly learned in therapy to stay put and observe herself, she has repeatedly found herself facing her core challenge: to believe in her ability to manage her life on her own without being swamped by the fear of being alone.

This is how she described her situation:

It's very hard to just say this. I want to get you to say it for me, or maybe just argue with me about stuff. If I can just hang onto you somehow, maybe I'll get through this.

It's like … it's like taking care of things all by myself gives me this sickening feeling. I'm like a little kid who's run away from home, and then I'm in the middle of a strange street and don't know my way back. It's horrible; it's in my stomach; I'm going to cry or throw up; maybe both.

This feeling takes me over, like the little kid. I want you to come and get me and make it stop. I know you're out there. I need you and I hate you for leaving me to maybe die. How can I tell myself I'm okay on my own when I have this feeling?

Ms. R's expression of her abandonment depression shows her outward grasp of two-person object relatedness, but reveals her struggle to create a consistent inner concept of that relatedness, with its shared sense of responsibility.

The Narcissistic Personality Disorder

In *The Narcissistic and Borderline Disorders* (1981), Masterson describes the abandonment depression unique to the narcissist: "Patients who are working through their abandonment depression or separation of the self from the maternal object report that the mother's withdrawal is experienced as a loss of a vital part of the self" (p. 20).

The narcissist's reaction is understood if Mahler's depiction of the practicing subphase child is recalled. The narcissist is psychically arrested at a stage where the infant's inner representation of self is still merged with the representation of the mother. In this state, the self is reaffirmed by a good-feeling sense of oneness with the other. Whether the child feels validated by the mother's delight in the child's happy self-importance, or confirmed by the approval of a mother felt to be the source of all perfection, the practicing child defines self in terms of a blissful mother–child unity. The narcissist's experience of the abandonment depression, therefore, is not (like the borderline) a disastrous feeling of loss of the mother, but a sense of fragmentation of the self *per se*. Masterson writes: "What differentiates the closet narcissist … is … the experiencing of the Abandonment Depression as the self 'falling apart' rather than as 'losing the object'" (1993, p. x).

Kohut, who speaks of this merged "selfobject" sense of being, holds that a "cohesive" sense of self is reliant on the firm establishment of this state. He believes that interruption of this maturational task – in childhood or later in analysis – leads to a dangerous "disintegration" or "fragmentation" of the self. Therefore, in treatment, he attributes the patient's experience of fragmentation as something to be avoided; it is the result of a failure in the analyst's empathy rather than the problematic consequence of the emergence of a distinct sense of self.

Masterson's concept of the abandonment depression marks a significant departure of his theory and practice from Kohut's approach to narcissistic personality disorder.

Ralph Klein notes this difference in his article "Masterson and Kohut: Comparison and Contrast" (1989). As Klein points out:

> *There is a fundamental difference in the concept of working through …. In my view, for Kohut (1971) the essence of the curative process … is to provide the "missing" psychic structure – to permit the grandiose self to emerge, be acknowledged, and gradually be brought into accord with external reality.*

(1989, pp. 326–327)

He continues: "For Masterson (1981, 1985), in contrast, the essence of the work … is the working through of the abandonment depression, the fundamental roadblock on the developmental pathway, which underlies all the disorders of the self" (Klein 1989, p. 327).

Facing and overcoming the circumstance that created the develop-mental arrest would seem critical to repairing the early psychic damage done to the self. As in the trauma model – first introduced by Breuer and Freud in *Studies on Hysteria* (1895), and now returning in contemporary analytic theory – the patient must regress to the unthinkable in order to heal. Within the containment of the therapeutic situation, and fortified by a now adult ego, the patient experientially transcends the repetition of the triad; in the case of the narcissist, the fear of fragmentation of the self is experienced and overcome.

Case Vignette: Fragmentation Anxiety in the Narcissistic Patient

Mr. S., a middle-aged realtor who had achieved notable success in his business, became first excessively active and then depressed as the hous-ing market fell through. At the same time, his wife of many years declared she was weary of supporting him emotionally, while his grown children had moved out of state. He entered psychotherapy seeking vindication for his conviction that he was being treated unfairly and disrespectfully.

At first, Mr. S. tried to transform his therapy into a cheering section. As his practical crisis intensified, however, he came to value the steady understanding he found in his treatment. He began to experience a basic affirmation in therapy that helped him find the strength in himself to face the sense of fragmentation that dominated his abandonment depression. He said:

> *This is almost impossible for me to talk about. I feel as if I am chok-ing in rage at you for making me say it. But then I ask myself why I am striking out like this. I'll fight, do anything, not to feel what I feel. I'm putting on a show of how tough I am when I'm falling apart. Nothing holds together if you won't tell me how good I am. Alone, I'm in pieces. I'm helpless. I'm a show without an audience, and the stage is falling apart under my feet. This is god-awful! But it's me, or what's left of me! Why do I feel this is your fault?*

Mr. R's inner concept of object relatedness is tenuous: he experiences him-self as complete only in the presence of an approving other. Consequently, he finds himself battling a chaotic sense of fragmentation, helplessness, and bewildered rage in encountering his abandonment depression.

The Schizoid Personality Disorder

In his last book, Masterson distinguishes different "core affects" in the triad for each of the major personality types. He observes that activation of the real self in the borderline evokes "abandonment," whereas this individuation in the narcissist calls up "painful vulnerability" and, in the schizoid, "danger" (2005, p. 149). In this statement, Masterson appears on the way to defining variations in the abandonment depression possibly in accord with the developmental paradigm. With each disorder, the challenge of the abandonment depression reaches an increasingly existential level – survival of a sense of self becoming ever more precarious. For the borderline, whose psyche is the most structured, abandonment depression calls up the fear of literal abandonment of a semi-independent child by a still-needed caregiver. However, for the schizoid as well as the narcissistic personality, loss of the other becomes more a threat to the formation of the self. The narcissist, who has not sufficiently established a cohesive sense of self, fears self-fragmentation. The schizoid, uncertain of a secure sense of inner reality apart from outer reality, fears loss of the self altogether – a loss of the sense of being.

To better understand the schizoid's sense of self, and so to understand the abandonment depression in that disorder, one must refer to the independent British object relationists, whose work defined the schizoid, and whose concept of the self and its vulnerability predated Kohut's.

Fairbairn, Guntrip, Winnicott, and Khan formed an interactive foursome that has profoundly affected the course of analytic thinking. In addition to placing the schizoid personality on the analytic map, they initiated the analytic shift in emphasis on the patient's wish for pleasure to the patient's need to relate to another; and they refocused the centrality of the ego to the primacy of the self (with the ego as its agency). Fairbairn, from his observing distance in Scotland, challenged basic analytic paradigms; Guntrip, the realistic preacher, organized Fairbairn's work into clinically useful formulations; Winnicott, the experienced pediatrician–analyst, provided understanding of the deep dynamic: the maturational deficits of the patient based on the unmet developmental needs of the infant. Khan, in addition to extensively organizing and editing Winnicott's writings, contributed the important insight that the deficit in relationship under-lying the schizoid personality can be a subtle one – gaining its effective-ness cumulatively over time. Clinically, Winnicott introduced an analytic process with the schizoid personality that is analogous to Masterson's working through of the abandonment depression: Winnicott called this "regression to dependence." To better understand this demanding clinical process, it is first necessary to describe the developmental basis of the schizoid personality, as understood by the independent object relationists.

Fairbairn first locates the origin of the schizoid personality using the Freudian developmental model: "There can be no question of the cor-rectness of relating schizoid conditions to a fixation in the early oral ... phase" (1941, p. 252). Then Winnicott uses his own terminology, based on his work with literally thousands of children and their mothers, as well as his knowledge of psychoanalysis: "The intimate study of the schizoid individual of whatever age becomes an intimate study of that individual's early development, development within and emerging from the stage of the individual-environment set-up" (1952, p. 222). Winnicott is referring to a time in the infant's first year of life that Winnicott's contemporary, Margaret Mahler, will soon identify as the "differentiation subphase." According to Mahler, the infant's major psychic task in the first six to ten months of life – the differentiation subphase – is the distinguishing of the inner subjective world from outer reality (Winnicott's "maternal environment"). The child's increasingly realistic and adaptive concepts of self, other, and relationship will be established on the basis of this first essential differentiation in the beginning of life. The British independent object relationists see schizoid personality pathology originating at this time.

As Kernberg considers Winnicott in the context of Mahler, "[Winnicott] ... described the pathology of early differentiation as related to excessive intrusion or impingement by mother with the subsequent consolidation of a 'false self'" (Grotstein and Rinsley 1994, p. 62).

Winnicott says that, for the schizoid personality, the mother's long-ago incapacity to psychically "hold" her infant resulted in a *"freezing of the failure situation"* (1954). This created a "fixation" that led to "The de-velopment of a false self ... one of *the most successful defence organizations* designed for the protection of the true self's core" (p. 292). Consequently, according to Winnicott, "For treatment to be effectual, there ha[s] to be a regression in search of the true self" (p. 280). In analysis with the schizoid,

Winnicott is speaking of personality disorder, in which the patient has a sufficiently organized psyche to enable a therapeutic regression to occur, and to tolerate the surrender of the false self within the analytic "holding" (p. 281).

In Winnicott's experience, the infant's psychic growth has been traumatically affected; has been "frozen" (fixated, arrested) by great anxiety aroused by the mother's inconsistent reception ("holding") of the first "spontaneous gestures" of the infant's true self. In "Primary Maternal Preoccupation" (1956), Winnicott describes how the mother of the early infant must provide "a good enough adaptation to need" for her baby. Reactions to the mother's inadequate holding "interrupt the 'going on being' of the infant, and lead to "a *threat of annihilation* ... A very real primitive anxiety, long antedating any anxiety that includes the word death in its description" (p. 303).

At the center of regression to dependency is the threat of annihilation, the "emptiness and void" of Masterson's abandonment depression. In the therapeutic situation, the safe "holding" of the therapeutic environment (relationship) is critical to enable the patient to transcend the terror of psychic nonexistence and find a new beginning for the self. As Kernberg summed it up in Masterson's 1978 exploratory conference: "A temporary regressive state reflecting this development may signify a potential for new growth, as Balint (1968) and Winnicott (1975 [1958], 1965) have suggested" (pp. 87–88).

Case Vignette: Annihilation Anxiety in the Schizoid Patient

Mr. T., a 45-year-old mechanical engineer, sought therapy following a recent divorce. He seemed to be falling into a state of functional paralysis that threatened his ability to work, or even his motivation to stay alive. Mr. T.'s intellect was a strong ally in his therapy, despite a tendency to obsessively reason himself into a standstill.

He reflected that he had never felt he had an existence on his own terms. He had been the designated "helper" in his family of origin: he had absorbed his mother's depression for her and, after her death, felt he no longer had a "use" as a person. His marriage temporarily restored a sense of identity, and he assumed a protective role with his wife until she left him, when he again felt "nonexistent."

As Mr. T. began to experience some feeling of existential safety in the therapeutic environment, he described a core horror sense of annihilation – a fear of being nothing. He compared himself to the astronaut in the film *2001*, who loses his umbilical connection to the mother ship, and floats away into space. He said: "I am slowly turning and turning in nowhere. There is nothing around me forever. I am nothing except oxygen that will soon run out. And emptiness. The emptiness inside me is the same as the space around me, and I am disappearing into it."

To overcome his core anxiety, Mr. T. must contend with a fear of loss of relatedness altogether – the sense of nonbeing arising from the absence of a sufficiently sustaining (maternal) environment. In the case of the schizoid, the patient's feeling of unmet dependency is so profound, and the psychic boundaries so fluid, that the constancy of the therapist's emotional availability is tested to an unusual degree through projective identification and the patient's somatic compliance to anxiety states. At the emotional developmental level of the schizoid, abandonment depression assumes a unique variation as annihilation anxiety. Without reliable "holding" (the "going-on-being" provided by the mother), the infant (still without the memory and experience needed to form a sense of process) feels to be no more than endlessly differentiating bits dispersing in space.

Summary

The concept of a developmental paradigm reminds us that each time we engage the abandonment depression in a different disorder we are meeting with a different affective experience. Also, that the developmental level of the patient will determine the existential level of the challenge, and the corresponding degree of sensitivity required of the therapist. However the abandonment depression may vary in feeling states related to different developmental levels, it is essential for the therapist to keep in mind that this is where the real self resides and can be found. Here, it is crucial that the therapist relate to the patient with the recognition and constancy that had failed to be provided by the mother.

As we trace the developmental paradigm back in time, we see that the less firmly established sense of self of the personality disorder, the more threatening the experience of the abandonment depression becomes to the sense of self-preservation. The degree of intensity too often reached by the abandonment depression can test our comprehension when we encounter it in the therapeutic process. Masterson and Winnicott both stress that the most elaborate defenses the patient can construct guard against this experience. In some cases, even physical death may be seen as preferable to facing the death of the self, which is a reason Masterson speaks of "suicidal despair" at the depth of the abandonment depression. This therapeutic phenomenon of abandonment depression, it would seem, essentially represents a traumatic situation: the facing of a nearly overwhelming threat to the patient's sense of survival.

Masterson's concept of abandonment depression is central to his Approach and, indeed, it seems crucial to attempt to address it for the therapeutic reconstruction of a personality that has been built on flawed assumptions.

Masterson and Winnicott, in the tradition of Freud, value regression in the service of psychic healing. Masterson proposes this as the working-through of the abandonment depression, and Winnicott describes this as a therapeutically "held" regression to dependency. Kohut's disagreement with this practice is perhaps explained in his stated concern with "the danger that a narcissistic injury could initiate an uncontrollable regression" (1971, p. 13). Although Kohut hesitates at this juncture, it would be well to keep his warning in mind, together with Winnicott's caveat that the patient's ego must be prepared to sustain this critical and profoundly destabilizing process.

It should be remembered that Masterson, Winnicott, and Kohut all were pioneers in the unknown territory of developmental arrest. They had no experienced guide who had gone before and could warn them of dangers, or even assure them that the dangers they encountered were survivable in mapping this region where the self waits to be found. To use Freud's metaphor, these originators had to have the zeal of a "conquistador" in order to explore the *terra incognita* of the human mind.

We are still testing their maps and trying to find our way.

It may also be noted that the abandonment depression may represent a pathological exaggeration of the natural sense of risk that is felt when making claim to the new. The thrill of assuming self-reliance is felt instead as fear of letting go that which has been sustaining, even defining one's existence. The mother–child relationship has failed to facilitate the transfer of the subjective task of taking responsibility for going-on-being from mother to child: the child doubts its capacity to maintain its own continuity.

Each developmental task incrementally tests the child's readiness to take on ownership of the maintaining of the self through time and environment. Adequate "mirroring" – the reciprocal and cumulative mother–child validation described by Fonagy – is essential for the building of the child's subjective readiness here. In this mutual process, the mother provides the balancing of decreasing directiveness and growing confidence that shifts with the child's increasing capacity for autonomy. But there is bound to be anxiety as well as anticipation even at times of desired change and, to use Mahler's images, the mother should be available for reassuring moments of "touching back," as well as carefully timed edge-of-the-nest nudges of encouragement.

Thus it may be that the abandonment depression, pathological though it is, has its roots in a healthy, even requisite, developmental passage related to Klein's depressive position and Freud's concept of transformative mourning. It may be based on an expectable hesitation preceding the taking on of what is, itself, a defining developmental task. It may reflect the desired risk and concomitant regret we must experience as we move toward taking charge of our own continuity.

Presented at the Fifth Biennial Conference of The Masterson Institute for Psychoanalytic Psychotherapy of South Africa: "Abandonment Depression: The Masterson Approach and Affective Memory." Cape Town, August 30–31, 2019.

CHAPTER 6

The Diagrams

It has become customary for those introducing Masterson's therapeutic model to illustrate the dynamics of the three personality types – borderline, narcissistic, and schizoid – with three comparative diagrams. Diagrams transpose the abstract into an immediate image that forestalls the qualifications and ambiguities of words: what you see is what it is. Masterson first introduced these pictograms to clarify his concept of borderline pathology, of the divided self still more divided against itself by faulty development. Later, he added diagrams picturing narcissistic, then schizoid pathology, based on adaptation of the original diagram of the borderline. This progression was compromised by the developmentally reversed order in which personality types were introduced. An earlier stage of maturation was pictured as derived from later development, instead of the other way around, that is, instead of building upon an earlier model, as it happens in actuality. Further, this visualization relied on an error in early object relations theorizing: the attribution of good/bad splitting of defined self and object concepts to the one-year-old psyche. Although this error was corrected by Melanie Klein's followers (notably the pediatrician/analyst Winnicott), and the correction reinforced by Kernberg (1994, p. 140), the attribution of the good/bad designation of the splitting defense in narcissistic and, especially, schizoid patients was maintained by Masterson. In the diagrams of narcissistic and schizoid pathology, what you see is not what it is.

The original diagrams appear singly in Masterson's books and lectures (as the theory itself evolves), and are gathered together in 2000, in a last volume, *The Personality Disorders: A New Look at the Developmental Self and Object Relations Approach*. They appear there with explanation in its third chapter: "Diagnosis: A Psychodynamic Approach to the Borderline, Narcissistic, and Schizoid Personality Disorders" (2000, pp. 59–74).

The developmental diagrams are at times out of step with predominating theory, also no doubt because the theory in itself was still much in the process of being determined and acknowledged (as indeed it still is). This applies especially to the schizoid. What follows is my attempt to re-formulate the diagrams with some theoretical reconsideration, especially that of Fairbairn, Winnicott, and Kohut, and in the order of childhood psychic development, as schematized by Mahler and her associates.

Clarification of terms – which are sometimes divergent, sometimes synonymous – is needed here. I venture the following, hoping it proceeds with some accuracy in the direction of contemporary psychoanalytic hypothesizing, and with the intent of the Masterson diagrams.

I venture the following, with italics for emphasis, that *dissociation* is the organizing mental process that governs the shaping of the preoedipal psyche, and is essentially a right hemisphere function (according to neuroimaging studies, it is induced by the early established, right anterior singular cortex). *Dissociation* complements the surge of psychic growth with a containing, boundary-making counterforce that shapes development to conform to the capacities of the gradual structuring of the self. This is what Freud referred to as "*primal repression*" (1915, p. 86), and Kohut as "*vertical splitting*" (1971, p. 185) – an ability of the mind to block out and segregate away from consciousness whatever threatens the integrity of the self. This is in keeping with Freud's inclusive definition of *repression*, "that *the essence of repression lies simply in the function of rejecting and keeping something out of consciousness*" (1915, p. 86, italics are Freud's).

In its constructive form, *dissociation* functions to *differentiate* the developing mind. In a detailed sorting, it first compartmentalizes self-states: "nuclei" (Glover) of the whole self to come. In the wider scope, it then defines coalescing parts of the emerging whole self – self and other, "good" and "bad" feeling – and then regulates their integration by titrating conscious awareness of their existence.

In its capacity to hold back premature or intrusive (internal or external) influences from overwhelming an immature self, *dissociation* can also be seen as protective; indeed, it always will be retained as a defense against traumatic events. In the early stages of mental growth, it acts as a *trauma mechanism*, creating *developmental arrest*, or perhaps what Freud described as *fixation*, in the service of survival. In the first year, *dissociation* halts the full actualizing of any self-states that would be unconsciously perceived by the infant as threatening the continued support of the life-sustaining other. For the same reason, *dissociation* holds back the integration of infantile self-states, which would otherwise gradually coalesce. What would normally evolve as flexible and evolving distinctions between components of the self become rigid, autonomous self-states – exclusive *splits*.

A significant distinction between the original diagrams and those I propose needs to be noted. The originals indicate that only one "side" of the self is defending against abandonment depression. My proposed diagrams picture an overall pathological patterning of personal relating, reflecting a characteristic freezing of spontaneity in order to avoid abandonment depression. Included at the close of this chapter for reference and comparison are the suggested modified diagrams (see pages 166-168), and the original Masterson diagrams (see pages 169-171).

The Schizoid

The primary dissociative division in the first year – Mahler's differentiation subphase – is the partitioning of the infant's sense of being into inner and outer "space." This is critical to the establishing of fundamental mental health. Outwardly, this begins the separation from the infant–mother symbiosis. Inwardly, it sets the boundary distinguishing outer perception from inner fantasy. While exploring the nature of both psychic alternatives, the schizoid must maintain the basic differentiation that holds the boundary between (essentially) reality-oriented personality disorder and the undifferentiated world of the schizophrenic. It is not surprising that the schizoid patient views the therapeutic relationship, with its prospect of change, with considerable caution. The differentiating boundary, still in formation, likely still oscillating, is not yet certain: things still threaten to disappear again into each other or cancel one another out. Annihilation anxiety, the characteristic inner terror of the schizoid, may be evoked.

Of major importance for this developmental subphase is the differentiation of numerous self-states (subselves, or ego nuclei). As they differentiate, these self-states (Fairbairn) are drawn toward their eventual "unification" (Winnicott) in the whole self. The experience of the schizoid-to-be, however, "freezes" (Winnicott) this process. Sensing the environment-mother's aversion to the spontaneous occurrence of certain self-states, dissociation protectively acts to "hide" these states. Representations of these self-states accumulate in the inner world (which will later become the nonconscious). A depleted, partial actualization of the self continues in the outer world, ever compliant with any accepting response from the environment-mother (and later object-mother). This functional but subjectively empty-feeling self-state was called the "false self" by Winnicott, and the "reactive self" by Khan (1974, p. 302).

A diagram of this situation would probably not be complete without the addition of Winnicott's hypothesized area of permeability that allows the rigid inner/outer division in the schizoid self to be accessible to psychic change. This receptive "transitional space" offers a tentative opening for experimental "play" with inner and outer relationship under the patient's guarded auspices (Winnicott).

It should be noted that the good/bad split in the original Masterson diagram is premature. As Winnicott says: "In regard to good and bad, I think it doubtful whether these words can be used before the infant has been able to sort out benign from persecutory internal objects" (1965, p. 177). The "master/slave" positions of the original diagram most likely reflect predominant self-states of the schizoid psyche.

The Narcissist

In the infant's psyche at the practicing subphase, inner and outer worlds are functionally distinguished enough, and even the fused self-to-be and pre-object are sufficiently differentiated so that there is no longer the fear of mutual absorption. In addition, increasingly differentiated and coalescing positive feelings are associated with this state, which reinforce it as the foundation for the continuing development of the whole self.

The narcissistic personality embodies a sense of self differentiating/cohering into a substantial subself that is aware of the other – although the other is not yet experienced as truly separate from the self and is only acknowledged in connection with good feelings. This is the RORU ("rewarding object relations part-unit") of Masterson, and the "selfobject" described by Kohut. The complementary negative part – the next major differentiation in the developing self – is still dissociatively held back, although it exists in potential. One speculates that this is a protective progression that keeps the negative part in abeyance until the positive is firmly established as the subjective location of the "secure base" (Bowlby) originally provided by the mother. Masterson's WORU ("withdrawing object relations part-unit") can only be tentatively represented at this point. That it is imperative that the good-feeling base be firmly established in this, Mahler's practicing subphase of development, will be abundantly clear in the next rapproche-ment subphase, when introduction of the negative part of the self creates ambivalence and disorientation in the self-system.

The Mastersonian diagram, I believe, would more accurately reflect the nature of the narcissistic split if the WORU were shown as potential only, with the patient exclusively invested in the RORU. Pathologically, the temporary division that delays incorporation of the negative is develop-mentally frozen. A problematic mother–child relationship (basically too much or too little attention) has left the self unprepared to maintain its "cohesiveness" (Kohut) under the psychic stress of maintaining the "good" while beginning to introduce the "bad." Such stress causes fragmentation anxiety and is resisted. Again, this would seem to be dissociation acting as a protective trauma mechanism, as it delays a psychically challenging de-velopmental step. The narcissistic patient, therefore, permits only empathic expression in the therapy, until a sufficiently positive therapeutic relation-ship has strengthened the patient's psychic capacity to tolerate the negative.

The Borderline

Even the original Masterson diagram, which so graphically illustrates his original concept of borderline personality disorder, requires some revi-sion at this point.

Some difficulty seems to have arisen in the attempt to collate Freud's pleasure ego and reality ego with the Mastersonian rewarding and with-drawing part-units of the pathological ego/self. It doesn't work. If the attempt must be made, it would seem more apt to relate both part-units to the pleasure ego, with the resolution of their combined defensive re-sistance enabling the consolidation of the reality ego.

There is also some question of dividing the part-units under the do-mains of the libidinal and aggressive drives. Masterson seems to make this distinction in keeping with Melanie Klein/Kernberg, but not in consonance with the "Independents," who understood aggression to be the product of frustrated libido. The latter seems to be a more accurate reflection of the rebellious borderline, who distorts the impulse toward independence into an endlessly oppositional form of attachment.

Although, with borderline patients, confrontation of the distorted re-lationship contained in each part-unit is critical, the confrontation of the (stuck) defensive alternation of the part-units – the intervention that brings them into a field of simultaneous awareness – dissolves the split. It is only then that the abandonment depression fully emerges, with its long-denied and devastating reaction to long-ago compromised relationship. Finally able to contain the traumatic impact of the feelings evoked by the failure of that relationship, the self is able to accept the past as contained within the reality of present time. The building of psychic structure in the therapeutic relationship now allows the therapist successfully to confront what was once unbearable, and so required splitting for psychic survival.

Dissociation acts distinctively in the rapprochement subphase of separation/individuation. At this stage of development, both positive and negative feelings have been accepted, and can be related to internalizations of self and other, but only when partial concepts of self and other are divided into separate "good" and "bad" feelings. The RORU of the narcissist now is joined by the WORU, but it would seem that their combined acceptance cannot initially be tolerated in awareness more than one at a time. Mutually conscious acceptance (mixed feelings) comes into being from an increasing oscillation of part-units, until they can be encompassed in a single field of observation. Until then, dissociation keeps one part-unit out of consciousness while its opposite is being experienced, and then the situation is reversed (in reaction to circumstance). This alternation is in part responsible for the "ambivalence" noted by Freud, the contrariness of the "terrible twos" generally witnessed by parents, and the "mood swings" typical of the borderline patient. One might also speculate that it exemplifies the extreme of the oscillatory action that accompanies psychic change in preoedipal states generally; it could perhaps be seen as the functional precursor to the psychic achievement of the capacity for conflict in the oedipal phase.

In borderline pathology, however, this developmental oscillation becomes stuck in an unresolving repetition. Now, dissociation works defensively to form a rigid split that delays growth in avoidance of negative feelings: blocking emotions evoked by impulses toward independence that are intolerably challenging to a tenuous positive attachment. The technique of confrontation within the therapeutic relationship begins to reinstitute the healthy developmental process. Mastersonian confrontation steadily brings the parts into the same field, and the defense of splitting is resolved and integration of the self resumed. A central insight of the Masterson Approach is the recognition of the abandonment depression that must be faced with the resolution of the split. Anxiety that the mother will be lost in reality accompanies the loss of the "good" mother of fantasy, and requires the containment of the therapeutic relationship for working through the abandonment depression.

In the rapprochement subphase, the self is now becoming able to operate independently, although maintaining an affinity for the now-separate other that will last a lifetime. Beyond the complexity of this integration, the self is undergoing a major operational change. With the emerging primacy of the left hemisphere and the conscious mind, dissociation will no longer be the preferred mechanism. Rational deliberation will permit the toleration of opposites within the same field of consciousness – the reality of conflict is discovered. As Kernberg observes in the 1977 Masterson symposium: "impulse-defense configurations cannot be carried out within a frame of intersystemic conflicts except in advanced stages of treatment" (Masterson 1974, p. 94). An argument will no longer have to be resolved by "disappearing" one alternative – or even the whole thing – by dissociation. This same argument can now be reasoned through to resolution. Consequently, repression now exists as a means for pre/unconscious storage of basic behavioral formulae available for instant emergency implementation (fight/flight/freeze), miscellaneous data ready for formulation, and (especially pertinent for the analyst) formulae for vital relationship and unresolved conflicts held for possible solution. Management of all these developmental issues is formidable, and the growing child struggles to assume a readiness to accept responsibility for being his or her own "holding environment." In this developmental "moment" mother–infant synchrony gives place to adult/maturing-child collaboration. Once this developmental task is accomplished, the memory of sufficiently accomplished developmental tasks will be stored away behind the repression barrier (Freud), and the oedipal self will prepare to build a conscious life.

Reliant on the achievements of rapprochement, the oedipal child is preparing to meet the social world with an open conscious mind working in bicameral co-operation with an unconscious mind that calls attention to unfinished business through dreams, symptoms, and quirks of character.

Diagrams benefit from the capacity of the mind to focus the complexities of an idea into an image. It should go without stressing, though, that the image gains force at the expense of the nuances captured by words. Also, although these particular images picture an aspect of the self that resists the flow of development, they do not show that the self is nonetheless moving ahead in other respects in its larger being. Similarly, the diagrams are occasionally stuck in Mastersonian time themselves, and fail to reflect the growth of his thinking. One example of this would be Masterson's trend away from drive theory, which gradually recedes from the foreground over the fifteen books.

Nevertheless, pictograms offer the clarity and persuasiveness of a single image. Diagrams convey a comprehension that brings a unique insight to pages and volumes of written words. I am venturing an updating of the Masterson diagrams out of appreciation and respect for their special pertinence in communicating his ideas.

Diagram 6.1 Divided Inner and Outer Worlds of the Schizoid Disorder of the Self

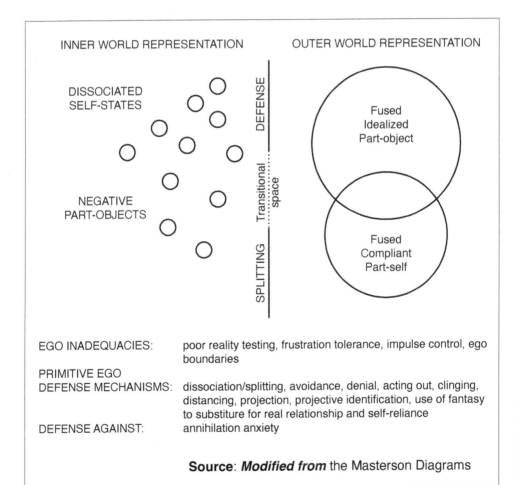

Source: *Modified from* the Masterson Diagrams

Diagram 6.2 Split Object Relations Unit of the Narcissistic Personality Disorder

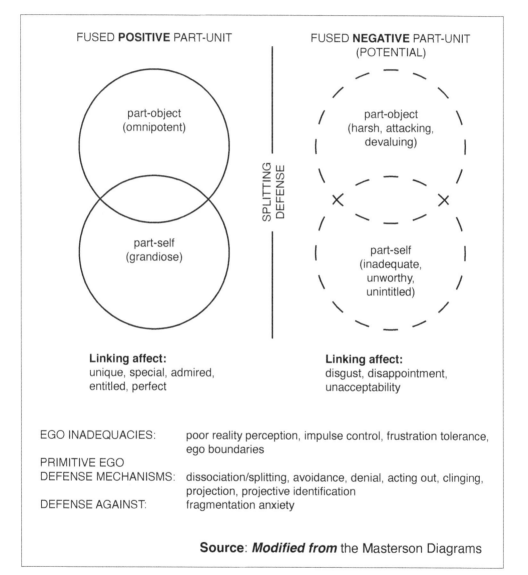

FUSED **POSITIVE** PART-UNIT

part-object
(omnipotent)

part-self
(grandiose)

SPLITTING DEFENSE

FUSED **NEGATIVE** PART-UNIT
(POTENTIAL)

part-object
(harsh, attacking,
devaluing)

part-self
(inadequate,
unworthy,
unintitled)

Linking affect:
unique, special, admired,
entitled, perfect

Linking affect:
disgust, disappointment,
unacceptability

EGO INADEQUACIES: poor reality perception, impulse control, frustration tolerance,
                         ego boundaries

PRIMITIVE EGO
DEFENSE MECHANISMS: dissociation/splitting, avoidance, denial, acting out, clinging,
                         projection, projective identification

DEFENSE AGAINST: fragmentation anxiety

Source: **Modified from** the Masterson Diagrams

Diagram 6.3 Split Object Relations Unit of the Borderline Personality Disorder

<table>
<tr>
<td colspan="2">

REWARDING PART-UNIT
REPRESENTATION (RORU)

Part-object representation:

maternal approval of
regressive, clinging
behavior

Affect: good feeling,
gratification

Part-self representation:

the good, passive,
obedient, ineffectual
child

</td>
<td>

WITHDRAWING PART-UNIT
REPRESENTATION (WORU)

Part-object representation:

maternal withdrawal,
criticism and anger at
independent behavior

Affect: bad feeling,
contentiousness

Part-self representation:

the bad, oppositional,
disobedient, angry,
worthless child

</td>
</tr>
</table>

SPLITTING DEFENSE

EGO INADEQUACIES: poor reality testing, frustration tolerance, impulse control, ego boundaries

PRIMITIVE EGO
DEFENSE MECHANISMS: dissociation/splitting, avoidance, denial, acting out, clinging, projection, projective identification

DEFENSE AGAINST: abandonment anxiety and depression

Source: *Modified from* the Masterson Diagrams

Diagram 6.4 Split Object Relations Unit of the Schizoid Disorder of the Self

MASTER SLAVE PART-UNIT

SADISTIC OBJECT-SELF IN EXILE PART UNIT

Part-object representation:

a maternal part-object which is manipulative, coercive, is the master and wants only to use, not relate to

Part-object representation:

a maternal part-object which is sadistic, dangerous, devaluing, depriving, abandoning

Affect:
In jail, but connected, existence acknowledged, relief in not being alienated

Affect - Abandonment Depression
Depression, rage, loneliness, fear of cosmic aloneness, despair

Part-self representation:

a part-self representation of a dependent, a slave who provided a function for the object and is a victim

Part-self representation:

a part-self representation of being alienated, in exile, isolated but self-contained to self-reliant

SPLITTING DEFENCE

EGO INADEQUACIES: poor reality perception, frustration tolerance, impulse control, ego boundaries

PRIMITIVE EGO
DEFENSE MECHANISMS: splitting, avoidance, denial, acting out, clinging, projection, projective identification, use of fantasy to substitute for real relationships and self reliance

SPLIT EGO: reality ego plus pathologic (or pleasure) ego

Source: *Based on* the original Masterson Diagrams

Diagram 6.5 Split Object Relations Unit of the Narcissistic Personality Disorder

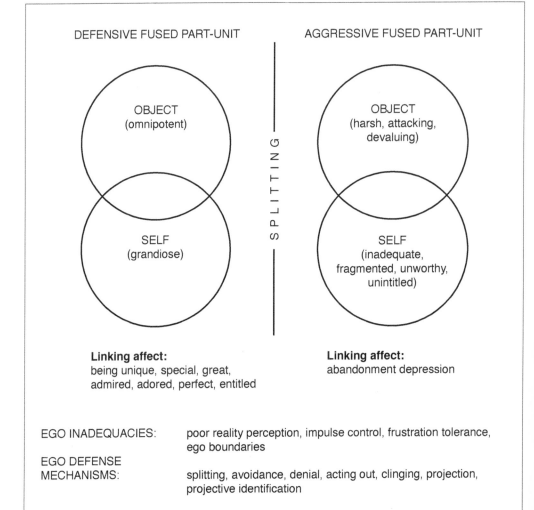

DEFENSIVE FUSED PART-UNIT

OBJECT
(omnipotent)

SELF
(grandiose)

SPLITTING

AGGRESSIVE FUSED PART-UNIT

OBJECT
(harsh, attacking,
devaluing)

SELF
(inadequate,
fragmented, unworthy,
unintitled)

Linking affect:
being unique, special, great,
admired, adored, perfect, entitled

Linking affect:
abandonment depression

EGO INADEQUACIES: poor reality perception, impulse control, frustration tolerance,
ego boundaries

EGO DEFENSE
MECHANISMS: splitting, avoidance, denial, acting out, clinging, projection,
projective identification

Source: *Based on* the original Masterson Diagrams

Diagram 6.6 Split Object Relations Unit of the Borderline

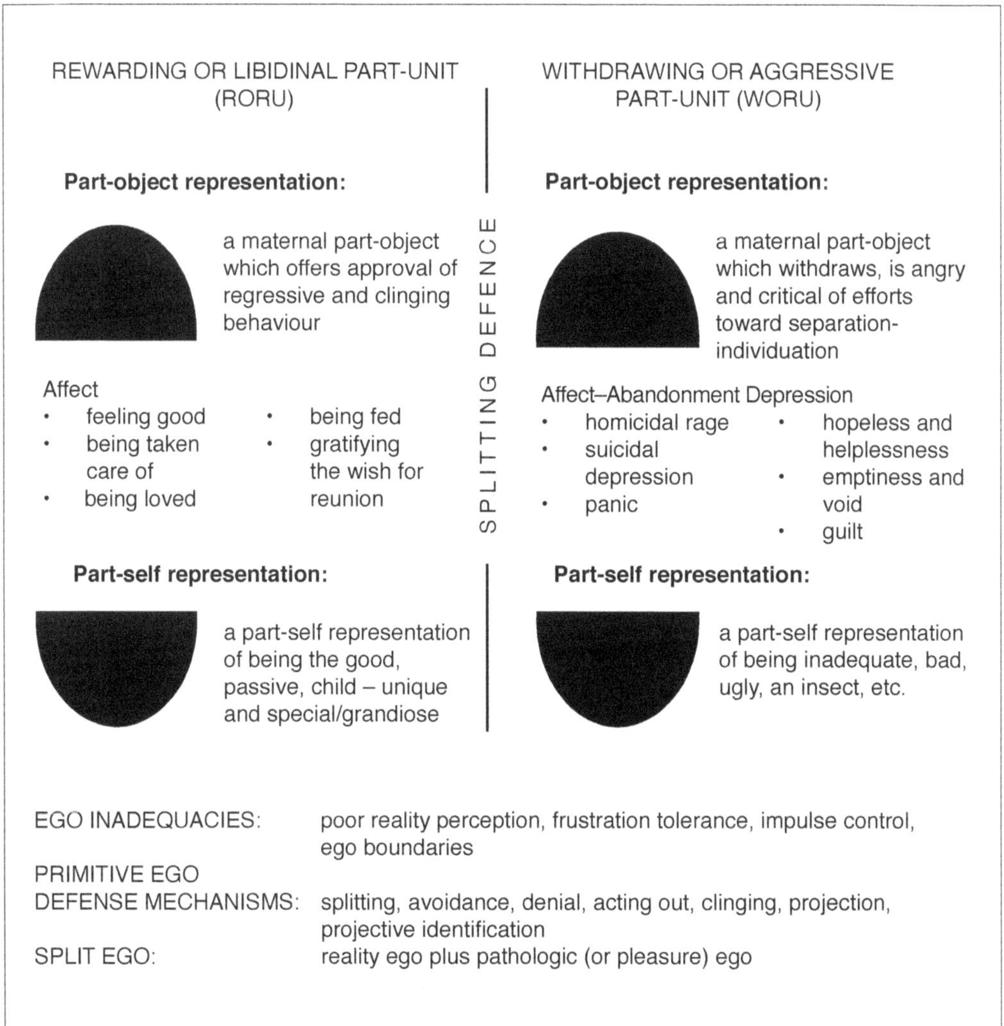

REWARDING OR LIBIDINAL PART-UNIT (RORU)

WITHDRAWING OR AGGRESSIVE PART-UNIT (WORU)

Part-object representation:

a maternal part-object which offers approval of regressive and clinging behaviour

Part-object representation:

a maternal part-object which withdraws, is angry and critical of efforts toward separation-individuation

Affect
- feeling good
- being taken care of
- being loved
- being fed
- gratifying the wish for reunion

Affect–Abandonment Depression
- homicidal rage
- suicidal depression
- panic
- hopeless and helplessness
- emptiness and void
- guilt

Part-self representation:

a part-self representation of being the good, passive, child – unique and special/grandiose

Part-self representation:

a part-self representation of being inadequate, bad, ugly, an insect, etc.

(vertical text between columns:) SPLITTING DEFENCE

EGO INADEQUACIES: poor reality perception, frustration tolerance, impulse control, ego boundaries

PRIMITIVE EGO
DEFENSE MECHANISMS: splitting, avoidance, denial, acting out, clinging, projection, projective identification

SPLIT EGO: reality ego plus pathologic (or pleasure) ego

Source: **Based on** the original Masterson Diagrams

CHAPTER 7

Masterson and Beyond: Trauma, Dissociation, and Self-states

The Building of a Self

In my maturing association with James Masterson, I learned increasingly more about the newly evolving understanding of personality disorder and its therapeutic treatment. Masterson was a leading figure in psychoanalytic psychotherapy of a mental dysfunction that was growing more central in clinicians' caseloads, and we apprentices and our patients were participants in an experimental approach to healing. Our clinical work drew upon Masterson's theory, and the theory in turn gained from ongoing clinical application. In addition to benefiting from this creative feedback loop, this Approach was strengthened by Masterson's constant inquiry into the therapeutic thinking and activity of other leaders in the field – other originating minds with experiences parallel to his own. Masterson invited comparison and contrast of conceptualizations of personality disorder in conferences that brought innovating opinions together with his own in search for definition. These conferences, preserved verbatim by Masterson (Daws 2021; Masterson 1978; Masterson, Tolpin, and Sifneos 1991), were forerunners of the two mainstays of the Masterson Approach: an overarching definition of personality disorder, and the distinguishing of subtypes of disorder that could be linked to stages of psychic development in early childhood. These conceptualizations were distinctively based on a synthesis of pertinent work of others, past and present, together with his own, and drew special effectiveness in providing specific clinical applications in an area noted for vagueness, confusion and contradiction.

Masterson's overall definition of personality disorder is in harmony with a steadily clearer, but still growing, dynamic definition. Together with many others concerned with the problems in the early formation of personality, he realizes that a critical shift in therapeutic perspective is needed. He observes that treatment has to be based not so much on interpretation of conflict over unexpressed childhood wishes and fears as on support of the healthy structuring of the "real self" in relationship. A more interactive effort is needed to reorient the patient blocked from adequate achievement of important milestones in psychic development. This goal is not primarily to make the unconscious conscious, but to release from psychic cold storage the growth potential that somehow has been inhibited.

The therapeutic process, therefore, requires the identifying of obstacles or deficits preventing the unfolding of a responsible, self-directed individual. Here, Freud's insistence on resistance analysis must take a new form: of resolving distortions created by what is missing in order to channel the flow of the process of psychic growth. Masterson's work contributes to the contemporary paradigm shift that views the average patient more in terms of developmental deficit than in terms of emotional conflict, and pathology as an issue for the personality as a compromised whole.

Masterson's uniquely synthesizing Approach integrates formerly "dissociated" categories of personality disorder, which he presents as partial but interconnected perspectives on an overall psyche – a psyche developmentally impeded at characteristic points. Masterson's theoretical base in object relations and Mahlerian developmental theory supports his theory of psychic damage arising from distortion in early interpersonal relationship, suggesting that traumatized child-states form the origin of personality disorder. Importantly, he suggests that the normal development of a specific child-state is the key to understanding what went wrong at a crucial developmental subphase. The therapy is provided with a guiding dynamic and developmentally appropriate technical "language" to communicate with and begin to heal that arrested part of the self's continuity. The Mastersonian Approach suggests that the relationship offered to the patient has to be specifically adapted to the presented disorder of the self, in order to provide in psychotherapy the interpersonal experiences required to establish new inner representations. These are representations of both self and other in the patient's psyche, which can, in turn, counter early emotional abandonment experiences by providing the "ground" from which the real self can activate despite overwhelming anxiety.

This addendum offers additional hypothesizing based on my thoughts about the interaction of trauma, self-states, and the formation of personality disorder. Masterson's openness of mind and collegial encouragement led to his incorporation into his books of the ideas of those who trained and practiced with him. His Institute prospered with this shared creativity, and now it comes to those who learned from him and worked under his mentorship to try to continue his contribution. One hopes to add to Masterson's pertinence by synthesizing, as he had, some of the more recent but diversified findings in the mental health field, and so benefit the treatment of personality disorder.

My line of thought in this addendum proceeds in a direction approved, and to a degree pursued, by Masterson, although I introduce hypotheses and other possibly controversial considerations not included in his works. It is appended in my belief that he would have encouraged this, although I cannot claim it as part of the formal canon. Creative thought leads irresistibly to further speculation, and Masterson's ideas, I believe, continue to draw together related ideas that provide new perspectives on the nature of personality disorder and its healing.

Developmental Trauma

In 1995, Masterson, in co-editorship with Ralph Klein, included my work on the impact of psychic trauma on the development of personality disorder in *Disorders of the Self* (Orcutt 1995a, pp. 181–254). In two clinical vignettes presented in detail, I described the emergence of previously dissociated childhood trauma, which followed the resolution of the presenting issue of personality disorder. In a chapter focused on theory, I hypothesized that "physical/sexual abuse sufficient to cause psychogenic amnesia … comorbid with a disorder of the self … may contribute to overall developmental arrest of the self." I speculated over a condition I named "developmental trauma," and wondered whether "developmental trauma will always be found in conjunction with a disorder of the self" (p. 188). I also noted that:

Where it exists, the situation is painfully compounded by the absence of conscious, corroborating memory of abusive experiences, and the patient is victimized not only by the original event, but also by the disruption in the formation and continuity of the self as the patient defensively refuses to accept the full impact of what has happened.

(Orcutt 1995a, p. 189)

I puzzled over instances of early traumatic episodes contained within disordered personality development, and possibly bearing some interactive connection with it. One thing seemed clear to me: in order to work therapeutically with such cases, it was necessary to limit interpretive interventions aimed at a neurotic condition in favor of not only the experiential, ego-oriented interventions appropriate for personality disorders, but also hypnotic methods often found to be effective in working with trauma. In different words, I found that technique addressed to neurotic repression became secondary to therapeutic approaches useful for therapy with dissociation.

In the mid-1990s, I based my hypothesizing on the general concept of psychic trauma at the time. I understood it to be based on an event or series of events too intense in impact (especially of an emotional nature) to be allowed full psychic acknowledgment. Pertinent to analytic inquiry was such trauma occurring in early childhood, and within the context of close interpersonal relationship. Sexual trauma, occurring within the family, was particularly relevant – as described in the seduction theory of Breuer and Freud. Sexual abuse was perceived by the patient as so psychically intolerable that the memory of the experience was closed off from consciousness, only becoming discernable in problematic symptoms that arose as the memory pressed to appear in symbolic disguise.

When I puzzled over the nature of what I called "developmental trauma," I was unaware of Masud Khan's concept of "cumulative trauma." First published in 1963, Khan's formulation posits that a mother–child dysfunctional relationship may not be "clinically detectable" – that is, superficially socially evident – in process, but can be recognized as "traumatic ... only cumulatively and in retrospect" (Khan 1974, p. 42). Beginning with the infant's first year, "cumulative trauma is the result of the breaches in the mother's role as a protective shield over the whole course of the child's development" (p. 46). Khan's concept is founded on the intensive experience and writings of the pediatrician–analyst, Donald Winnicott, which focus on the importance of the maternal "holding" of the infant's psyche – especially in the first year. This containing presence is needed to protect the infant both from imposition of external pressures and from overintensity of internal states. This maternal "auxiliary ego" (Spitz) sets a model for gradual internalization, as well, as the young child steadily becomes able to assume protective capability for himself or herself.

In a detailed tracing of the history of the psychoanalytic understanding of trauma, especially in Freud's writings, Khan refers to the culminating work: *Beyond the Pleasure Principle* (Freud 1920g). He cites Freud's hypothesizing over the need of "living organisms" to develop a "protective shield" to moderate the effects of both inner and outer stimuli, a forerunner of the "system Cs" with its mediating ego. Khan quotes Freud's definition of "traumatic" as "excitations from outside which are powerful enough to break through the protective shield" (Khan 1974, p. 45). Khan, extending this concept to Winnicott's depiction of "infant in care," concludes: "The infant in care has for his protective shield the caretaking mother" (p. 46).

The consequences of cumulative trauma are dealt with more specifically in a companion article (1974, pp. 59–68). Khan addresses the way in which analytic discussion "has extended to the larger issues of identity formation … and the establishment of self." He continues:

> I shall here restrict myself to that type of ego distortion which derives from cumulative trauma. It is my contention that the breaches in the mother's role as protective shield and the consequent impingements on the infant-child's emergent ego-integration become visible through what in Freud's idiom are said to be "inconsistencies, eccentricities and follies of men", that is, in character and personality disorders.
>
> (p. 62)

Khan retains the tendency of the independent object relationists to interchange the terms "ego" and "self," and to maintain the theoretical focus of this group on the schizoid self. This noted, he is clearly proposing a dynamic describing the origin of personality disorder (or "disorders of the self," as Masterson eventually came to say). This definition posits a traumatic outcome resulting from a persistently dysregulated mother-child relationship, and sees a traumatic mechanism at work in the formation of personality disorder.

At the same time that Masterson & Klein (Eds.), 1995 edition incorporated the issue of psychic trauma into his Approach, the neuropsychoanalyst Allan Schore was beginning to introduce a body of work that included his concept of "relational trauma" (Schore 2009). Like Masterson, Schore is a synthesist, and he articulates "an interdisciplinary model of attachment trauma and pathological dissociation, an early forming defense against overwhelming affect that is a cardinal feature of self-pathologies" (Schore 2009, p. 189). Schore meticulously integrates neurobiological data (especially data pertinent to right-hemisphere activity) with psychoanalytic attachment theory and self psychology (notably the work of Heinz Kohut). He concludes: "the essential task of the first year of human life is the creation of a secure attachment-bond of emotional connection between infant and primary caregiver" (p. 192). Relational trauma occurs when "in a growth-inhibiting relational environment the primary caregiver induces traumatic states of enduring negative affective arousal in the child" (p. 196). Although he does not refer to it, Schore empirically validates Khan's concept of cumulative trauma – incorporating the extensive pediatric observations of Winnicott with the scientific data that Freud longed for ahead of his time.

Masterson's last book, *The Personality Disorders Through the Lens of Attachment Theory and the Neurobiologic Development of the Self: A Clinical Integration* (2005), is focused on incorporating Schore's studies into Masterson's developmental, self, and object relations model. Masterson makes a succinct summation of Schore's contribution:

> *a center emerges in the right prefrontal orbital cortex in the right brain for the control of emotion and emotional relationships, and is, therefore, a neurobiologic center of the self. Prior to this emergence, the child is unable to regulate his or her own affect, and thus the primary caretaker's interaction with the child becomes the principal regulator of emotion, and also the creator of the background from which the prefrontal orbital cortex will emerge, grow, and mature.*

(Masterson 2005, p. 10)

Through the face-to-face, nonverbal "transmission of reciprocal mutual influences," the right hemispheres of mother and infant achieve "affect synchronicity … fundamental to the ongoing affective development of the orbital prefrontal cortex, and, therefore, of the [infant's] self" (p. 10).

Pertinent to analytic understanding of the maladaptive patterns of personality disorder, he continues: "These attachment experiences of infancy are deeply internalized in the right brain to become unconscious working models of attachment relationships" (p. 10). Critically important for the therapeutic reshaping of personality, he also states: "The growth of the right brain is experience-dependent, and its wiring can change after it is fully grown" (p. 9). The creation of neural synchrony is scientifically posited to support belief in the necessity for therapeutic relationship in fostering intrapsychic change. Masterson assimilates into both the theoretical and clinical aspects of his model Schore's emphasis (2004, 2014) on the importance of right-hemisphere synchrony for the healing nature of the therapist–patient relationship as well as for the nurturing ability of the mother–child attachment.

Since the 1970s, another synthesist, the psychiatrist Bessel van der Kolk, has drawn worldwide attention to trauma through his researches. His trauma center in Massachusetts, founded in the mid-1990s, is dedicated to the understanding and treatment of trauma, combining the discoveries of neuroscience, developmental psychopathology, and interpersonal neurobiology. His book *The Body Keeps the Score: Brain, Mind, and Body in the Healing of Trauma* (2014) has become pre-eminent in the field of trauma studies. Politically active as well, van der Kolk spearheaded the attempt to include "developmental trauma disorder" as a category in the American Psychiatric Association's *Diagnostic and Statistical Manual-V* (the widely adopted guide for the definition and classification of mental disorders). Stunningly, in 2009, the proposal was rejected, and a letter from the DSM subcommittee included the statement: "The notion that early childhood adverse experiences lead to substantial developmental disruptions is more clinical intuition than a research-based fact" (van der Kolk 2014, p. 159). This is demonstrably incorrect in view of the studies conducted by van der Kolk, Schore, and others. In this instance, perhaps dissociation and growing reliance on and profit from the use of medication as a cure-all have reinforced the expectable human reluctance for assimilating new knowledge. Since the 1990s, van der Kolk has encouraged the profession to "remember to remember," but many seem hesitant.

The now often-used term "developmental trauma" seems not so much attributable to one person as to the zeitgeist of a collective. It seems the result of convergent thinking that has found the term descriptive of a newly conceptualized phenomenon.

"Developmental trauma," however, tends to refer to overt traumatic events, or a sequence of these events, rather than the subtle process hypothesized as "cumulative trauma." Khan notes this sort of distinction when he refers to the writing of Ernst Kris: "Kris in his paper 'The Recovery of Childhood Memories in Psychoanalysis' (1956) has distinguished between 'shock trauma' and 'strain trauma'. The latter he has defined as 'the effect of long-lasting situations, which may cause traumatic effects by accumulation of frustrating tensions'" (Khan 1974, p. 52). A clear distinction should be made between the specific acts of commission that define child abuse and the more elusive acts of omission that may create attachment disorder, although both occurrences are often found unhappily blurred together in actuality.

The exploration of trauma as a psychic mechanism capable of shaping the early development of the personality seems well in process. Schore's concept of "relational trauma" offers psychoneurological findings that provide a context for both "cumulative" and (overt) "developmental" trauma, showing them both as instrumental in disrupting psychic growth (it often seems likely that, like the tip of an iceberg, the overt acts of developmental trauma are imposed on underlying cumulative trauma). Masterson's incorporation of Schore's theorizing advances his Approach in terms of an increasingly scientific base. This is work in progress, and points to much to be learned, in addition, in the understanding of dissociation and self-states.

Trauma and Dissociation in the Masterson Approach

In the resurgence of interest in trauma in the 1990s, Masterson himself increasingly incorporated this dimension into his Approach. In 1997, he had established a contact with the Institut Victoria in Montreal that led to a five-day conference offered by Masterson and the Institute faculty, and which included a day-long presentation by myself on "Trauma and Dissociative Problems." At the same time, my article "Death, Trauma, and Personality Disorder: Thoughts on the Inability to Mourn" had been accepted by *Frontières*, a periodical published by the University of Montreal (Orcutt 1998).

The Canadian connection continued with a teaching program established between the Masterson Institute and Traumatys, a clinic in Montreal specializing in resolving post-traumatic stress disorder (PTSD) and the training of psychotherapists in treating this problem. Notably, most patients treated at Traumatys also presented with a disorder of the self. I was the Mastersonian representative in this undertaking, and the collegial sharing and personal friendship initiated there continue to this day. In particular, the publications of Louise Gaston, Ph.D., founder and director of Traumatys, have steadily increased the field's store of rigorously researched theory and moving clinical studies (2015, 2017). In addition, personal conversations with Louise Gaston on the internet have provided me with professional support at sometimes challenging times.

Somewhat earlier, in 1994, Masterson and I had collaborated in writing an article, "A Theoretical and Classical View of Multiple Personality Disorder in the United States in the 1990s," for publication in *Kokoro no Rinsho* (*Clinical Mental Health*, Tokyo, vol. 13, no. 4). Even as psychotherapy with trauma and dissociation was entering Masterson's Approach, it was becoming part of a widespread reinterest in the topic. Although this attention was to encounter a setback, typical of the history of this problematic therapeutic undertaking (Orcutt 2018), this time the resistance would be fairly brief. It is pertinent here to recall Judith Herman's observation that "the conflict between the will to deny horrible events and the will to proclaim them aloud is the central dialectic of psychological trauma," and "these moments occur in the histories of societies as well as in the histories of individuals" (1992, pp. 1–2).

In keeping with the persistent resurgence of interest manifested in the field, the Mastersonian focus of the 1990s on trauma resurfaces in Masterson's last volume, where the faculty of his Institute continue the theme. Steven Reed pursues the clinical concern of psychotherapy when personality disorder and trauma combine (2005). Other faculty members examine still further theoretical avenues newly open for exploration, especially those concerning the effect of trauma and dissociation on the formation of the developing mind, relationship, and the shaping of consciousness (Beattie 2005a; Pearson 2005; Short 2005). With this volume, the Masterson Approach is poised to incorporate a fundamental reconception of personality disorder, based on newly pertinent understanding of trauma and dissociation.

Before considering some future possibilities of trauma understanding and treatment in the Masterson Approach, it might be useful to review the sometimes elusive historical context surrounding this inquiry.

Dissociation Instrumental in the Emerging Study of the Mind

The ability of the human mind to adaptationally limit its self-reflective capacity is the hallmark of dissociation.
(Bromberg 1998/2001, p. 7)

After a tentative yet failed resurfacing in the 1900s, the topic of dissociation seems again to be resuming its place in the consciousness of mainstream psychoanalysis. This may be in part because of its pertinence to the now more socially topical issue of trauma – a connection that first accompanied dissociation and analysis itself into scientific focus in the late 1800s.

The opening history of the science of the mind (scrupulously narrated by Henri Ellenberger [1970]), having more or less freed itself from adherence to paranormal possession as causative, came dramatically into being with the hypnotic demonstrations of Jean-Martin Charcot (Ellenberger 1970, pp. 89–102). Part scientific experiment, part show, Charcot's display of fainting women patients and hypnotic suggestion brought together issues of current interest, both professional and popular: altered states of consciousness, suggestibility, dual and multiple personality, and the erasing of the memory of all of these. This exploration of "hysteria," promoted by Charcot to a subject of scientific inquiry, was further elevated by two young adherents: his student, Pierre Janet, and his translator, Sigmund Freud. Initially moving along parallel investigations, these two young innovators would lead the developing science of the mind along significantly diverging pathways. Charcot had proposed that the "hypnoid" states of his subjects had been evoked by trauma. Janet and Freud continued from this point, but in different ways.

Janet maintained, and further scientifically objectified, the exploration into "dissociation" of these traumatic states. Freud followed a different progression, eventually displacing trauma and dissociation with unconscious fantasy and repression. For a while, the two had seemed on the same quest: Janet introducing "psychological analysis," while Freud was constructing "psycho-analysis." Janet's "subconscious" was paralleled by Freud's "unconscious;" Janet's concept of trauma-based subconscious "fixed ideas" that achieved symbolic expression in hysterical symptoms, found a similar formulation in Breuer and Freud's *Studies on Hysteria* (1895); Janet's "automatic talking" was similar to Freud's "free association."

A point of divergence, however, was Janet's assumption of an underlying predisposition for "neuroses," while Freud was developing a theoretical basis for the psychological origin of mental illness. Any possibility of collaboration was consistently eliminated by a growing mutual resentment. Janet expressed regret that Freud had given no credit to his ideas, while Freud took umbrage and eventually refused to even meet. Janet's less assertive professional presence began to fade with time, taking the developing exploration of dissociation, trauma, and hypnosis with it; his death in 1947 went almost without notice. The conviction of Freud's internationally organized mental science took hold, and the dissociation of dissociation took place in the analytic field (Ellenberger 1970, pp. 372–374, 487).

Freud at first had been fascinated by the contemporary involvement with hysteria, and he contributed the critical default opinion that the issue under examination was an illness of the mind, not a biological peculiarity. After that, however, he left the exploration begun by Charcot, Janet, and Breuer to continue independently as best it could. Despite attempts to integrate psychology with neurobiology, beginning even in Freud's own time, it is only fairly recently that the goal has been in sight. For after all – despite the dramatic diversity of some of its manifestations – it was always the same human mind under investigation.

Perhaps the whole reason for the Freudian shift in theoretical orientation will remain hidden in an obscure place in Freud's psyche. Freud's letters to Fliess reflect an ambivalence that never seems altogether resolved, nor is it, even in *The Interpretation of Dreams* (1900a). It also has been observed that Freud never fully relinquished the causative effect of trauma – along with "preoedipal" concerns, it may have had to give prominence to the Oedipus complex for political as well as theoretical purposes (Gay 1998, pp. 475–476). Perhaps, as well, Freud was influenced by a shift in the communal psyche, that then as now shows hesitation over examining dissociation and the veil that it places over the abuse of humankind by humankind.

In any event, it is interesting that, one hundred years after Charcot, Janet, and Freud, there was a significant resurgence of interest in dissociation, trauma (combat-related PTSD and child abuse), and hypnosis. A small library of literature (often biographical) was available by the 1990s, with a substantial shelf devoted to the once-focal subject of dual personality and multiple personality (e.g., Casey and Wilson, 1991; Schreiber 1973; Sizemore and Pittillo 1977; The Troops for Truddi Chase 1987). Curiously, following a popular as well as a scientific fascination reminiscent of the 1890s, the topic once again met with a countersurgence of skepticism. Political efforts of such groups as the False Memory Syndrome Foundation even made pursuit of dissociated (or "repressed") recollections of trauma professionally risky (Orcutt 2018). A scrupulous and even-handed assessment of these recent "memory wars" may be found in the comprehensive *Memory, Trauma Treatment, and the Law*, by Brown, Scheflin, and Hammond (1998). However, the rule of "two steps forward, one step backward" would seem to have been in operation, and perhaps a need to correct our shortcomings still drives humanity hesitantly ahead. An increasing tolerance for addressing the reality of child abuse and the emotional damage of war has now reintroduced consideration of dissociation and trauma, and has resumed the psychic exploration of Charcot's day.

Freud's emphasis on repression and the oedipal phase of psychic growth does not contradict the importance of preoedipal development and the use of dissociation in shaping the evolving personality, especially in regard to traumatic influence – it skips over it. It is as if the psychological revealing of the vulnerable early self has had to be gradually released from protective forgetfulness: a dissociative regulation of theoretical insight itself.

From the outset, dissociative responses have been attributed to traumatic causes, especially human abuse of humans; hypnosis, always the black sheep of the scientific family, has been related to traumatic reactions and their possible remedy. Social awareness and civilized responsibility, aimed for and to a degree despaired of by Freud, have managed to progress to the point where trauma and its accompanying forgetfulness can no longer be blurred out in the portrait of human society. If we can now permit ourselves full acknowledgment of this symptom and the deeply disquieting illness it signifies, are we ready to take the next step – the one followed by Masterson – in exploring the possibility that healthy, even universal, mental processes underlie unhealthy human tendencies?

"Conflicting" Concepts of the Psyche

Although, in *Studies on Hysteria*, Breuer seems to be collaborating with Anna O in an intuitive clinical application of the French approach to hysteria, Freud initiates a reconceptualization of the data in the service of theory building. As Giovacchini observes:

> [Breuer] dealt with clinical phenomena every day and his thinking must have been primarily that of the clinician, not that of the scientist who examines every step in the process leading to his conclusions. Freud, on the other hand, was young, enthusiastic, and dedicated to establishing a new system of thought.

> (1982, p. 64)

As described by van der Hart (2016, pp. 45–46), Janet defined the basic characteristics of dissociation as: (1) retraction of the field of consciousness; and (2) dissociation of phenomena – doubling of personality. The manifestation of these characteristics in "hypnoid" states and dual/multiple personalities remained central to Janet's investigations, but became only a stepping stone to Freud's ambitious project of defining the human mind.

Freud's undertaking began with replacing dissociation with a new concept: repression, which he claimed to be "the foundation-stone on which the whole structure of psycho-analysis rests" (1914d, p. 297). Dissociation is in part subsumed under the larger context of repression, which Freud defines as *"the function of rejecting and keeping something out of consciousness."* His description of "primal repression," in particular, is reminiscent of the activity of dissociation in what now would be essentially identified as the brain's right hemisphere: "a first phase of repression, which consists of a denial of entry into consciousness to the mental (ideational) presentation of the instinct. This is accompanied by a *fixation*" (1915, p. 86). Primal repression, like dissociation, forestalls conscious awareness, and, suggestive of the later concept of developmental arrest, can create a "fixation" in psychic growth. Freud states that "anti-cathexis is the sole mechanism of primal repression," and adds: "here we may substitute for the term 'cathexis' that of 'libido'" (1915, p. 114). Freud seems to be describing an unconscious counterforce that can restrain the love-impulse that drives growth forward. This would be a forerunner of the conscious capacity to say "no" as well as "yes," for there is no "negation" as we know it on the unconscious level: "In the Ucs [unconscious] there are only contents more or less strongly cathected" (1915, p. 119). Here, primal repression could be seen as analogous to the developmental activity of dissociation, which tempers the expression of subjective impulses within the maternal environment in Mahler's differentiation subphase; which restrains a premature introduction of bad feelings in Mahler's practicing subphase, or prevents a too-sudden integration of good and bad feelings in the rapprochement subphase. This counter-cathecting force seems congruent with Freud's formulation of a balancing function of the mind, his "principle of constancy," where the "mental apparatus endeavors to keep the quantity of excitement constant" in the psyche (1920g, p. 9). Might not a contemporary restating of Freud's concept of "primal repression" – dissociation – conceive of it, as Freud perhaps might, as a basic neurobiopsychological process? As a shaping, limiting complement to the expansive, incorporative impulse of our psychic being, enabling the progressive structuring of the self?

The doubling of personality in hypnoid states, and the usefulness of hypnotic technique, however, meet with Freud's almost complete rejection. In "The Aetiology of Hysteria," the "so-called *hypnoid state*" is dismissed: "often there are no grounds for presupposing such hypnoid states. What is definite is that the theory of hypnoid states contributes nothing to the solution of the other difficulties" (Freud 1896, pp. 187–188). He also replaces the use of hypnosis with his personally devised technique of free association (which, like Janet's automatic talking, actually is itself an evocation of an altered state of mind – a hypnoid state).

In transforming the "doubling of personality" into a defensive operation of the ego, Freud renames as "splitting" what is left of the original concept of dissociation:

> *The known causes of "double conscience" (splitting of consciousness) prove nothing against our view. They may most accurately*

be described as cases of a splitting of the mental activities into two groups, whereby a single consciousness takes up its position alternately with either the one or the other of these groups.

(Freud 1915e, pp. 103–104)

Dissociation of primal personality states has been subordinated to the later operations of the structured psyche. This redefinition may be reconceptualized as differing, even competing, psychological operations between the preoedipal and the oedipal states of mind. A contributing motivation would seem to be that Freud's focus is less on the healer's concern with how pathology disrupts the functioning, even the formation, of the individual mind, than it is on the scientist's interest in defining the nature of the fully operational, fully constituted mind of that individual, and how pathology makes this more observable.

Given another lifetime and the advance of brain science, would Freud have extended his inquiry beyond its oedipal focus? "Some Character-Types Met with in Psycho-Analytic Work," written in 1915, suggests that this might have occurred. Here, he reflects that, although the analyst's technique is directed toward neurotic symptomatology, nevertheless it "soon constrains him to direct his immediate curiosity towards other objectives. He observes that his investigation is threatened by resistances set up against him by the patient, and these resistances he may justly attribute to the latter's character, which now acquires the first claim on his interest" (1915, p. 318). Freud understands that the character resistance of such patients "was connected with an event or painful experience from which they had suffered in their earliest childhood" (1915, p. 320). Furthermore, this resistance derives from early relationship: "love is the greatest teacher; and it is by his love of those nearest him that the incomplete human being is induced to respect the decrees of necessity and to spare himself the punishment attendant on any infringement of it." In this context, Freud even implies the healing nature of the therapeutic relationship itself: "let us say that the physician in his educative work makes use of one of the components of love. In this work of after-education, he probably does no more than repeat the process which first of all made training of any kind possible" (1915, p. 319). Freud is clear that symptom work can only be approached after the resolution of resistances intrinsic to the patient's character; that such character ways were learned in childhood as a necessary part of a loving compliance required by "those nearest him"; and that the "after-education" of analysis itself makes use of a similar "loving component." Unfortunately, this contention by Freud was not emphasized, by himself or others, until Fairbairn, Winnicott, Bowlby, Kohut, and Masterson came along.

Work with personality disorder seems only to be waiting for the future studies of child development and attachment and, especially, brain studies, to advance psychoanalysis toward hard science. Freud will continue to maintain an unyielding focus on the Oedipus complex, at least in part out of concern that extension of his still abstract theory will dilute its persuasiveness. He also continues frustrated by the scientific limitations of the time, which had prevented the realization of "The Project"– his ideal goal described by Strachey as "a highly complicated and extraordinarily ingenious working model of the mind as a piece of neurological machinery" (Freud 1900a, p. xvii). Freud the scientist once more has had to give way to Freud the metaphysician.

The Self and Structuralization

The purpose of psychoanalysis, as stated by Freud in the *New Introductory Lectures*, "is to strengthen the ego, to make it more independent of the superego, to enlarge its field of perception and to expand its organization so that it can appropriate new pieces of the id. Where id was, there ego shall be" (1933a, p. 80). In accordance with the structural theory, the oedipal mind is engaged in completing its healthy formation. The preceding three years or so of childhood have been a time of preparation, of a steady introduction of impulse and perception to the modification of conscious awareness. Fixation to early libidinal stages has significance for the oedipal mind primarily as a place of defensive regression from a still inadequate capacity to manage mental conflict.

For Freud, the mind of the three- to five-year-old has achieved sufficient object relatedness to provide a clinically useful contrast to transference distortion: the misunderstanding of present-time relationship in terms of past unconscious fears and wishes. Looking at the patient from this point of view seems to provide a workable basis for treatment, as long as the difficulties experienced by the patient are being processed by the patient's predominantly mature mental structure. But what if the structure itself is at issue? What if, for instance, anxiety cannot be attributed so much to the failure of the ego to mediate the conflict between an impulsive desire and the sense of its impropriety, as the relative absence of a capacity to even recognize the validity of an ongoing inner argument: for instance, a contention between an insistent child-part of the mind and an equally unyielding but opposing parental identification. In the latter instance there is a representative for the id, as well as a spokesperson for the constraints of the outer world, but where is the ego? Where is the therapist's structural ally-to-be in the therapy?

To a greater or lesser extent, in work with the preoedipal patient, the ego is a product of the process. In the therapy of personality disorder, we speak of "building an observing ego" and "strengthening the ego's adaptive defenses" in hopes of furthering the growth of a healthy "executive ego." We facilitate the reorientation of the patient, from a predominant reliance on external direction, to implementation of a guiding locus within the individual. Here, we are addressing the major distinction between the therapy of neurosis and the therapy of personality disorder: not so much the interpretation of what is there and shouldn't be, as the provision of something that is expected to be there, but isn't.

Freud's topical model hypothesizes a brain with interactive levels, foreshadowing the contemporary understanding of a brain that is actually two cooperating hemispheres. We now recognize the right hemisphere (roughly equivalent to the unconscious) as the brain that regulated our prehistoric personal existence and operates (now as then) in accordance with basic formulae governing rapid reactions optimizing survival. Although, to a degree, learning these patterns was part of mother–child training, they were essentially built in, having been genetically established by the ongoing survival of those who practiced them: the "fittest." Communication was nonverbal, relying to a degree on brain synchronicity, in part on gestures and behaviors that were self-evident or, perhaps, could automatically cue essential formulae stored in the collective mind. This is a speculative summary, but suggests a tenable conclusion: the right brain, with little time to waste in a primitive environment, is able to direct the individual's practical activity with a minimum of preparation.

The uniquely complex human mind, however, further evolved to make use of what little activity did not have to be defined purely in terms of survival. With the right hemisphere standing guard, the left hemisphere not only was also able to maximize the use of available opportunity not focused on survival, but was able to maximize the extent of such opportunity itself in the process. Consequently, while the individual could contain the right-brain capacity for split-second ("unthinking") reaction in a crisis, the left hemisphere could increasingly take its time to consciously think things out, even developing a useful concept of time in so doing. Thus, the logical left brain might organize a detailed perception of a situation, assess it in a context apart from instant assumption, regulate an expression of feeling suitable for the situation (especially what might be carried into action), and communicate intentions specifically in spoken words to another for possible further modification. However, unlike the right-brain mode, which requires only a brief and unambiguous imprinting to operationalize largely inborn instructions for survival, the left brain needs a teacher to learn how to think for itself. The complicated human mind not only needs about three or so postpartum years to physically develop, it must spend those years with a constant caregiver to learn the use of that mind. More than any other species, the human being is able to make choices – an ability that even allows the individual a certain independence from the group. While the mind is developing, though, such "freedom of choice" is chaos without the protective, guiding containment of another. In fact, it is this very containment that serves as a model for the management of things, and will be internalized nonverbally preceding the more specific instruction of words. We may have common sense, but we require relationship with another to learn how to use it.

Our ego – our ability to differentiate, define, modify, and operationalize our feelings and perceptions – takes form through our relationship with another. This will include the formula for relationship itself, which will guide us on a level of assumption below consciousness. This process, distinctively created within each new mother–child dyad, has remarkable present-time flexibility. Not only is there room for consciously directed adaptation to others, but there is the additional ability, within a sufficiently conducive relationship, for the individual mind to change the basic formula. It would appear that the readiness of the human mind to take shape within a relationship of a parenting nature also makes possible the reshaping of that mind within the reparenting context of psychoanalysis.

(It might be noted that present brain studies show that the amygdala, the basis for the drives, is fully mature at birth, although it can be triggered into higher or lesser activation in time. We also know that the hippocampus, the basis for the observing ego and its recording of biographical data in an unemotional fashion, matures within the first three to four years of life – unless the amygdala's activity interferes with its activity via secretion of too many neurotransmitters, which can shut it down and even destroy many of its neurons. These findings offer a neurological basis for the effect of trauma on the psyche in the developmental years, suggesting both a neuropsychological definition of dissociation and, by extension, of personality disorder itself.)

The ego, "das Ich," is the representation of a successful effort: the conscious, civilized achievement of an individual presence ready to consciously coexist with others like itself. Although Freud rescued childhood from a "blank slate" existence, evidence of the old bias still remains in the Freudian image of the untamed, inwardly absorbed, barely conscious child-being. Do the parents hold the bits and pieces of this being together until an "Ich" can take shape? Or is something like an ego there all along, waiting to become "present" when able to manifest itself in ways we consider socialized? Is the ego the equivalent of who the person is, or is it the agent of something more comprehensive – something often referred to as the self – that may have preceded formation of the ego?

Defining the self has been an ongoing undertaking of psychoanalysis. This effort has been reflected in psychoanalytic language since the time of Freud, who tended to use the terms "ego" and "self" interchangeably. For a while (even now), the two have maintained competitive, governing separate schools of theory, although recently they sometimes can be found occupying the same field of inquiry. A question increasingly pertinent to analysis is "Did the self have a structure of its own preceding that containing the development of the ego?"

Frank Putnam, psychobiologist, describing the self as "who we are," refines his definition of self in terms of "identity" and "personality." He writes: "We each have a number of identities that we activate as called for by different life situations. The result of our efforts to integrate our various identities together into a more or less unified 'self' is expressed by other people as our personality" (2016, pp. 15–16).

Donald Winnicott, the pediatrician–analyst, relates the essence of the self to the individual's sense of reality: "The True Self comes from the aliveness of the body tissues and the working body-functions, including the heart's action and breathing. It is closely linked with the idea of the

Primary Process, and is, at the beginning, essentially not reactive to external stimuli, but primary." The true self "quickly develops complexity, and relates to external reality by natural processes." Maturing over time, "the infant develops an ego-organization that is adapted to the environment … because of the mother's good-enough adaptation to the infant's living needs" (1965, pp. 148–149). Generally implied, but critical for Winnicott's thinking, the self depends on relationship for its full realization.

John Sutherland, psychoanalyst and Fairbairn's biographer, proposes that the self is "the overall dynamic structural matrix." It is "a supraordinate structure of great flexibility and perhaps in the nature of a 'field force', its primary function [being] the container of motives from all the subsystems which have differentiated from it" (1989b/1994, p. 59).

Undoubtedly, a full definition of self at least has to account for a range of possibilities, some ineffable. These possibilities extend from a specific, observable part, or summation of parts, of one's being, to a presence that energizes, structures, and transcends what is manifest. It would seem that the self encompasses a combination of Freud's ego ("I") and psyche ("soul").

Masterson's definition of the self is a pragmatic one, in line with his emphasis on the clinical. In 1995, he refines his Approach to consider "the developmental arrest of the self as primary" in the therapy of personality disorder. He defines the mature, healthy self (which he names the "real self") as follows:

> the real self is experienced as a sense of self that feels adequate and competent, a feeling derived mostly from reality, with some input from fantasy. The sense of self includes appropriate concern for others, and its self-esteem is maintained by the use of self-assertion to master challenges and tasks presented by reality.

> (Masterson and Klein 1995, p. 12)

Masterson emphasizes the importance of ongoing exchange of inner and outer self-experience. He sees relationship as critical to the understanding of the self, both developmentally and therapeutically, and the real self as focal for the experience of human "aliveness."

In important ways, self theory is both intrapsychic and relational. Fairbairn, who probably can be considered the originator of analytic self theory, questions the tenet of drive theory that motivates the ego as initially pleasure-seeking, and proposes that the ego/self is primarily object-seeking. Further, he holds that the self both gains and creates structure from relationship. Richard Rubens sums it up accordingly: "In the relational/structure model of Fairbairn, the shape of the self grows and changes from its experience in relationships, while at the same time the nature of the relationships it has is being shaped and changed by that self" (1994, p. 153).

Taking some liberties to extend Fairbairn's hypothesis, it could be posited that the preoedipal mind develops through increasingly complex degrees of self-structure. Formed within a consistent relationship, this self-structure makes use of dissociation (splitting) to set aside aspects of itself that are not favorable to that relationship. This is the early mind, essentially guided by the right hemisphere, that relies on the protection of relationship for survival, and consequently divides and structures much of its being in keeping with learning and following the ways of the other.

The human mind, however, has evolved its biological and psychological capability to advance this early structuring toward a more independent level of organization. Over the first three years of life, the right brain gradually shares operation with the left brain and its ability to consciously assess a situation and think it through according to its own resources. In a qualitative move, the three- to five-year-old mind has acquired its own capacity for self-containment and direction, based in part on an internalization of its environmental model. The individual can now initiate independent relationships, acting in part on a template provided by a representation of group values (the superego) that is challenged by subjective impulses (the id) and regulated by a highly adaptive and functional part (the ego). This new, more conscious structure will no longer rely entirely on the closely formulated dissociative process that enables emotionally based, rapid-fire, either/or decisions, but will use a conscious, rational management of conflicting issues, with repression storing away outdated considerations.

In this advanced (oedipal) level of structure, the self has more of a supervisory capacity, with its agency, the ego, operationally in charge of directing a psychic mechanism able to function on its own. But although this structure actualizes a considerable degree of separateness from the other, Fairbairn might argue that it is still governed by the self, which places the need for others even before the need to pursue pleasure. Even the separate and individual self, highly organized according to Freud's structural theory, is still guided by its first structuring, which was founded on relationship.

I would propose that the definition of the self, or at least the self in its more evident aspect, seems to change with two significant levels of development. At the more sophisticated oedipal level, the self seems more directive – maintaining identity and motivation – while the ego is in charge of regulating a balanced and operative intrapsychic–interpersonal psychic mechanism. In the earlier "primal" level of development, the self is structuring its own nature. On this earlier level, the self undergoes differentiation and then integration (or lack of it) in ways that will define the eventual personality style of the individual, especially after the individual is no longer under the regulating influence of another. Psychological problems tracing to each of these two levels are different in kind: they are problems of neurosis and those of personality disorder.

To return to a consideration of Fairbairn's work, it shows its further departure from drive theory in emphasizing the importance of psychic development in earliest childhood. This theoretical shift places a focus on personality disorder (although it is not specifically named as such) on a par with the attention given to neurotic conflict (Grotstein and Rinsley 1994, p. 11). Even distinguishing personality disorder from neurosis is a relatively recent theoretical pursuit, and whether, or how, to vary technique from one to the other is still in debate. Contributing to the lack of clarity is the tendency to divide patients into either/or categories, rather than understanding that we are all complex beings with predominating issues at various stages of our development, and even that these issues may shift in importance given a change in circumstance (including therapeutic process).

Kernberg, whose dynamic approach contributes to the basis for Masterson's, describes a confluence of self-building and ego-building processes. He traces a consistent psychic progression from early self-states through oedipal structures: "The gradual integration of the self-components of early internalized object relations permits the concept of an emerging self that ... gradually leads to the simultaneous organization of drives and internalized object relations to form the tripartite structure" (Kernberg 1994, p. 63). Kernberg believes that the integration of analytic thought from Fairbairn and Bowlby through Jacobson and Mahler leads to a natural relating of "the psychoanalytic concept of the self and the object world to the structural properties of the psychic apparatus" (p. 63). This theoretical progression not only has a commonality with Masterson's "developmental" spectrum of personality pathology, but also can be understood to extend the paradigm to include neurosis. It seems feasible to think of neurosis and personality disorder as neither oppositional nor mutually exclusive as categories, but as psychic difficulties arising from different but sequentially related phases of psychic maturation. These phases at first seem unrelated because a quantum shift in mental capacity and ability occurs in the transition between rapprochement and object constancy. A shorthand definition of this shift would include the increasing influence of left-brain thinking.

It would seem reasonable to consider that there could be an inclusive "developmental" model for mental disorder, basically following the general model for healthy psychic development. Like the healthy mental schema, the less healthy one should not present a definitive progression of time-limited tasks that demands completion of each task prior to undertaking the next. Human development is, and must be, sufficiently adaptive to continue despite the inadequacies and importunities of various contributing factors. Lack of complete achievement is not the issue, but rather the degree and decisiveness of that lack. Given the opportunity and resources, the human psyche can accommodate, compensate, and even rebuild itself to maximize its chances for realization. We are presently inclined to view the mind as a complex networking of simultaneous possibilities, all timelessly accessible, and so therapeutically reachable in a present-time clinical environment. However, since unfinished psychic business from a particular developmental phase to a degree is caught in a presentation of the self characteristic of that time, it is most effectively addressed in language that respects the thought processes and emotional expression of that phase. For this reason, the "language" of technique needs to speak to the emotional ear of the developmental level being addressed in the therapy. In the gradations of personality disorder, the voice of acknowledgment communicates with the schizoid personality, while mirroring reaches the narcissist, and confrontation, however contended, models the borderline's sought-after resolution. The neurotic, on the other hand, can better tolerate, and so better benefit from, the insight evoked by interpretation and even dialogue. As Bromberg points out, the neurotic has achieved tolerance for conflict: the containment of opposing concepts within the same field of thought. The neurotic is more prepared to modify emotional reactiveness in the service of reason, whereas work with personality disorder requires that the therapist to some extent assume responsibility for this function.

Masterson's Approach potentially advances an inclusive theory of personality that synthesizes progressive concepts of self-realization, presenting a shadow-side of unfolding psychic process that takes its distinctive nature from the levels of development that it shadows. This Approach draws special clinical relevance from its application of phase-specific techniques guided by understanding of the communication that both speaks to and facilitates the evolution of a specific stage of psychic development. This developmental Approach can probably be extended beyond personality disorder to include neurosis, although technique must further adjust to match communication that reflects a quantum shift in the maturation of mental functioning.

But how can it be that therapeutic relationship retains a sense of collaboration with the patient's overarching sense of self even while addressing a problematic part of that self? The answer is to be found in the theory of self-states, a currently evolving concept that addresses the paradoxical nature of the self as simultaneously one and many – a concept not taken into consideration by Masterson, although it advances his model.

As described by Sutherland, "all organisms" are:

> *wholes which cannot be made from the aggregation of parts. Their constant exchanges with the environment mean that constant transformations are proceeding, despite which they maintain their own characteristic form by a process of self-regulation. What is essential in these continuous self-renewals and self-expressions are the self-bounding processes rather than the changing structures.*

(1989a, p. 166)

Or, as more recent neurobiology contends, the mind is composed of "a pattern of constancy and variation leading to highly individualized networks" (Edelman 2004, p. 29). In psychotherapy, we must address the collaboration of whole and parts in the patient – in particular, the dysfunction in that collaboration.

The Theory of Self-states

We need a terminology to express this inner disunity, not an instinct terminology but one that clarifies the strongly persisting differences of attitude and reaction within the over-all ego, which prevent it from expressing a unified front to life and undermine self-confidence.

(Guntrip 1971, p. 170)

Self-states, also called subselves, are formally introduced into analytic theory by Fairbairn, whose evolving concepts – rather like documented thinking aloud – benefit from the clarification provided by Guntrip and Sutherland. As often in his time (and in contemporary usage, as well), Fairbairn tends to use "ego" where "self" is increasingly intended, condenses the earliest levels of development, and uses "repression" and "splitting" interchangeably with "dissociation." That kept in mind, Fairbairn describes the self as beginning as a pristine whole that divides when the sought-after object it seeks frustrates its outreach. The self splits off representational parts of itself and other in order to maintain an idealized object to which an idealized core self may remain attached, and so avoid separation anxiety.

In 1943, contemporaneous with Fairbairn, Glover questions the belief that the "ego" evolves from a state of pristine oneness. Instead, he proposes that "the ego develops from a cluster of primitive islets until about the end of the second year it becomes definitely unified" (as quoted by Khan 1974, pp. 242–243). Pertinently, Glover's time frame for ego/self consolidation follows the now-established range for basic child psychic development.

Winnicott's thinking, while related to Fairbairn's, is closer to Glover's. Fairbairn and Winnicott both see defensive splitting as resulting from an inadequate emotional connection between mother and child. But, while Fairbairn sees fragmentation of wholeness as the consequence of failed mother–child relatedness, Winnicott sees a healthy developmental process of differentiation subsequently distorted by that failure. Winnicott understands the infant to be in a normal state of "primary unintegration," which would steadily achieve integration unless maintained out of a defensive attempt to modify the self to meet maternal needs (1975, pp. 149–150). For him, the "bits and pieces" represent a normal condition in the very beginning of the manifestation of the self.

For Winnicott, the concern is more with the mother's intrusions into the differentiation process. As Ogden writes: "when a mother substitutes something of herself for the infant's spontaneous gesture (e.g. her own anxiety over separateness for the infant's curious exploration), the infant experiences traumatic disruption of his developing sense of self" (1994, p. 95). Winnicott describes a strategic defensive activity, picturing a conciliatory "false" part-self positioned to deal with the antipathetical outer world, while problematic part-selves are withheld (though sometimes available for limited tactical use), all in the service of preserving the "true" self, with its essential "aliveness." In this strategy, the creative protectiveness of dissociation is shown as it sets aside in forgetfulness aspects of the self that are perceived as a danger to survival – as a threat to the relationship that sustains life. As described by Bromberg: "Dissociation … is distinguished by the presence of a selective amnestic state. As a global defense against ongoing trauma or the fear of potential trauma, it represents as adaptive hypnoidal capacity of the personality" (1998/2001, p. 184). Further, however, as Bromberg continues: "Paradoxically, the goal of dissociation is to maintain personal continuity, coherence, and integrity of the sense of self and to avoid the traumatic dissolution of selfhood" (p. 182). Sacrifice of a part of the self is not to be questioned, if the alternative is loss of one's total being. "Psychological trauma occurs in situations, explicitly or implicitly interpersonal, in which self-invalidation (sometimes self-*annihilation*) cannot be escaped from or prevented and from which there is no hope of protection, relief, or soothing" (1998/2001, p. 12). With the capacity to psychically "disappear" the part of the self that evokes existential terror, dissociation, as Putnam says, is "the escape when there is no escape" (1992, p. 104).

The price to pay, however, is some compromising of the development of the whole. Glover, cited by both Winnicott and Khan, proposes that "the concept of fixation can be extended from its customary instinctual reference to include fixation of the total ego to any one period of development" (Khan 1974, p. 243). Or, according to Khan, the degree of dissociation may reach "a state of developmental arrest where something has not been allowed to grow to its second stage as it were" (Willoughby 2005, p. 97). The self continues, but takes on a distinctive coloration – a defining character style formed by unfinished developmental business.

Since Fairbairn, analytic thought has tended toward "a view of the mind as a configuration of discontinuous, shifting states of consciousness with varying degrees of access to perception and cognition" (Bromberg 1998/2001, p. 225). As might be expected, this "discontinuity" was first defined in its dysfunctional aspect. Predictably, the dissociative phenomenon first caught the fascination of early mental practitioners through its highly dramatic pathological forms, especially dual and multiple personality. The curiosity they observed we now believe to be a radically protective structuring of the personality:

> *What was formerly normal dissociation, the loose configuration of multiple self-states that enables a person to "feel like oneself while being many," becomes rigidified into a dissociative mental structure (the most extreme form of which we know as "multiple personality" or "dissociative identity disorder"), each self now uncompromisingly boundaried within its specific pattern of interpersonal engagement that gives its self-meaning the cast of truth.*

(Bromberg 2001, p. 12)

Steadily, as Putnam describes, extensive clinical observations and research studies have explored the psychological mechanism of state-dependent learning and memory (SDLM), as it influences our sense of identity. This linkage "is most apparent when the person's identities regard themselves as in the psychiatric condition known as dissociative identity disorder (DID). In these cases, the different identity states report separate memories for the individual's life experiences" (Putnam 2016, p. 16).

The originating cause is a familiar one. "Traumatic identity fragmentation" occurs in varying degrees when "recurrent childhood mistreatment … Undermines the development of healthy metacognitive/executive/observing ego mechanisms that integrate the different states of being into a more global sense of self" (Putnam 2016, p. 248). Extreme conditions create the more observable results, whereas the less obvious causes of cumulative trauma result in a more subtle distortion of personality. As vital as what is there – mistreatment – is what is not there: the consistency of maternal presence to assure and model the continuity of the developing self.

This leads us back to early mother–child relations and the establishment of relational patterns. In particular reference to Sullivan, Laing, and

Fonagy, Bromberg observes: "the engagement of minds constitutes an act of recognition that allows the child to accomplish the developmental achievement of taking his own state of mind as an object of reflection" (1998/2001, p. 10). Further, Bromberg, referring to Laing, points out that when the other systematically "*dis*confirms" a child's state of mind, "the child grows to mistrust the reality of his own experience." With this "precipitous disruption of self-continuity," disconnection, or dissociation of that state, "becomes the most adaptive solution to preserving self-continuity" (1998/2001, p. 11). The more extreme the need, the more extreme the solution.

Subsequent theorizing strengthens a fundamental contribution of the independent object relationists. To quote Ogden: "Fairbairn (1944, 1946) replaced the Freudian dichotomy of ego and id, structure and energy, with a notion of 'dynamic structures.' These dynamic structures are conceived of as aspects of the mind capable of acting as independent agencies with their own motivational systems." Ogden then makes the critical addition: "Donald Winnicott's major contribution to the development of a theory of internal object relations was his theory of multiple self-organizations functioning in relation to one another within the personality system" (1994, pp. 94–95).

The undistorted, healthy picture of this situation reveals a personality system with many different, adaptable, and movable parts working interactively within a consistently identifiable, ongoing, and encompassing host. This allows the individual to present as a recognizable totality capable of fulfilling a personal goal or social role, while at the same time being composed of interoperative parts representing diverse possibilities modifiable to meet the demands of changing circumstance. The neurons of the brain, increasing or diminishing according to the needs of relationship, follow a mental "selection of the fittest" to influence a personality style in the individual or even, given intergenerational repetition, family character.

Dissociation and Trauma in the Mastersonian Context

Freud taught us (among many such lessons) that the successful working of a mechanism is made more observable through seeing how it goes wrong. When *what is* runs smoothly, its nature is simply assumed, but erratic operation catches our interest, and breakdown demands our attention, even our need for definition. As well as dreams, mental illness, for Freud, provides a *royal road* to our understanding of the mind itself. Fairbairn took the next step by directing inquiry to the need for and response to relationship in the very beginning of life. In the instance of dissociation and self-states, normal developmental processes as well as pathology brought on by trauma may point to an understanding of the very nature of the structure of the personality.

Bromberg proposes that personality disorder "might be usefully defined as the characterological outcome of the inordinate use of dissociation and ... it constitutes a personality structure organized as a proactive defensive response to the potential repetition of childhood trauma" (2001, p. 200). Quoting Peter Goldberg, he carries the function of dissociation to its ultimate role in psychic process, as "a fundamental organizer of personality structure" (p. 190).

Although it is observably protective and constructive in situations threatening to self-continuity, can dissociation still further be seen as a normative process intrinsic to healthy human development? Might it be hypothesized that the formative action of dissociation aids in shaping the early individual to the ways of the family/group it will be part of, even before later adaptive learning takes place? In subtle but consistent ways, does the degree of the mother's responsiveness nonverbally "teach" the infant which aspects of the self are more or less favorable for belonging in the family/group, and does the limiting action of dissociation conform to that guidance? Does dissociation serve as a restraining counterpart to the unqualified energy of psychic growth, and is it at work even before the regulation of society and the conscious self become explicit? Is this possibly another view of Freud's hypothesis of the balancing of cathexis and counter-cathexis? Freud would most likely find reassuring such contemporary neurological thinking as Edelman's (2004) theory of neural Darwinism.

Referring to Mahler's subphases of psychic growth, and the specific tasks each presents, one can see a possible role played by dissociation in normal development. Dissociation may provide an adaptive modifying effect on the subphase-specific styles not favored by a particular mother (or social group). Unfortunately, it also stands to reason that, given the need to adjust to a more problematic maternal relationship, this containing function may increase until it actually impedes individual expression and identity.

Considering Mahler's differentiation subphase, there is positive value in dissociation holding back aspects of the self that do not resonate with the maternal source of continuity. There will always be some degree of adjustment required from both sides to facilitate the mother/infant "fit." As previously discussed, some editing of the spontaneous flow of the self toward the outer world not only strengthens compatibility with the maternal source of survival, but may also initiate adaptability to the family/culture. However, steadily dividing off expressions of the self that meet with (for instance) anxiety or neglect from the mother may lead to a schizoid inhibition of self and false compliance with the outside world. As Fairbairn implies, the most basic defense against separation anxiety also can be the most basic foundation for personality disorder.

Next, the major task of the practicing subphase is the beginning of a perception of personhood, which is associated with increasingly specific feeling. This task is undertaken with enthusiasm because the emerging sense of self and other is experienced as "good" and mutually affirming. The complementary emergence of "bad," divergent possibilities is delayed. Dissociation may function here to assure that the positive state of being has been securely enough established to maintain its coherence (as Kohut would say) when the negative is introduced. However, dissociative delay of the negative becomes rigidly set if acceptance of disagreement and frustrated feelings is either prematurely insisted upon or indulgently underprepared for, and the opinionated, defensively outraged narcissistic personality begins to emerge.

In the next subphase of rapprochement, both positive and negative states of personhood and affect have been accepted *per se*, but their further definition into separate whole self and whole other, each associated with both good and bad feeling, is a maximum undertaking. Good and bad part-selves are introduced into the same psychic field, but only in alternation at first. This seems to require an oscillation that allows increasing proximity, toleration, and eventual synthesis of opposites into a new complexity. Dissociation works distinctively in this subphase, to slow the speed of integration by splitting of alternative states. Mastery of this subphase necessitates a shift in mental capability itself – the transition in primacy from emotionally directed right-brain formulae, to rationally considered left-brain judgements; from decisions reliant on instantaneous access to set assumptions, to conclusions motivated by a calculated weighing of opposites; and, finally, to the increased assuming of responsibility on the self for all this mental processing. Then there is the fine-tuning: ability to consider a complexity of variables – to transition from either/or thinking to something more comprehensive but systematic – takes time to process; pacing is needed if new mental functions are not to become mental chaos. Parental modeling is vital in this always somewhat disorienting adjustment to a new way of thinking. Without the presence of another to patiently "hold center stage" (Masterson) and demonstrate the capacity to maintain contradictory feelings within the psychic field, dissociation (splitting) is maintained to permit the alternating needs for dependence and independence to exist without prolonged sense of too much loss of one or the other. Unresolved alternation of opposite states can then become entrenched in borderline acting out.

Mahler's open-ended on-the-way-to-object-constancy will see the ongoing (lifelong) consolidation of the rapprochement transition, including the refining of bicameral coordination between the two hemispheres (shown at work in dreams and psychoanalysis). It is notable that dissociation, having done its developmental job, defers to new methods of managing conflict (rather than "disappearing" one or both sides of it), such as reason and repression. The defensive capacity of dissociation – limited to absolute, instant moves – remains for handling issues that approach or reach crisis or even traumatic proportions.

In each of Mahler's subphases, dissociation may temper the pacing of quantum changes in psychic growth to maintain psychic balance. The containing, regulating influence of the mother-child relationship, however, is essential for the process. Lacking sufficient maternal moderating and modeling, dissociation may overcompensate in order to assure stability of the self. This may result in developmental arrest, with the resulting personality disorder taking a rigid characterization from the specific developmental task that could not be completed. For instance: the schizoid cannot trust to opening the self to the outside world; the narcissist cannot tolerate negative and differing opinions; and the borderline cannot resolve the alternating pull toward vital but seemingly unreconcilable goals.

An additional perspective on the nature of dissociation needs consideration: one that provides validity for the field of dynamic psychotherapy itself. In addition to helping shape the self into set patterns of feeling and functioning supporting survival, it seems that dissociation also leaves an allowance for future reconfiguration. The parts that are dissociated are not destroyed, but are, as the term indicates, "split off" and encapsulated away from the integrated, conscious aspect of the self. Here, the formation of personality follows a recognizable trauma mechanism. Aspects of the self, which could not be allowed full recognition without threatening the self's dependence on mother–child connectedness, have been stored aside for the greater good. However, these self-parts remain dormant to allow for possible future integration when and if this becomes both desirable and tolerable. Like the casebook traumatic experience, the "trauma" and the aspect of the self containing it will not disappear, but will wait – even sporadically press – for possible processing under more favorable circumstances. This affords the basis for psychoanalytic psychotherapy itself: the potential, cybernetic capacity of the self to heal itself, given the context of the therapeutic relationship.

Masterson's concept of abandonment depression (fragmentation anxiety; annihilation anxiety) at the motivational center of developmental arrest in each subphase works in conjunction with a trauma model of personality disorder. Personality disorder is understood as a defensive configuration of the forming self, established in early childhood, that has been frozen in place to protect against the traumatic threat of maternal loss – even of existence itself. Individuation, the psychic move away from the mother, can be felt as threat-provoking as psychic separation, and often is perceived as disobedient and punishable. Any point in the "psychic birth" process of separation-individuation can be susceptible to anxiety, but points of task consolidation at the major subphases seem especially vulnerable; the traumatic freezing brought about by abandonment depression leaves the self prone to dividing off the unintegrated "character" of the troubled subphase. Later attempts to resolve the defense of personality disorder can only re-evoke existential panic and depression and reinstatement of the defense; the resolution must be accompanied by a new relationship capable of supporting the self to move through this crisis and continue its growth. Masterson's "triad" is critical to process here. He cautions that resolution of the maladaptive personality defense will lead to abandonment depression and unexpected resumption of that defense – that this should be understood as part of the therapy to be worked through, not its unfortunate outcome. The supporting "other" internalized from the therapy will remain, even when the "other" of the old pattern is relinquished and mourned. Throughout, the essentially unspoken but containing therapeutic alliance, personified in the therapist's "real self" (as described by Masterson) stays constant to sustain the patient's self through its transformation.

Masterson teaches that work with personality disorder is founded on a therapeutic relationship that can assure an alternative experience of growth despite fear of abandonment. His Approach includes a technique that will speak to the arrested part of the patient: the language that addresses the emotional level of the traumatized child-state, whose developmental arrest requires this style of communication for an experience of mutual understanding. Simultaneously, however, the therapeutic alliance more or less implicitly maintains a consistent and mature containing presence. The self-correcting capacity of the human mind can be activated by a relational attunement with another that ensures the sense of safety and continuity necessary to facilitate psychic change.

Self-states – Working with the Cast of Characters

Self-states can be found clinically represented throughout psychoanalytic/therapeutic thought. At one prestigious extreme stands Freud's superego, a semi-personification of internalized parental values, and the inspiration for Fairbairn's punitive internal saboteur. On the other extreme, perilously attractive to popular fiction, are the dual and multiple personalities – embodiments of psychic states prepared to directly interact (favorably or otherwise) with manifestly integrated therapists. In this last instance, there is the example of the too brief, but exciting, interchange between Jacob Breuer and representatives from the self-system of "Anna O." These representatives first appeared as a "normal"/"bad" duality, were then joined by a third calm observer, and engaged in a unique relationship with the analyst. Following "Anna O's" instructions, Breuer listened while the "hypnoid states" spoke randomly and began to realize once deleted memories of a traumatic paternal relationship, thus initiating what "Anna O" named "the talking cure." This historic account was interrupted, however, first by Breuer, who was overwhelmed, and then by Freud, who redirected the telling of the story in his own terms. "Anna O" herself persisted, predominantly in the dedicated self-state that was to make her a founder of professional social work.

Analytic thought has been steadily attracted to the inclination of the human psyche to illustrate its nature by means of inner personification. Somewhat more psychologically engaging than the superego (which is more compatible with communal ethics and morality), the ego has increasingly attracted analytic thought as the personal representative, defender, and social diplomat of the individual psyche. Even so, the ego has never quite managed to exceed its role as agent for some greater personal context, and was first equated with, but then superseded by, the containing, always somewhat indefinable, self. Ego psychology, object relations theory, self psychology all have sought to fill the inner world of the mind with a population variously based on feelings, experiences, capabilities, attitudes, responsibilities, and imitations (and more) that strive to compose an independent balance-of-being ready to interrelate with other composite beings like itself in the outside world. The concept of self has emerged as the overarching, guiding psychic presence: a unified sense of *being* paradoxically composed of a multiplicity of parts. The parts, in their turn, have made themselves persuasively known through personifications.

When the overall sense of being, the self, is troubled, why not (when possible) follow Anna O's advice and hear what its personalized elements – its subselves – have to tell us? Work with multiple personality disorder/dissociative identity disorder (MPD/DID) suggests that all it seems to require basically is a relationship that provides mental synchronicity – a "hypnoid state," perhaps – to open the communication. After that, resonant listening may become therapeutic if the right questions are asked ("Can you tell me about yourself?"), understanding is confirmed by accurately reflective acknowledgment ("It sounds like you've decided you don't have much choice"), and occasionally needed information is provided ("I don't think you were ever taught that feelings come in different sizes"). Josef Breuer and Morton Prince, and more recently Richard Kluft, Bennett Braun, and others, have demonstrated how to communicate with self-states in their most vocal form, that of MPD or DID. Closely allied is John Watkins' "ego-state" therapy (Watkins and Watkins 1997). Why wouldn't we welcome the chance, if possible, to find ways to speak directly with less dramatically defined parts of a damaged self in order to be informed "where it hurts"?

Interestingly, the idea of clinically relating to a psychological system of self-parts has been more readily accepted in family therapy than in individual treatment. The contemporary list of systems-based family therapy models is substantial. The reader is referred to Richard Schwartz, himself creator of Internal family systems therapy, for a succinct review of the subject (1995, pp. 5–7). The pioneering work of Murray Bowen (1978), of structural family therapy, systems family therapy, and the strategic approach with its highly sophisticated input from Ericksonian hypnosis (Erickson 1980), have proven particularly effective in repairing the interaction of complementary family roles. The liveliness of the work, plus the personal immediacy of the therapist who becomes therapeutically interactive with the family system, has further brought popular appeal to family therapy.

But why is therapy with a system of part-selves or self-states so limited to its application for social groups only? Freud himself might have experienced some curiosity while in his *Totem and Taboo* (1913) mood, noting the dynamic parallel between the individual and the group psyche. As quoted by Schwartz, Gregory Bateson (a prime contributor of cybernetic systems thinking to family therapy dynamics) wrote: "The ways of thinking evolved by psychiatrists in order to understand the family as a system will come to be applied in understanding the individual as a system. This will be a fundamental change within the home territory of psychology" (Bateson 1970, p. 243).

Self-states are so integrated within ordinary daily adult experience that we tend to pay them no special notice. We more or less perceive our personifications as a familiar embodied consciousness moving from one thing to the next. Occasional sensations of unfamiliarity or detachment from our "own" persona or surroundings are remarked upon as uncanny. At the same time, we casually accept routine shifts in self-state, especially those connected to a particular relationship, role, emotion, or memory. We hear this in everyday talk: "I can never speak up to authority figures"; "I have to be in the mood for that"; "When I'm with her, I can really be myself"; "I got so angry, I was beside myself"; "Back in the old neighborhood, it feels like I'm still ten years old"; "Give him a compliment, he's a different man"; "I'm not myself today"; "This makes me feel like a new person."

As the severity of personality disorder increases, not only does personality style become more rigidified and pronounced, but the self-states are delayed in unification. Discontinuity as a defense against separation anxiety becomes increasingly pronounced. With the carry-over of right-brain thinking, for example, there are irreconcilable either/or, all-or-nothing, attitudes that may manifest themselves in endless internal arguments. The persistence of these arguments is often a matter of patient concern, and too often a matter of defeat for patient and therapist alike, who try to bring about an impossible resolution of seemingly "neurotic" conflict in oppositional personality states. I have found that my experience with MPD/DID is instructive here, as therapy with the more pronounced condition can guide the technical approach to the more subtle self-states.

What I learned repeatedly from the "alters" (alternative inner subselves) in a multiple self-system, is that the issue is one of acknowledgment, not conflict. It is recognition and respect for all parts of the self, and their place, however superficially questionable, in the system of the self, that promote psychic progress. It is the patient's interpersonal experience of this acknowledgment on the part of the therapist, far more than various interpretations, that counts. An example of this in my experience of MPD/DID dealt with the treatment of an abused child alter, who first "told," of her abuse, and then gradually began to enjoy play for itself, until one day she was "gone." When I made inquiries, I learned "she had been acknowledged enough," and had unified into another alter who, surprisingly, was businesslike and intellectual (see also Orcutt 1995b, pp. 250–251; 2012a, pp. 229–231). This contributed to my understanding that changes in psychic structure are, as Freud held, subject to a "principle of constancy," which strives to maintain a balanced nature of the personality. Elements of the self, allowed sufficient expression and recognition with another, seek a complementary position in the whole. The maturing self begins to manage conscious conflict once a capacity has been established for a comprehensive consideration of the range of elements involved.

How does this translate to therapeutic treatment of self-states in personality disorder? As mentioned, typical of personality disorder is the persistence of inner arguments. First, I assume that the arguments are fundamentally based on an insistent need to be heard. I find it useful to propose that the patient describe, or even "quote," each side of the argument in detail. I sometimes make an attempt (with the patient's permission) to speculate how that "part" of the patient might argue: "I guess this is a pretty relentless point of view, like, 'Why don't you do what I tell you; you don't do what you should do; you don't do anything right.'" If this is on target, there will be some degree of feeling response – often rueful, but with luck somewhat amused. If the therapeutic relationship is in place, and the timing is right, there is a potential for playfulness. There is no interpretation, criticism, or disagreement, but simply space for expression. I then may reflect that this part of the self doesn't have much of a problem speaking up, but how about the other side of the argument? What would the other part of the self say? This may require a little coaching – hopefully playfully – and some speculation from me, based again on what I have learned in previous sessions: "From what you tell me, there's probably a part of you that feels obligated to do what's expected of you even if you don't want to. Right?" With the patient's assent, I continue: "I bet you've just learned to try harder and not complain." ("Yes.") "Maybe it feels too risky to disagree." (Tacit assent.) "But there wouldn't be an argument going on if this other part of you really agreed." (Curious attention.) "I see this in a lot of people I work with. This part of you probably never entirely bought into this and even may be plotting rebellion." (A slight smile followed by disavowal.) "All right. It's smart to say the right thing and keep your plans to yourself." (Another slight smile and silence.) "Maybe it's good to play safe. Any chance you can speak for that part of yourself and tell me what that smile means?" (After a pause, "I don't want to do what you say, but I'm smart enough not to tell you.")

It is important to allow expression for both points of view. Since it is the nature of parts, or self-states, to assume their point of view is the only one, opposing parts see no prospect of compromise, but have a desire to be understood. Each needs full acknowledgment, including the therapist's spoken recognition of the validity contained in each. Thus (in the above example), the resourcefulness of the child-state is credited, while the consistency of the parental identification is noted. As consideration is afforded both, a gradual complementarity is initiated, as the energy of one is juxtaposed with the reliability of the other, and vice versa. This and similar interludes are entertained in a simple therapeutic context: all inner arguments represent reality as it was dealt with long ago, but need to be updated to be useful in present time. All parts of the patient will have validity if understood in terms of the time they came into being.

Working with self-states in personality disorder is not a recommended frontal approach, as in Bradshaw's "Inner Child" therapy

(1990), or Berne's "Transactional Analysis" (1961). It is a technique to be introduced selectively, and preferably playfully. However, the uncritical acknowledgment of even contradictory set attitudes and behaviors within a single containing field of inquiry distinguishes the experiential approach with personality disorder from the insight-oriented, conflict-focused treatment of neurosis. It characterizes therapy across the range of personality disorder, from Winnicott's holding of the schizoid patient, to Kohut's mirroring of the narcissist, to Masterson's confrontation of the borderline. Especially with patients receptive to considering "parts" of themselves, initiating dialogue with the parts can open the process to a new level of feeling. It also can bring an interactiveness into the therapeutic relationship that tests the stubborn humorlessness of the transference.

It is important to keep in mind that this is a concept with its basis in the normal psyche. As Putnam says, it is "a big idea: that our conscious-ness is chunked into basic units we call states of being/consciousness/mind and that all of these states, despite their many apparent differences, share common principles" (2016, p. 24).

The Masterson Synthesis

The reason that developmental trauma (also termed relational trauma) is of such significance is that it shapes the attachment patterns that establish what is to become a stable or unstable core self.

(Bromberg 2006, p. 6)

Issues of attachment in early childhood may result in structural arrest that skews the healthy progression of the self through its developmental positions. The steady integration of a core self with the unified subphases of psychic growth does not take place. Instead, there is a personality struc-ture overinfluenced by a particular subphase of psychic development still in need of adequate processing. Masterson's Approach to the healing of personality disorder is founded on a therapeutic relationship that gains its effectiveness from what we have increasingly learned of the nature of relationship and development itself. Consequently, his Approach has gained effectiveness from an ongoing synthesis.

Masterson's Approach to the psychoanalytic psychotherapy of personality disorder is a cumulative undertaking. Like the subject of its concern, it is a growing project that takes quantum steps forward as it assumes new capacities. Masterson does not compartmentalize the expert knowledge of others in territorial domains, but synthesizes their work within an expanding whole. His first melding of psychoanalytic object relations with Mahler's developmental model (the rapprochement subphase) created therapeutic insight critical for guiding his own extensive experience with borderline patients. The promise of extending this developmental framework further seemed likely when Kohut's definitive experience with the narcissist was clarified by correspondence to Mahler's model (Kohut himself noted a parallel consideration, while Masterson focused it specifically on the practicing subphase). A linear conceptualization of personality disorder seemed to be forming, with specific diagnoses having their origin in specific stages of psychic growth in early childhood. Dysfunction of the mother–child relationship at those stages seemed an essential consideration, in combination with the internalization of corresponding part-self and part-object representations.

Masterson began to have second thoughts, however. Although (for example) the narcissistic patient is so entrenched in his characterological mindset that one must speak in a particular way to establish common contact, there are times when the patient's functioning seems to have moved past that limitation. How can the personality be stuck in its development and also not be stuck?

This developmental doubt persisted when Ralph Klein contributed his invaluable addition of the schizoid dynamic to Masterson's canon, but at the expense of a linear formulation. Klein favors the more networked, multidimensional model proposed by Daniel Stern, where an expanding sense of self supplants Mahler's more regulated time frame. Klein's presentation is persuasive – it has conviction and clinical perception – but it largely eliminates Mahler's contribution. Mahler's guide to understanding the distortedness of the analytic enactment in contrast to healthy relationship is lost, along with the developmental basis for technical "language" with different personality disorders.

But why not at least consider the possibility of a correspondence between the schizoid disorder and Mahler's differentiation subphase? Masterson emphatically describes the schizoid situation as the "third major dimension of psychopathology," stating that it "takes its place alongside the narcissistic and borderline disorders of the self." (Masterson & Klein (Eds.), 1995, p. ix.) But why should the schizoid assume any greater significance than (for instance) the depressive or the masochistic ways of being? Is it not worth considering that the schizoid, together with the narcissist and the borderline, completes a "progression" of pathological types that shadows the advance of the healthy growing psyche: a specific pathology that demonstrates the traumatic interruption of consolidation of a major developmental sub-phase. There is a validity to the linear model that intuitively "feels right." But Masterson's initial inclination to pursue a linear premise based on Mahler appears to have been discarded for two main reasons: a synthesis of expert theory on the schizoid was not attempted and, even if it had been, a completed linear model would not have been enough.

It is puzzling that the considerable body of theory devoted to the schizoid – its developmental, intrapsychic, and interpersonal elements – was not fully taken into consideration by Masterson. The theory of Fairbairn and Winnicott explicating the schizoid condition is specific in locating the origin of the schizoid condition in the early mother–infant relationship as well as the growth of self in the first year of life. The theory is further supported by Winnicott's extensive pediatric as well as analytic experience, and organized, focused, and clinically expanded in substantial publications brought forth by Guntrip and Khan. In addition, it is contemporaneous, and sometimes overlapping, with Mahler's work. And it is the contribution of the very object relationists who form a cornerstone for Masterson's Approach. The difficulty of recognizing and integrating this work seems to have been a general issue in the field, however, and is not exclusive with Masterson. It is hoped that a synthesizing of theory of the schizoid to Masterson's original developmental model may bring it new relevance.

The restoration of a linear model of personality disorder is not enough, however. Although the manifestation of arrested development may seem to consume the therapeutic encounter, the "real-life" situation is more complex than that. Although in some ways the patient remains stubbornly in the psychic world of the two-and-a-half-year-old or younger, in many ways the patient is functioning well beyond the demands of early life. The view of the psyche as a system seems as pertinent as a linear progression.

The Masterson Approach need not make an either/or choice here, especially since the linear can be interwoven within the systems model of the self. Indeed, Masterson's synthesizing of the latest scientific data brings new relevance to the linear relational model. With the incorporation of the neuroanalytical thinking of Allan Schore, and the elaboration of attachment theory by Fonagy, Gergely, Jurist, and Target (2002), Masterson is once more on the way to accepting the developmental importance of the first year of life: study of the brain now reinforces the psychic oneness of mother and infant as crucial to the secure establishment of a beginning sense of self. Mahler's observations still hold, especially when free from drive theory metaphysics. Shore's synthesis of neurology and Bowlby's attachment theory of personality development make understanding of the evolving relationship of mother and child more important than ever in creating the healing relationship of dynamic psychotherapy of personality disorder.

A subphase origin of personality disorder might once again be considered, but how can the personality be "stopped" at a specific stage of development while maturing in other ways? Masterson's exploration does not continue to consider a networked concept of self that could encompass this complex view of personality. Such a view is contained in self-state theory, however, and, if Masterson had lived to pursue his interest in Schore's work, it is not difficult to imagine he would have synthesized this exciting theory to make a further integration of the Masterson Approach possible.

Especially through the combined effort of Schore and Bromberg (2011), we see how a self-state distorted at one point in the early mother–child relationship may freeze through "relational trauma." Other inner representations of parts of the self can persist, however, compensating to maintain a psychic balance adequate enough to carry forward a relatively consistent and crucial sense of being. Given this, one can see how this "holding" aspect of the personality can tacitly form and retain a therapeutic alliance with the therapist while, simultaneously, the therapist uses specialized language to reach the rigidly defended self-state at its developmental level. The treatment continues: to establish the alternative experience of relationship needed to address the problematic deficits and distortions of the self-state, to address relational trauma (abandonment depression), and to facilitate integration of the self-state with the greater whole.

A fundamental shift in psychoanalytic perspective has been highlighted by self-state theory. As Bateson observed, it would be a matter of time before systems theory expanded from family therapy to treatment of the individual patient – but understanding gathers slowly. It has been nearly a hundred years since Glover (1930) suggested a theoretical basis for this view in psychoanalysis, and now hard science is beginning to actualize the undertaking. Freud's *Project* is growing closer to realization, and Masterson's Approach can claim the theoretical, clinical whole implied at the very beginning of his major work of synthesis of psychoanalytic models.

CASE STUDY

These sequential accounts – originally published in separate collections – are brought together here as a demonstration of the complexity of the self and the necessity for a circumspect clinical approach that respects that complexity. By therapeutic process and over the passage of time, strengthening of the "holding" personality makes possible the reorganization of the underlying, adaptive self-components. An integration then may follow of these continuously containing and contained, complementary elements of the whole individual self.

It should be added that, twenty-five years after the publication of these studies, "Gerda" continues settled in her work life and in a close, established marriage that has nourished now-grown children.

Part I: Psychotherapy with a Borderline Adolescent: From Clinical Crisis to Emancipation

Gerda, fifteen years old, came to her first regularly scheduled appointment with her hand in a cast. She had punched a wall during a frustrating discharge process from a psychiatric inpatient unit. It also occurred to her that she might have needed to create a crisis to relieve the anxiety she felt upon leaving the unit.

A month before, while leaving a party alone at night, she had been forced off the street and raped. Subsequently she overdosed twice and was admitted to the hospital.

Gerda, a sophomore in high school, was a well-groomed, overweight girl with long, Alice in Wonderland hair. Her manner was engaging, although she described herself as "untrusting." She was intelligent and perceptive; her speech was articulate and fluid except for periodic silences. The silences occurred when she felt sad. She said she didn't like to talk about sadness but, rather, would wait until it was "over." She believed that her problem had to do with "character," which she thought was not such a bad thing, since character could be changed.

I had already spoken separately with Gerda's mother, an author of children's books who constantly traveled in search of ethnic source materials. The mother was attractive, thin, and dressed like a fashionable bohemian. She was quick, intelligent, and intellectualized. She told me she felt as if her life had been "knocked out from under her" by her daughter's hospitalization.

It occurred to me that Gerda seemed like one of her mother's fictional creations – even her name had a storybook quality. "I hate my name," said Gerda. "It isn't a real name, and nobody ever pronounces it right."

Gerda's childhood was described to me by her mother. Gerda was the more reliable historian about her own adolescence.

Gerda had been a healthy baby who was weaned at nine months and had loved to eat. Her developmental milestones were achieved early, and apparently she toilet trained herself. She developed asthma at about two to three years of age, a year before her parents were divorced. When Gerda was four, her mother decided to move to Quebec to allow herself "time to think." Gerda, uprooted from her home and friends, began to withdraw. Her mother sent her out to buy bread and milk so that she would have to deal with people and learn French Canadian, and somehow Gerda managed. A year later, they moved again to New York City, and the mother's career took priority. At seven, Gerda was a latchkey child, with the door key on a string around her neck so that she could come and go by herself. When her mother arrived home from work exhausted, Gerda tucked her into bed. Gerda used to have "intricate, beautiful dreams" for her mother's benefit, and would recount them in the morning to cheer her mother up.

Gerda's latency period was fragmented by multiple moves, the mother's changing romantic attachments, and extensive trips abroad.

She was the clearest about her early adolescence. At eleven, she had begun what she called her "symbolic year," a period of expressing her anger at her mother in all possible indirect ways. For instance, she wrote "I hate you" in tiny letters on the walls in back of the furniture. By age twelve, she had declared open war, and she and her mother fought constantly.

By the time therapy started, Gerda had had one surrogate father as well as a series of surrogate mothers who took over her care when her own mother traveled. In school, she was maintaining an A average despite her troubles. Her compliance, social skills, energy, and humor helped her to keep up the appearance of a model, outgoing, all-round student. Actually, she was constantly surprised to find that others perceived her this way. Her sense of herself was tenuous, and she told me that she had hid under her desk during her earlier school experience. Her relationships with both girls and boys had an intense, dyadic quality. She was offended at the idea of discussing her sexual activities with anyone of my generation, but she said that she believed intercourse should be saved for a deeply committed relationship.

On the night of the rape, she had left the party early when a girlfriend had unreasonably grown angry at her and had ordered her to leave. Gerda, upset, was searching for a cab when she was caught from behind by a man with a knife, who forced her into an empty lot and raped her. She walked home in shock and found that her mother was out. The phone rang, and it was an obscene phone call. Overwhelmed, she swallowed No-Doz washed down with rum, and eventually began to vomit. Her mother arrived home and called the police, but Gerda locked herself in her room and refused to come out. Later, her mother took Gerda to the gynecologist for persistent vaginal bleeding. Gerda then overdosed again on flurazepam (Dalmane) and left a suicide note. This time, her mother got her to the hospital, where her stomach was pumped, and she was admitted to the psychiatric unit.

Course of Treatment

The treatment – shorter-term and crisis-oriented – was of two and a half years' duration. For the first nine months, Gerda was seen individually twice a week and with her mother once a week. After that, she was seen individually three times a week for a year, then twice a week for the last nine months. Treatment ended when, at age eighteen, she graduated from high school and went away to college. From the outset, it was understood that her treatment would probably be time-limited by her college plans.

The first phase of treatment focused on the crisis in Gerda's individual and family life. Although the work was heavily confrontational, it became increasingly insight-oriented – especially when the family sessions ended, and Gerda took increasing responsibility for her therapy.

In the family sessions, the mother and daughter argued, and they could be verbally devastating. At home, these arguments escalated into dramatic scenes with screaming and slamming of doors. Enmeshed in each other's anger, they could go on endlessly over such matters as the care of the cat's litter box.

I pointed out that, although they were both concerned with the issue of responsibility, neither was taking it. I labeled the arguments phony and nonproductive and wondered what it was they would have to face if they stopped arguing. Gerda agreed that the fights were useless and would surely put her "in her grave." Her mother said she feared there would no longer be any communication between them if the fights stopped. The theme of separation emerged (and, of course, the fighting had started when Gerda had begun to move toward adolescent independence). My job, then, was to promote constructive communication and confront phony litter-box talk until, one day, Gerda exclaimed: "We're running the session without you!" With a workable-enough truce declared on the home scene, it was possible to end the family sessions and give Gerda full attention and responsibility for her therapy.

In her individual sessions, Gerda avoided her feelings by chattering entertainingly, more or less nonstop. I confronted this by asking how keeping me entertained was going to be helpful to her. In response, she told me about her "Pollyanna routine," which she had invented to minimize painful feelings in her social interactions. I said I was receptive to all her thoughts and feelings, and that she would be maintaining herself at an impasse by leaving part of herself out of therapy. She then told me that she had always felt safer keeping her feelings "in little boxes," and was afraid of losing control if she didn't.

My confrontations then focused on the silences that increasingly interrupted the "Pollyanna routine" – and each of these silences turned out to be "a little box" containing an unexpressed feeling. Gerda began to see how she inhibited her spontaneity by these silences. I began to realize how sensitive she had learned to become to meet her mother's need for constant cheering up.

Once Gerda began to observe her patterns of avoidance, she began to cautiously test how I would receive her expression of feeling. Anger came first, but obliquely. She began to criticize my office in fine detail. I responded to this in a light way, saying, "How can I help you get it together when I can't even put together my own office?" She became a little more direct, noting that I was from the suburbs, with "all those little polyester people living in little polyester houses." I asked if she was worried about my being synthetic – a fake therapist. She then expressed her annoyance more directly, saying ruefully that I left her to take the initiative and have painful thoughts and feelings when she talked about herself. She also resented not having a choice about being in therapy. So, I pointed out that she had made a kind of choice through her suicide attempts, and that she could make it easier for herself in the long run if she would learn to say what she wanted instead of doing it.

She told me she would rather feel angry than feel "betrayed." It seemed that the feeling of betrayal related to separation, since she immediately spoke of her discharge from the hospital. The night before her discharge, she was both angry and afraid of her anger. She had dreamed that she was taken from the hospital in a coffin, although she wasn't dead. She sat up in her coffin with her eyes burning "like a character in a horror film." In her dream, she fell through to hell, where she searched endlessly through dark caves. That night she woke up terrified, with no one to comfort her, and felt as she had when she had nightmares at six years of age.

She next began to bring in her poems and short stories, which she read to me. One story had been written between the time of the rape and her second suicide attempt. It told about a grotesque circus – which was really the world – in which a woman behind a curtain of white silk was "the main attraction." In the story, the curtain is drawn aside, she "makes her one plea to the crowd," and then "a razor-sharp knife descends upon her." Gerda said she was frightened by the feelings in the story and of the feelings aroused in therapy. She was afraid she might be crazy and that, if she told me too much about herself, I would hospitalize her. This was more of a conviction than a fantasy and let me know how persuasively she had been taught the unacceptability of her feelings.

At this time, she grudgingly admitted that the family sessions were going well, and sadly remarked, "My mother is not a grown-up." She spoke of finding it difficult to have her mother lean on her emotionally, and then began to feel guilty. She then wandered off the subject. I confronted her avoidance, wondering why she chose to create a diversion rather than accept her own feelings (a repetition of pleasing her mother rather than expressing herself.) She got mad at me, saying she did not want to get depressed again, as she had after the rape – that she wouldn't be able to put the feelings away and would be stuck with them. I said, "You're stuck with them anyway; why not learn to manage them?" She got mad at me again, and I asked her why she was angry at me for believing she could handle her own feelings.

She next brought in an article on child molestation that stressed the importance of the child's being able to talk about what had happened. This was followed by an attack of laryngitis (the first of many), but she was able to whisper to me that she had had a "flashback" and recalled the face of the man who had raped her.

The borderline triad (individuation leads to depression, which leads to defense) was getting clearer: when Gerda began to express her feelings, she would become depressed and anxious and would defend against these feelings by reverting to the "Pollyanna routine," or an angry outburst, or a physical illness.

On the other hand, the more she was able to tolerate her feelings, the more she was able to remember, and to integrate a sense of continuity of herself. She noticed how discontinuous her memory was and began to mend the gaps, reviewing her life back to age three, where she had vivid memories, happy and unhappy, of her parents.

She was looking forward to celebrating her sixteenth birthday.

She told me that she was beginning, for the first time, to cry about the rape. She reported having nightmares and difficulty concentrating and began to cry painfully in sessions. Then she told me of a family "secret" she had forgotten. When she was seven, she had gone camping with her father and his current girlfriend with her fourteen-year-old son. The teenager sexually molested her, and persuaded her not to tell her father, because their parents would not then be married. Eventually, she did tell her mother, but the matter never went beyond that.

She allowed herself to express anger toward her mother in my presence. She was "a fake person who liked to play mother." Gerda began a catalog of adults who had let her down, and I was included for going on vacation. She also told me that sometimes she hated me for making her feel. Words increasingly carried the burden of her self-expression.

She began to act more for herself. She completely redecorated her room at home, painting over the little-girl-pink walls with a sophisticated gray, and displaying her collection of crystal objects. Her toys were given away or put in the attic (except for the doll's house, which the mother took off to *her* room).

She began to lose her voice again but continued to prepare herself to talk about the rape. She said it now seemed only to be a part of her, instead of all of her. But she said she still was not ready to trust me enough to begin.

Then she had a series of cancellations because of an earache, a toothache, a cold, laryngitis, and a strep throat. And, when she came in, she came in fighting: she said I was intrusive and made her feel stupid and sick. She said she hated therapy and wanted to be independent. I said she was expecting me to be like her mother, and that she was letting this get in the way of using her therapy to help herself become independent. She then decided to tell me about her "secret criminal life," where she hated her mother and had dreams that she was watching her mother being killed. She decided that she had invested me with the "power" to make her feel sick or criticized, and now realized that I actually had no such control over her.

At this point, I was unexpectedly called away by a family illness. At the same time, Gerda underwent an overdue tonsillectomy. When we both returned, she said she had felt betrayed by my absence, but had also discovered that she missed me and cared about her therapy.

The work had been deepening in intensity since family sessions had ended and Gerda had been coming in three times a week. She had internalized my confrontations, catching herself when she began to avoid her feelings. And she was becoming more observant about the borderline triad, noting: "I'm now going to take one step backward because I've taken two steps forward."

One year into treatment, she began to report her dreams regularly. She dreamed she was watching a bright, cold maze of mirrors, and then she was in the maze, with a giant shouting at her. Next, she had a dream in which she was looking out a window through a white gauze curtain. She watched a girl go down a road that divided into two paths. One path led to a spindly house of ice with a cold light in it; inside was a closed box with a padlock. The other path led to a "plump gingerbread house with bright red geraniums living in window boxes"; inside was an open box. (What a picture of the withdrawing and rewarding split! Remember, gingerbread houses contain witches who eat little children.) As she stood at the window, she held a key that was so cold it burned her hand, and she dropped it.

She associated the cold of the key and the icy house to the mirror in the maze in her first dream, and to the cold she felt during her tonsillectomy, when she came out of the anesthesia screaming for her mother – or when she woke from her nightmares on the psychiatric unit – or from her nightmares long ago when she was six. She felt she was in the cold, crying for her mother who wasn't there.

She had a similar dream, and I was in it. She was looking through the same window, and someone drew back her arm, which in turn drew back the curtain. She couldn't remember what she saw, but it was terrifying. She felt I was helping her to remove the curtain that veiled painful memories.

She then picked a phony fight with me. Catching herself, she regained her perspective and began to joke about "feeling like a killer." She told me: "Go to your corner and die!"

She said that she had picked the fight because she had made up her mind to talk about the rape but was avoiding getting started.

She reflected that she was experiencing "a new sadness" beyond terror and anger. The sensation of "coldness" she had been describing to me had something to do with the rape but perhaps had been there even before. It was a feeling of coldness inside – an emptiness. She thought of all the times she had set aside her needs to care for her mother, and of the cold house in the dream. She said: "Dreams really do have a meaning!"

She began to reconstruct the memory of the rape. At first, she did this by drawing fragmentary, half-symbolic pictures which she brought to her sessions. The drawings contained certain repeated elements: malevolent eyes, a religious medal on a chain, a knife, a stuffed bear being torn apart, dissociated gears, and mechanical parts. The paper the drawings were done on was cut in an elongated, hexagonal shape.

She said that the drawings had to do with evil and the destruction of innocence. The rape was "the ultimate deceit that confirmed all other deceits." She said, "These are pictures of my head, filled with broken gears." She felt "fragmented, in pieces that don't fit together." It occurred to her that the paper was cut in the shape of a coffin.

She had more nightmares and a fear of being overwhelmed by a sense of guilt; she said that was why she had attempted suicide. She said she wished she had been beaten, because people didn't believe she had wanted to resist. I said, "Your life was in danger. If you had resisted, you might have been killed." She said she recalled being grabbed from the back. When she started to run away, her sweater was torn off, and she experienced a brief amnesia – perhaps when she saw the knife. She next remembered being in the empty lot and gagged with her own sweater. She thought she was going to be killed and just wanted it to be over. At that point she gave up.

Her recollections of the rape itself were fragmentary, "like pieces of a jigsaw puzzle that don't match." She began to recall the empty lot: a discarded automobile tire, a license plate. She fixed on her assailant's religious medal – how it turned, and how the light fell on the gold (afterward, she often felt panic when she spoke with a man wearing a gold neck-chain). She thought the medal had a mother and child on it. She was aware of how cold she felt. She said, "His breath was hot, and his pendant was cold."

More nightmares followed. In one dream, she was observing herself in the form of a transparent doll. An arm kept putting gears inside her. Finally, the arm produced a key and wound up the gears. Then she dreamed she was on fire.

In another dream, she was in a glass case locked with a key. She tried to smash the glass, but, instead of breaking, it burst into flames.

She began talking about the rape again, saying that her recollections had a feeling of coldness, deadness, like a glass wall or ice. She told me that she never felt angry about the rape – just cold. In the hospital, she had made lists of reasons why she deserved the rape. However, she had felt angry at God.

Gradually, she also became angry about the rape and at her assailant. She said her pictures did not have enough anger in them. At home, she concentrated on drawing the rapist's face over and over.

Her seventeenth birthday passed. She went up to visit her dolls in the attic, but they were no longer a comfort, and she felt all alone.

Recollection of the rape evoked one further memory (probably a screen memory, because it also seemed dreamlike to her). She said that the feeling of cold went back to her early childhood when her parents were still married and living together with her in the country. She thought she remembered looking out the window on "a shining day." It was the window of her dreams, and it was closed and curtained because it was winter, with the cold snow shining outside. Her father entered, filling the doorway "like a great bear." She could not get hold of the "other half" of the memory, which involved "something frightening." However, this persistent theme or lifting a veil ended here; its implications went beyond the scope of our time-limited work together.

She began for the first time to discuss dating. At first, she felt embarrassed and uncomfortable: "Things are getting out of their boxes ... things are in messes." I commented that she had felt freer about talking about dating since she had decided to talk about the rape. She agreed there was a connection, in that she now felt better about the dating itself. She said she had gone through a period of having "flashbacks" while dating, but these experiences had lessened the more she was able to talk about the rape.

She completed her junior year with flying colors. She had maintained her high average, scored high on her Scholastic Achievement Test, was busy in school activities, and enjoyed being a seventeen-year-old.

As she approached her senior year in high school, her appearance changed, as well. Her hair was trimmed to shoulder length, and her dress was more tailored. Her poise seemed to come from an inner balance rather than from a defensively imposed manner. She agreed that she had changed, and that she felt "seventeen, not two or thirty-two."

At the beginning of the school year, she decided to reduce her sessions to twice a week. She said she felt she could get on without the "security" of so many sessions, and that she needed a little more time to be "a teenager with other teenagers" after school. I saw reality in this, especially with termination drawing closer, and with the stepped-up activities and responsibilities of her senior year. So, I said it was her choice. She had been prepared to fight me or be directed by me and said that taking responsibility for making her own choice was much more difficult. She did decide to reduce her sessions to twice a week, with the result that she felt for the first time that her therapy was fully her own choice and responsibility.

She also regressed somewhat in the beginning of this brief but important phase of treatment. Her increased independence (and probably the impending termination) led her to perceive me as withdrawing from her. She accused me of growing distant: I didn't talk like a person; my face was painted on; I had been transformed from a human being to a Pod Person (disguised alien). She was going to retaliate and stop coming, because there were no problems left to discuss, anyway. I asked her how she could say this when, as yet, she had no steady boyfriend. This confrontation evoked the angriest response I experienced from her. It also put the last phase of therapy on the track.

The next session she came in, very poised, and said that it was true she gets into an argument with me when she is resisting a turning point in therapy. Actually, she said, she no longer experienced the rape or suicide attempts as so important and needed to talk about her present life.

She said she had had a steady boyfriend for the past three weeks and, although she cared very much for him, she was worried whether or not to have intercourse with him. She was still concerned about flashbacks and wanted to be sure not to do such an important thing perhaps out of peer pressure in the senior year. She also spoke about fears of maturing sexually – the shift in the attitude of boys toward her, and feelings of disgust about her own body that she had tried to hide in being overweight. She was bewildered, then resentful of her mother's reaction to her increasing attractiveness: her mother kept creating scenes about Gerda's clothing being too provocative (it wasn't so at all).

But now she had internalized confrontation to the point where she remained self-activating while experiencing whatever feelings were being evoked. Consequently, she became increasingly depressed and, I believe, was able to work through the first layer of her abandonment depression.

She felt very alone, without a family, and realized she had always felt this way. She began to weep because she felt that no one in her family had ever cared for her as a person, only as an extension of themselves. She felt cheated that she couldn't even mourn the loss of a family, because there had been no family to begin with (what family there was was geographically scattered as well as emotionally distant). She said she believed she must be utterly worthless to have driven them all away. Her guilt helped her to maintain the illusion that she could have some effect on their feelings. As long as she could indulge in self-blame, she would not have to relinquish some hope of changing the situation. I said that she must have felt helpless indeed to believe the only way she could get her mother's attention was to attempt suicide, but wouldn't it make more sense to acknowledge the feeling than let it take the form of such a desperate action? Gerda said, "I really feel great hate for you for pointing out what I already know."

The depression that was expressed in her sessions was also contained by them. Outside, her life was increasingly stable, and she made dramatic improvements in assertion and communication.

One day she announced that she and her boyfriend had become lovers. No flashbacks, she said, but no fireworks or roses, either. Just real lovemaking, and she was in a good mood about it.

She even came to the conclusion that her mother wasn't so bad after all – a decent person, though scattered.

Termination

Just before her eighteenth birthday, Gerda had one more fit of anger at me. She said I did not understand her, and that she felt like putting her fist through the wall. When I reminded her that this was what she had actually done when she left the inpatient unit, she realized she was having a reaction to the impending close of treatment.

She used the remaining time well, calling upon her increased capacity to observe, to make responsible decisions, and to follow through despite difficult feelings. Her last accomplishment was to face up to the illnesses she used as an avoidance. She confronted herself, observed her actions, and saw that she exhausted herself by overwork or overplay in order to get sick and avoid feelings.

Her individuation, as well as her integration of confrontation and management of separation feelings, was exemplified in her final sessions. The next-to-last session had been so right – such a healthy balance of sadness, happiness, direct expression of feeling for me, and thoughtful anticipation of her future – that I worried she might waver and miss the last session. With great effort, I said nothing and left it up to her. To my relief (and joy), she came in, and told me that she was proud of herself because she had foreseen that she would try to do something to miss the session and, when the impulse came, she contained it and faced the separation.

Epilogue

When Gerda reviewed this account of her early history, she felt that more needed to be said. The following is her reflection on the work she did and still continues to do:

> I am twenty-one now, and it is six years since I was raped. My initial treatment, which was time-limited and crisis-oriented, succeeded in that it taught me how to survive. Recently I returned to therapy with Dr. Orcutt, but my goals have changed. I am now willing to make a commitment to become whole, not pieced together. It is time to find out why I am so filled with self-hatred and why my answer to difficult events in my life has been to try to kill myself. I have resumed my therapy because surviving is no longer enough. I want to learn how to live.

Candace Orcutt (1989c). Psychotherapy with a borderline adolescent: from clinical crisis to emancipation. In: J. F. Masterson & R. Klein (Eds.) Psychotherapy of the Disorders of the Self: The Masterson Approach (pp. 185–196). New York: Brunner/Mazel. Copyright 1989 by Brunner/Mazel, Inc. Reprinted by permission of the publisher.

Part 2: Integration of Multiple Personality Disorder in the Context of the Masterson Approach

In *Psychotherapy of the Disorders of the Self* (Masterson and Klein 1989, pp. 185–196), I described the case of a borderline adolescent who came to the Masterson Group in crisis and remained to work through important characterological issues. The chapter was subtitled "From Clinical Crisis to Emancipation." When the patient returned to therapy after a two-year absence, I thought I might title any follow-up of the work "From Clinical Emancipation to Crisis." It seemed that the first two and a half years of therapy had prepared her to uncover a level of conflict that tested both the patient and the therapeutic process itself.

Underlying the character pattern that had acted as a defensive false self from her infancy was a second line of protection – an elaborate dissociative shield of multiple inner personalities that contained and compartmentalized a lifetime of traumatic experience – a failsafe barrier that prevented the flooding through of devastating information should the characterological defense give way. At the most, this dissociative barrier would permit only a fragment of past experience to emerge, "held" by an inner personality whose presence, even when made known to the therapist, might not be acknowledged by the patient consciously.

Initial Phase of Therapy

Gerda (her pseudonym when earlier described in the 1988 Masterson and Klein edition) was fifteen and a half years old when she first entered treatment at the Masterson Group. She was discharged to the group from a psychiatric inpatient unit, where she had gone as a result of two suicide attempts. The attempts were precipitated by a rape in a deserted city parking lot. It was almost immediately evident that Gerda's problems had not begun with the rape: she had lived a life of surface charm and excitement, while feeling essentially uprooted and neglected. Her parents, both of whom were bright and talented, divorced when Gerda was four years old because of the father's physical abuse of the mother. Gerda had lived a nomadic life with her world-traveler mother, and her closest relationships were with the mother and her own world of fantasy. She was creative, highly intelligent, and attractive, but she was an isolated only child.

Although the crisis issue was focal in many ways, the main focus of her therapy was her borderline self-style. Avoidance and hostile outbursts characterized her approach to relationship, offsetting the clinging she both desired and feared.

Essentially, she recovered from the rape crisis, worked through many of her borderline issues (mainly by discovering that the use of words could have value), and graduated with distinction from high school. I worked with her on a three-times-a-week basis, later diminishing to twice a week, until she left the city for college.

At the time of the initial termination, I believed there was some earlier trauma connected with her father that she was not ready to approach. Her character work had been done so well that I had felt satisfied to see her more in charge of her life and moving forward.

Impasse and Transition

There was a two-year hiatus while she was away at college. These were troubled years during which she developed severe anorexia nervosa and then bulimia nervosa, which resulted in a leave of absence. She returned to therapy when she learned that her father was dying. She resumed college attendance and commuted six hours (round trip) for a weekly double session with me.

The next two years were marked by puzzling symptoms: fugue states; during which the cigarette she held burned down to her fingers; extreme fluctuations in blood pressure that sent her to the hospital but received no diagnosis; severe ongoing disturbances in sleeping and eating. She was able to graduate, although she was preoccupied with suicidal wishes.

Back in the city, she found an apartment, secured a position as a decorator's assistant, and worked creatively and responsibly. However, her symptoms worsened. She would abruptly lose consciousness and fall down in the street. She reinstituted (deliberately) once-rejected defenses, such as cutting and bulimia, which seemed to relieve the new symptoms. She seemed to be in a terrible dilemma, able neither to submerge some central trauma nor to bring it to the surface. I wondered if she might be helped through hypnosis and sought a local hypnotherapist to try a catalytic intervention.

The patient herself located a hypnoanalyst who worked with dissociative states. I accompanied her for three sessions, during which she was helped to transcend her anxiety and find an "inner child" – a three-and-a-half-year-old – who was deeply intimidated and expressed fear of her father.

At that point, I incorporated hypnosis into my sessions with Gerda, following the hypnoanalyst's initial guidance and seeking regular consultation with a colleague in the Masterson Institute who was experienced in the use of hypnosis. A primary technique I learned helped the patient to construct a "safe place" in her inner world – a containing induction used routinely in the treatment of post-traumatic stress disorder.*

Gradually, "Little Gerda" began to meet with me in the safe place. We took time to get acquainted, as Little Gerda introduced me to the world of the three-year-old and four-year-old. We went for inner walks and had a tea party with her cat and pet rabbit. After several weeks, she asked me cautiously whether I could keep a secret. When I assured her that I would honor her confidence, she began to tell me about Daddy.

I recognized the event from a dream she had told me years earlier, a dream that had made me wonder about the possibility of child abuse. She often had dreams about a particular window, and in this dream she looked out on cold snow shining outside. She watched as her father approached, "like a great bear," and the dream ended with "something frightening" that she could not remember.

Now, Little Gerda kneeled on her bed, watching Daddy in the window, and then was terrified as someone roughly took her arm from behind. She had been watching her father's reflection in the window at night, and he had actually been entering the room behind her.

The traumatic experiencing of a savage rape followed. For the first time, I witnessed the unfolding of an abreaction – muted but disturbing to see. The patient spoke and looked like a little child in fear and pain; she broke into perspiration, and her body twisted beneath the blanket in which she always wrapped herself during these sessions.

*"The author wishes to express her gratitude to Robert S. Mayer, Ph.D., and Diane Roberts Stoler, Ed.D., for their tutelage and support during this challenging, often overwhelming initiation to her work with multiplicity.

Another eerie thing occurred. In order to complete the experience of the rape, Gerda divided her awareness into three consecutive personalities. The first "went into her garden" (dissociated) when the rape began; the second endured the rape ("that's my job") but resisted when Daddy tried to force her into telling him she loved him. He burned her hand on the radiator. and would have broken her spirit, except that another child, meek and sad, took her place and reassured Daddy that she loved him, and said she was sorry that it took her so long to say so. When Daddy finally left the room, the tough little child re-emerged and smashed the window that had held his reflection.

At this point. I hypothesized that Gerda was using a dissociative defense – diluting the impact of the traumatic experience by dividing it into different segments of her personality. It was clear that the abreaction was not complete until the three inner children had linked their stories, like pieces completing a puzzle. I was too amazed by the revelations of Gerda's inner world to be able also to grasp that I was working with multiple personality disorder (MPD).

I thought at the time that MPD was very rare and had never observed an overt case in a clinical setting. Additionally, I had known my patient as an apparent nonmultiple for nearly six years and could not absorb such a different concept of who she was.

Gerda, also, was too disoriented to consider fully the possibility of multiplicity. She was too upset by the revelations of her inner world, especially when they began to involve shattering recollections of abuse by a religious cult.

The multiplicity had to be faced. She began to abreact outside of sessions, to lose time, to find her apartment mysteriously torn up, or discover herself perched alarmingly on the windowsill or on the edge of the roof. "Someone" managed her job for an entire day. I knew I would have to check for an internal alter ego.

I "went inside" to ask if I could speak with someone who could provide me with facts and figures – someone who, without stirring up more emotion for the patient, could inform me about the lost time and other matters.

I felt a shock as Gerda changed before me into a cold, pragmatic person who indicated that she had taken over Gerda's job one day when the patient was too distraught to function. This was Paulina, who had rebelled against conforming to the cult that had abused "us." She was co-conscious with Gerda and "others inside." Through her, I met a group of alters: Penelope. who was socially charming, avoided the negative, and was present for much of early therapy; Meg, who cut the body to "let out bad things"; and others.

"I feel as if I'm living in a grade B movie," said Gerda grimly after she had filled in the blanks in her conscious recollection with the information I retained. If I was shaken as I reperceived my familiar patient as a system rather than as an individual, how must she have felt? At least I had a continuous conscious recall of the session and did not have to rely on someone else to be my auxiliary memory (a holding function of the therapist, I believe, that is crucial to the therapeutic process – it is internalized by the patient).

What is Multiple Personality Disorder and How is it Treated?

Diagnosis

The *Diagnostic and Statistical Manual of Mental Disorders* (DSM) conferred official recognition on MPD in 1980. *DSM-IV* (American Psychiatric Association 1994) changed the name of the disorder to Dissociative Identity Disorder (DID – although MPD remains the internationally used nomenclature). In the 1994 edition, the diagnostic criteria were somewhat expanded:

    A. The presence of two or more distinct identities or personality states (each with its own relatively enduring pattern of perceiving, relating to, and thinking about the environment and self).

    B. At least two of these identities or personality states recurrently take control of the person's behavior.

    C. Inability to recall important personal information that is too extensive to be explained by ordinary forgetfulness.

    D. The disturbance is not due to the direct physiological effects of a substance ... or a general medical condition.

                                      (p. 487)

This certainly would suffice to identify such overt multiple personalities as "Anna O," described by Breuer and Freud in *Studies on Hysteria* (1895/1995), and other pioneering cases, such as Morton Prince's (1906), about a century ago.

The criteria would not have helped in diagnosing Gerda, or any other patient in a less than unmistakable state requiring no reference to any manual. Colin Ross (1989, p. 102) has listed several nonspecific diagnostic clues for the disorder, which, when they occur together, make it by far the most likely diagnosis. They are:

1. History of childhood sexual and/or physical abuse

2. Female sex

3. Age 20 to 40

4. Blank spells

5. Voices in the head or other Schneiderian symptoms

6. DSM-III-R criteria for borderline personality are met or nearly met

7. Previous unsuccessful treatment

8. Self-destructive behavior

9. No thought disorder

10. Headache.

These criteria would have been more helpful in diagnosing Gerda's problem. What would have helped the most would have been a capacity on my part to even consider MPD as a possible diagnosis for Gerda, or any other patient.

(Incidentally, Gerda herself reported additional symptoms that seem to occur frequently with MPD patients: periods of dizziness and disorientation; a persistent ringing in the ears. With regard to evidence of physical abuse, well into her treatment of multiplicity, Gerda suffered from recurrent back pain. It was the policy of her treatment to check out physical symptoms medically before attempting to treat them as body memories. In this instance, Gerda underwent a technologically advanced bone scan that revealed startling results. Her neck had been fractured more than once, and her pelvis and limbs showed evidence of breaks dating back to childhood. Some of these breaks appeared to have healed without treatment. In any case, nothing in her medical history provided any record of or explanation for the data that confronted her chiropractor. Toward the close of treatment, when Gerda had become engaged, she worried that her past sexual abuse had made it impossible for her to bear children. She and her fiancé were relieved when the gynecologist reassured her that she would be able to carry a child to term. However, the doctor shocked them with the observation that her uterus had been torn and stitched. Again, there had been no formal medical history of that event.)

Etiology

Richard Kluft (1988) has described MPD as a chronic post-traumatic dissociative disorder characterized by recurrent disturbances of identity and memory. He observes that the condition is no longer thought to be rare, but now is understood to occur in the wake of overwhelming early experiences, usually child abuse. The besieged child who has nowhere to find protection or hide in external reality retreats to the inner world to "establish alternative self-structures that allow intolerable circumstances to be disavowed or otherwise mitigated" (p. 212).

Breuer and Freud (1895/1955) were very clear that disorders such as Anna O's were based on trauma. Freud refined the concept, holding that the psychic illness came from a conflict between the conscious and unconscious parts of the self, rather than from congenital weakness. Freud also acknowledged the importance of actual parental abuse in the creation of this disorder. However, "MPD fell into disrepute following Freud's rejection of dissociation, the seduction theory, and hypnosis" (Ross 1989, p. 147).

Frank Putnam (1989) proposes a developmental substrate for MPD.* He emphasizes the work begun by Prechtl and his colleagues in

* Dr. Putnam, in addition to writing a major text, *The Diagnosis and Treatment of Multiple Personality Disorder* (1989), [was] chief of the Unit on Dissociative Disorders, Laboratory of Developmental Psychology, Intramural Research Program, National Institute of Mental Health, Bethesda, MD.

the 1970s, and notes that behavioral states of consciousness have emerged as the essential ordering principle for all infant studies. He hypothesizes:

> I think that the evidence suggests that ... over the course of normal development we more or less succeed in consolidating an integrated sense of self ... At birth, our behavior is organized into a series of discrete states ... The transitions between infant behavioral states exhibit psychophysiological properties that are highly similar to those observed across switches of alter personalities in MPD.

(p. 51)

As this sequence of normal developmental states is frozen by trauma, it becomes the ground for the development of subselves:

> One can conceive of these dissociated states, each imbued with a specific sense of self, being elaborated over time as the child repeatedly re-enters a specific dissociative state to escape from trauma or to execute behaviors he or she is unable to perform in normal consciousness. Each time the child re-enters a specific dissociative state, additional memories, affects, and behaviors become state-dependently bound to that state, building up a "life history" for the alter personality.

(p. 54)

Treatment

Freud and Breuer, basing their approach on the therapy of Anna O and others, stressed what Anna had described as the "talking cure" as the treatment of choice. Breuer, in particular, developed the cathartic method of therapy, using hypnosis to access a traumatic event, but requiring that the patient fully describe the event, until verbalization and behavioral repetition merged to create an affective conscious experience. With the entry into consciousness, the trauma was transformed into a memory that, like all memories, could be relegated to the past and released.

However, Freud abandoned the cathartic method; his substitution of the Oedipus complex for literal incest led to the de-emphasization of trauma as the basis for his neurotica. Free association, interpretation, and working-through (incrementally connecting pathology with infantile antecedents) became the hallmarks of psychoanalytic technique.

I believe it would be a theoretical error to dismiss analytic input into the treatment of multiplicity on the basis of this shift. The concepts of the influential inner world, and of working-through, are essential to the dynamic therapy of MPD. The lonely and courageous pioneer work of Cornelia Wilbur (Schreiber 1973) advocated an essentially psychoanalytic framework for the treatment of MPD. The overall work of Braun, Kluft, and Loewenstein stresses the importance of retaining a dynamic basis in the treatment of MPD, synthesizing it with the dissociative techniques that are more familiarly used.

Although hypnosis is surely *a* treatment of choice for MPD, it addresses only the dissociation, without helping the patient to place the enormity of his or her experience in the context of the history of the self. Resolution of the distortions of character that are built on the foundation of dissociated trauma is necessary if the self is to become whole.

As Karla Clark has noted elsewhere: "Freud's disavowal of his original trauma theory was a necessary precondition, ironically enough, for the development of theories that are comprehensive enough to treat trauma victims" (1993, p. 256).

Treatment of MPD by conventional dynamic therapy typically reaches a stalemate, if, indeed, the condition emerges at all. Abreactive work alone, however, floods the patient when little or no attention is paid to establishing the containment good character work provides. Casualties of either one-sided approach are prevalent. As Braun (1986) sums it up:

> *Gathering facts or emotions is useless if they cannot be integrated. Abreaction, without cognitive structure, can be dangerous in an MPD patient because it can activate traumatic memories for which the patient has no defense or coping skill. This in turn can lead to an escalation of acting-out behavior and psychological or physical collapse.*

(p. 14)

MPD and the Masterson Approach

Gerda has told me repeatedly that the initial work she accomplished, focusing on the Masterson Approach to her borderline self-style, was essential in finding the strength to face her real self. The revelations that came with trauma work would have been insupportable (they would have retraumatized her, or worse) without the character work and the beginning of the working-through of her abandonment depression. In this phase, she began to access and strengthen her real self to grapple with the trauma. The phase was marked by a more observant and adaptive ego, and a strong alliance with the therapist, supplementing areas where her ego still struggled to mature.

The unfolding of the work with Gerda demonstrates a therapeutic phenomenon I have since witnessed numerous times, both in my own work and in the work of others trained in the Masterson Approach: with patients with a character disorder and MPD, the effective resolution of character (personality) defenses opens the self to another level of dissociated conflict, and the working-through must then include an additional area of dissociated trauma.

It appears, then, that the self protects itself in ingenious layers of defense. On the basis of my work with patients at the Masterson Institute, I would propose the following configuration of early defensive groupings in the genesis of MPD.

First, there is a defensive operation that deals exclusively with the early and relentless onslaught of traumatic experience. It would seem that, through splitting, the part of the self that experienced the traumatic episode is divided from the main self and dissociated. Since multiplicity is generally conceded to have its origins in early childhood, repression (as it is defined as a major defense of the mature self) is not available as a means of psychic protection. Instead, the primitive defense of dissociation must be utilized. Freud (1915d) referred to this level of dissociation as primary repression, saying that its "essence ... lies simply in the function of rejecting and keeping something out of consciousness" (p. 86). (Freud substituted the term "repression" for "dissociation" to distinguish his dynamic concept from the then more commonly held concept of dissociation as the result of genetic weakness.)

Second, developmental forces and the dyadic interchange begin to shape the emerging early defenses that form the infant's character (projection, projective identification, denial, acting out, and so on). When the interrelationship with the mother (or a consistent caregiver) fails to be emotionally supportive (or is abusive or allows others to be abusive), the pain of this situation is circumvented by a rigid configuration of early defenses. The character (or personality) becomes set and stereotyped in order to evade, as automatically as possible, the kind of self-expression (related to separation and individuation) that is likely to evoke a response from the mother that will trigger the abandonment depression. Acting out, especially, becomes a major character defense, as it permits some lessening of tension by demonstrating in behavior the dyadic impasse, while keeping the actual understanding of it outside conscious awareness. This forms the intrapsychic structure, which is an encoding of the misalliance with the mother and is repeatedly projected onto all subsequent relationships of importance, including the therapeutic one.

Finally, infantile amnesia, or the repression barrier, further seals off the painful experiences of childhood to prepare the psyche for the new learning tasks of latency.

What brings the patient to the therapist is the failure of these protective barriers to withhold the pressure of excessive infantile pain or the defensive system's being so maladaptive that it presents a difficulty as great as, or greater than, that it defends against. Thus, in good-enough character work, the patient relinquishes old ways of being in order to be more adaptive. This releases a front level of defense, and the patient is faced with underlying traumatic issues, whose primitive dissociation had been doubly fixed in place by the character structure.

When the trauma experienced by the infant has been great enough to create multiplicity, the dissociative level is unique and differs from the dissociation found in more encapsulated experiences of physical or sexual abuse. It is a highly elaborate structure that acts to partialize and contain such a degree of trauma that even a moderate rupture in the multiple system could let through enough traumatic material to break down the psyche. This system not only has its own defensive and executive functions but exhibits other sophisticated specializations that amaze one with the resourcefulness of the self to persevere, and also with the ability of the self to divide into subselves indefinitely, to both the gain of safety and the loss of conscious continuity.

One realization becomes increasingly clear in the work with MPD: this elaborate dissociative work is not with defensive mechanisms only, but is also with a lost part of the patient and, in talking and interacting with the inner alters, the therapist is in touch with a part of the self that has been divided from consciousness since that part's inception. The real self of a multiple can never be established unless this defensively hidden part of the self integrates with the conscious part.

Dynamic Psychotherapy with Gerda and Her Inner World

Introduction to the Patient's Inner World

Since the time of Morton Prince (1906), representations of the inner world of the multiple have provided diagnostic guides for the therapy. My first tentative entrance occurred spontaneously when I asked Paulina to introduce me to others she knew in the inner world, and when I asked them to tell me about themselves. Since then, I have learned to elaborate on that process. I first introduce myself (partly to set a standard of order and courtesy, partly to allow for occasional inner unawareness of my identity), and then, basically following Bennett Braun's guide (1986, p. 19), I ask:

1. *What can I call you?* Giving a name may be considered dangerous, and certainly a sign of trust, so I may settle for "the one who is angry" until enough trust has been established for me to learn the proper name.

2. *How old are you?* This tends to identify the age at which an especially traumatic event or the need to perform some task in order to survive led to the creation of this alter. However, other reasons may determine the age of an alter, or an alter may have a range of ages (reflecting chronic trauma of a state-bound nature over time). So, I also ask: What was the age of the body when you were created? And: Do you have more than one age?

3. *What is your job?* Alters exist for specific (state-bound) reasons. If an alter addresses the therapist more or less directly, this is a useful question to ask, since the alter is likely to have a specialized function ("I get the body to the

office," or "I keep the records for the system," or "I'm here to deal with fools like you who ask too many questions"). These typical answers, followed by as full a discussion as is allowed, begin to identify the alters who are concerned with functioning and helping, or who guard the secrets of the perpetrators or are identifications with them.

4. *What is your story?* Alters who "hold" traumatic material – most typically (although not exclusively) victim children – may appear in an abreactive state and need encouragement to tell the event (release the event from dissociation to the consciousness). Because talking is considered dangerous, the story may have to be told through drawing or symbolic play, or even in sign language or by ideomotor signals.

In this initial phase of the dissociative work, I was becoming aware of the dynamic balance of the inner world and beginning to realize how the dissociative level had its own dynamic principles that required systematic conceptualization and specific approaches. For instance, the principle of containment was critical: the conscious, nondissociated part of the personality had to be healthy enough to manage the no-longer-divided-off memories and accompanying feelings that were released into awareness by the abreactive work. This meant that characterological work preceded abreactive work whenever possible, and that abreactive work had to be followed by a period of working-through, allowing the once-disavowed past to become part of the aware self.

I also discovered that inner victims and perpetrators had to be kept in balance. After the sequence of inner children had told the story of the father's abuse, the inner father emerged to threaten the system, saying that Gerda, or myself, or both, would be hurt if any more secrets were revealed. The presence of the internal abuser needed acknowledgment, and the system had to be helped to overcome and contain the terror evoked by the internal abuser before resistance to further abreactive work could be resolved.

Hospitalization

Gerda decided to enter a hospital specializing in treatment of dissociative disorders. The decision was based on concern for her safety and the need for both therapist and patient to understand more about the nature and treatment of multiplicity. We were worried about the increase in her suicidality and about the management of the violent alters (formed through identifications with her aggressors), and looked forward to contact with practitioners experienced in this work.

I visited the hospital weekly and attended sessions during which Gerda was held in restraints (cf. Braun 1986, p. 14). Gerda found the restraint sessions a relief, describing them as her first experience of being positively held, no matter how violent she needed to be. These sessions also provided the basis for her mastering of internal (or hypnotic) restraints, a skill we relied on thereafter. (There is an informal consensus in the field that internal restraints suffice when the patient's ego strength and the therapeutic alliance are in place. I would agree, with the added comment that multiples are overcontrolled people who can benefit from a safe surrounding fully to vent a depth of pain and rage that has only been permitted to be turned against the self or channeled into a mindless repetition of abuse. Perhaps a technique can be found that is less suggestive of past bondage.)

Resumption of Outpatient Treatment

After a month, Gerda returned from the hospital. By that time, we had both gained some sense of balance and direction. We relied on a well-established therapeutic alliance to combine the knowledge gained about multiplicity with her therapeutic work in the past, and to evolve a concept and a strategy that would guide her to integration of her real self.

I believed that Gerda could only be healed if I were able to find an overall way to conceptualize the therapy. Incremental abreactive work with each traumatic episode that appeared would be an impossible task; by definition, MPD is created by years of unremitting abuse, and would take years to undo piecemeal. I was also wary of the evoking of alters indiscriminately – what I call a body count. Both of these approaches seemed repetitious and interminable, and threatened to flood the patient. (There is an analogy here with the therapist who countertransferentially attacks a patient with deep interpretations, when the patient's ego is not strong enough to contain the feelings that are dredged up; or to the patient's perpetuation of a crisis state in order to avoid managing accompanying feeling.)

It was clear that the dissociative level had come forward when the character work had strengthened her ego enough to permit the management of a deeper level of conflict. It followed that the synthesizing of the trauma work with the character work, and subsequent inclusion of dissociative material in the working-through, was a step toward integration of the real self. Each time this step was taken, the self became stronger and ventured another forward move.

(It also seems likely that, as the patient's self matures, a wider range of defenses, including repression, diminish the need for dissociation, which had become the predominating means for managing psychic pain. The therapist should be aware of this transformation of the defensive structure, and so not unintentionally encourage the patient's inclination to detach and personify reactions to stressful challenges that can be handled in other, more conscious, ways.)

As I have already mentioned, the dynamic principles of resistance analysis could be readily applied to the treatment of MPD. In addition, therapy with Gerda's inner alters in many ways seemed to resemble work with both adaptive and maladaptive defenses. Acknowledging and understanding the alters sometimes seemed analogous to a second level of ego work. The increasing cooperativeness among alters released warded-off perception and feeling about the past, just as the healthier alignment of characterological defenses had opened the way to a similar understanding of individual depth and continuity. Combined, the character work and trauma work led to complementary aspects of the working-through.

Richard Kluft, who is a hypnoanalyst, has initiated much valuable psychodynamic guidance to the treatment of MPD. Gerda, by Kluft's definition, was a highly complex multiple with innumerable subselves. According to Kluft's dynamic approach, these subselves could be grouped variously, in levels and in types, and these aggregates often could be treated with collective interventions. Kluft also emphasizes resistance analysis; for instance, he is concerned with understanding the alter who is blocking the progress of the therapy, and who may represent a source of danger if bypassed. In addition, Kluft (1988, following Braun 1986, pp. xiv–xv) has conceptualized integration in a dynamic, whole-self way. He departs from the old idea of the forced merging of alters (equivalent to an overriding of major emotional issues) and sees the unification of alters as a basically spontaneous process that (with occasional strategic facilitation) takes place as the need for dissociative barriers dissolves. He understands integration within the larger context of what might be called self-actualization, as he describes the synthesizing of the unifying alters into the maturation of the overall personality: "Integration [is] a more comprehensive process of undoing all aspects of dissociative dividedness that begins long before the first personalities come together and continues long after fusion until the last residual of dissociative defenses are more or less undone" (Klufte 1988, p. 213).

Perhaps the following could sum up the contemporary approach to the understanding and treatment of MPD. Multiplicity is a complex reconfiguration of the self, intensively relying on dissociation to defend the fundamental integrity of the self from the disorganizing effects of ongoing traumata. Trauma originates in the developmental years and is directly associated with the family of origin, so that the infant has no recourse but to utilize inner resources of the psyche. The infant who is able to access these resources has probably found a way not to go mad or not to fail to thrive. Dissociation, and the elaboration of the splitting defense to contain dissociated material in discrete subself compartments, continues to be the defense of choice in subsequent years, particularly when the abuse is unabated. The treatment of MPD, therefore, is especially challenging, since it not only requires the loosening of the dissociative defense but calls upon the patient to manage pain and conflict in a unified, conscious manner, and to establish a basis of consistent trust with a valued person in the external world.

The treatment of MPD, as I have learned it within the context of the Masterson Approach, involves what Loewenstein (1990) has referred to as an ecology of therapies. Character work, with its ego-oriented interventions, gives place to interpretation and working-through. However, in the case of multiplicity, as early childhood material emerges into the consciousness, specifically traumatic issues also surface, and in a highly elaborate form that is best treated with some knowledge of hypnotherapeutic technique.

In addition, adjunctive nonverbal interventions, such as drawing and play therapy, may prove invaluable in maintaining communication with the patient's inner world (the use of sand-tray "worlds" is a specialized form of nonverbal therapy devised for work with MPD [Braun and Sachs 1986]). A primary skill, in both the assessment and implementation of the therapy, is knowing when to shift technique, and also knowing how to incorporate that shift into a consciously acknowledged and unified approach. This dynamic psychotherapy relies on the most steady therapeutic alliance, and the synchronization of the work, I believe, provides the basis for that desired dimension of treatment – the real relationship. (In retrospect, it seems essential to note that the patient's effective containment of the work may ultimately rest on the capacity of the therapist to hold an inclusive model of the process that can be internalized by the patient.)

Resumption of Outpatient Treatment: Inner Alters and Mapping

When Gerda returned from the hospital, she had a working relationship with a number of her alters and was constructing highly schematized maps (with the assistance of her inner world) that included all known alters, along with their relationships to one another. The maps changed with the progress of therapy.

Putnam (1989) has described such sophisticated mapping as follows:

> In essence, the personality system is asked to produce a map, diagram, or scheme of the alters' best understanding of how they fit together or their sense of their inner world. The exact form of the map should be left up to the discretion of the personality system. I have received Mercator projection maps, pie charts, architectural blueprints, organizational personnel charts, target-like arrangements of concentric circles, clock faces, lists, and some totally unclassifiable documents. What is important is that all of the personalities be represented on the map in some fashion.

> (pp. 210–211)

Gerda's alters primarily conformed to the two main types described by Putnam (1989): those created to protect the system from trauma, and those able to supplement the functioning capacities of the normally conscious self (p. 54). Other subselves, or partial subselves, also made themselves known (see Braun 1986, pp. xii–xiii). These included personifications of defenses, identifications with perpetrators, representatives of a spiritual state, and fragments. The work with Gerda emphasized four fundamental categories: Victim Children, Perpetrators, Protectors, and Helpers.

The inner alters, under ideal conditions, make themselves known to the therapist after a therapeutic alliance has been established with the Host personality – the part of the multiple system that represents the system as though it were unified.

- *Victim Children.* These alters "hold" abuse memories and are the primary abreactors.

- *Perpetrators.* These alters are mainly identifications with actual abusers. In doing the therapy, it is very important to remember that these alters are not the external abusers but represent identifications with those aggressors – identifications that had to be made to survive in an environment where someone else held the power. "If you can't beat them, join them," would be an accurate statement of their rationale. Perpetrators can be arrogant, contemptuous, and even violent, depending on the nature of the original model, but they become more accessible as they are acknowledged and the child behind the identification is found. As Gerda said of the Perpetrators: "They are all children with masks on." Perpetrators are really outdated Protectors, whose capacity to coexist with the external abusers may have saved the patient's life. However, the Perpetrators, like maladaptive defenses, live in the world of the past, and are traumatically fixed to reacting in old, self-defeating ways, unaware that new ways have become available.

- *Protectors.* These alters mainly represent adaptive ego states and preserve the impaired real self. Their basis for being seems to lie in a determination of the self to survive, sometimes formed around brief (but deeply significant) contacts with people who showed caring and values. It is often a Protector who is the first representative of the inner world to contact the therapist.

- *Helpers.* These are highly controversial inner selves, first described in detail by Ralph Allison (Allison and Schwartz

1980), and later by Christine Comstock (1991). There is often a sequence of Helpers, and the central one, the Internal Self Helper (ISH), poses the controversial concept. The ISH represents the spiritual aspect of the self and has been credited with paranormal abilities. Without entering into the controversy, I would like to define my sense of Gerda's ISH as the function of this Helper affected treatment. This alter understood the nature and possibilities of the entire self-system, and willingly worked with me to educate and guide me. The ISH did not claim to be a spirit but protected the unifying spirit of the self. The ISH could relieve other alters from pain, especially through dissociation, but could not effect psychic change in the system without the presence and concern of a significantly allied outside person.

- Although the ISH may have extraordinary influence in the entire multiple system and is able to perform acts that seem magical in the inner world (such as constructing protective force fields), it is interesting to note that dynamic change in the multiple system happens within a therapeutic, dyadic relationship. Again, the form taken by multiplicity is elaborate, but the psychotherapy of multiplicity follows familiar, well-established rules common to the containment and working-through of all types of personality disorder.

The Host Personality

This part of the self, named and described by Bennett Braun (1986), is in its own category. The Host personality has the special function of presenting the multiple system to the daily social world as if the system were a conscious unity (that is, a non-multiple); the Host, apparently to carry out this task more effectively, is convinced of its own oneness. As Gerda's transition to conscious awareness of her multiplicity demonstrated, probably the first major task of integration of the multiple self takes place as the Host begins to acknowledge the inner world of alters. (Since human individual consciousness may be a relatively new achievement in our evolution, and since modern scientific culture demonstrates antipathy toward the concept of the unconscious, the dilemma of the Host personality suggests correspondences with the larger, evolving social self.)

Braun specifically defines the Host as "the personality that has executive control of the body for the greatest percentage of time during a given time period" (1986, p. xiii). The fact that the Host must give place to inner alters that push through, that these alters may be at cross-purposes with the Host or consider the Host inconsequential, and that the Host may not even be aware of having been displaced, but only aware of having lost time, tends initially to create animosity, or at least much anxiety, in the Host's attitude toward the inner world. Well into the last stages of integration, it was my task to encourage Gerda's Host personality to work with her inner world, and to facilitate the cooperation and adaptiveness of the inner alters in supporting the Host's increasingly mature goals and actions. I found it especially important to strengthen an alliance between the Host and the "Front."

The Host, as I understand that part of the self, could probably be described as an outer alter. In Gerda's case (which I have found to be typical, both in my experience and as mentioned in the literature), there had been more than one Host. A child Host had committed "suicide" when she lacked the strength to act as container for an increasingly embattled system. She had been replaced by a stronger Host. During the process of therapy, Gerda (the Host carries the daily name) often came to the edge of despair, and the ISH once quietly remarked: 'We may have to make a new one." However, this Host personality was able to maintain herself, and then strengthen herself enough to integrate the younger Host who had "died." (Death, madness, illness, disfigurement, and dismemberment all may be found in the multiple system. These conditions are reversible as long as the body remains alive and intact and the total system is not overwhelmed.) Braun (1986) mentions the importance of finding the "original personality," which "is often difficult to locate and work with, but ... [this] needs to be done to achieve a stable and lasting integration" (p. xiv). In Gerda's case, the finding of the Host and the integrating of the entire Host line, back to the original personality, who had had the potential to contain a united self, were difficult, but essential for healing.

It is my experience that the Host, when first encountered in therapy, is a type of false, defensive self. The Host keeps up social appearances and carries the personality disorder that initially may bring the patient into treatment. Gerda, the Host, carried the borderline personality disorder. When the character work advanced, the Host was adaptive and strong enough to begin to acknowledge the inner world of alters. As the trauma work and the working-through progressed, Gerda held steady enough (although severely tested and often suicidal) to accept into consciousness the knowledge previously held in compartments by the inner alters. (It is interesting to note that the inner alters often had very different diagnoses than did the Host and had to be addressed by the style of intervention suitable for that diagnosis. The Perpetrators were almost invariably narcissistic, whereas certain of the Victim Children were psychotic. The ISH was normal neurotic, if neurotic at all, and demonstrated conflict only briefly over the acceptance of sexual maturation.)

As the therapy progressed and the personality disorder of Gerda's Host was resolved, the Host gradually became the conscious, adaptive container for the unifying real self. Gerda's impaired real self was inherent in her inner world, but had to overcome seemingly endless inner division, as well as support the Host's struggle with inhibiting defensiveness in order to emerge. The result of Gerda's integration could be described much as Masterson (1985) describes the real self:

> The term real self refers to the normal, healthy, intrapsychic self and object representations and their related affects. It functions along with the ego to effectively adapt and defend in order to maintain a continuous source for the autonomous regulation of self-esteem as well as to creatively identify and articulate or express in reality the self's unique or individuative wishes.

> (p. 30)

The more the Host was able to become continuously, consciously aware and to manage a full range of feeling, the more the real self was able to find a focus and a container for growth.

The Front

Scattered throughout the literature are references to an inner executive committee or team of specialized alters who are aware of the Host personality's problems and seek to maintain the functioning of the self by supporting, or even temporarily co-opting, the Host. This group may be co-conscious and constructively cooperative when first met by the therapist, or they may need to discuss with the therapist the advantages of clarifying and pooling their adaptive capacities for the safety and growth of the self. In Gerda's case, the Front, represented initially by Paulina, needed recognition and guidance from the therapist to form a working coalition. Once this coalition was established, the Front was indispensable for creating inner structure for safety, setting up warning systems for inner and outer dangers, shoring up the Host, and offering a rounded assessment of the progress of the therapy. In Gerda's situation, the Front was especially helpful in maintaining her daily functioning, protecting the inner children, and finding ways (especially hypnotic restraints) to modify the destructive impulses of alters who still operated according to past rules of power and abuse.

The Front, when united, operates as a sort of ego within the dissociated part of the self: it facilitates healthy functioning and defense. It is my impression that a number of multiples decide on a good-enough termination of their treatment when the Front operates in a highly coordinated way with the Host personality. This would be the equivalent of the patient who is satisfied to stop psychotherapy on the adaptive level and not venture into the revelations and emotional stress of the working-through, and it has its own validity. (It seems likely that the Front, a primary executive agency, is the forerunner of the ego in the structuring of the self-system. As Kernberg describes in the 1977 Masterson conference, it seems representative of "the fantastic, early object relations derived structures that are the building blocks of the later tripartite system" [1978, p. 83].)

The Inscape

I have borrowed a term used by the poet Gerard Manley Hopkins (1918, p. xvii) to identify the geography of Gerda's inner world. This Inscape, depicted through a series of evolving drawings, charts, and verbal descriptions, symbolized the patient's conscious acknowledgment, understanding, and gradual unification of her inner world.

Much of the Inscape was vague and uncharted. Even when the area was fairly well mapped, new regions sometimes appeared that demanded attention. (It was my impression that the full extent of this area, call it the subconscious, probably cannot be completely charted by contemporary psychic cartography.) However, one characteristic of the Inscape was dramatically familiar.

Gerda's inner world showed a split in the structure and evolution of the self that appeared to illustrate Kleinian psychology. The Inscape was divided between the Perpetrators and the Protectors, who established separate domains and vied over influence on the multiple system. In the course of the treatment, the creation of the "Safe Place" helped to establish a base for the "Safe People" that supported the building of more adaptive ways of being. As the good side of the split strengthened, the bad side – the "Tunnel Folk" – could gradually be acknowledged and educated. Translated into object relations terms, Gerda's sense of herself as good became coherent enough to begin to allow her acknowledgment of herself as bad – to integrate memories so ugly that only a mature sense of self, ready to manage ambivalence, could maintain her. (Importantly, the therapeutic process must aim toward actualizing the ability of the patient to sustain the mutual existence of the positive and negative in the psychic field.)

In this strange work, where one literally talks with the subordinate elements of the self, it has become clear to me that psychotherapy provides critical interpersonal elements necessary for psychic growth. The negative part-self, monolithically based on a past of consistent, ongoing abuse, needs the modification offered by a concerned other, while the positive part-self needs a dyadic presence therapeutically supportive enough to help build and reinforce inner structure that can facilitate the balancing and eventual integration of the negative.

The Safe People occupied the good side of the split, in a stone tower surrounded by picturesque, but carefully guarded grounds. They formed a sort of executive committee, a Front, that seemed analogous to the adaptive ego on the dissociative level. They were Protectors who supported functioning, managed feeling states, helped Victim Children to come to the Safe Nursery to release their stories to consciousness, and were vigilant against intrusions from the Tunnel Folk. The Safe People represented a part of the ego that had survived abuse and indoctrination and believed in the possibility of a life of individual worth and choice. Over the course of the therapy, this group became more interoperative, flexible, and receptive, and even learned to assist the evolution of the Tunnel Folk.

The Tunnel Folk occupied the bad side of the split in a labyrinthine, multileveled structure. There were many rooms representative of locations where the traumatic events of Gerda's life had happened; for instance, the bedroom with the father's reflection in the window was there. The Perpetrators – introjections of and identifications with Gerda's actual abusers, or with times when she, herself, had been forced to abuse – lived in the tunnels, endlessly repeating their hurtful activities. The Perpetrators sought out Victim Children, to return them to the replicated scenes of their victimization. The frozen, redundant nature of the Tunnel region, and the preoccupation of its inhabitants with power (either wielding it or obeying it), demonstrated the fixated and pathological nature of that part of the Inscape.

Only the ISH was able to travel throughout the entire system with some degree of safety (although with anonymity and caution in the tunnels). She seemed most at home in an area of bright fields that she said provided a region of spiritual protection for the system. In Gerda's schematic maps of her Inscape, these fields maintained a buffer zone between Safe and Tunnel territory, and steadily decreased in size as the Safe, conscious territory increased, and elements of the Tunnel territory were gradually made safe or neutralized.

Integration

Although the term "integration" is generally used to describe the merging of inner alters, it probably should more accurately refer to the inclusive therapeutic process that culminates in the emergence of the real self. Braun (1986, pp. xiv–xv) and Kluft (1984, p. 35) make this distinction, referring to the merging of alters into one as unification, and the post-unification working-through as integration of the no-longer-multiple personality.

Gerda's psychotherapy involved this ecology of therapies. The emergence of the self – of containment, insight, and psychic transformation – was held in a progressive balance. Confrontation (ego-oriented intervention) was used primarily in the first stage of character work. As the working-through phase began, interpretation was used more, until the surfacing of the dissociative level called for the use of hypnotic techniques. Although hypnotic techniques were especially helpful in the dissociative phase, interpretation of the working-through continued, and return to confrontation was often necessary as the patient regressed under the stress of increasing abandonment depression and decreasing recourse to dissociation to manage it.

Another kind of balancing act was required of the therapist in the shift from the essentially linear, cause-and-effect progress of ego work to the nonlinear processes of classic analytic working-through (free association, evenly hovering attention) to the dramatically spatial and systemic development of the dissociative work. In the last, equilibrium had to be maintained between the Host and the inner alters, and between the system (outer, inner, and as a whole) and the therapist. Even in the inner world, the acknowledgment of Victims, of Protectors, of Perpetrators, and of the Helper demanded equal weight.

Character work with the Host personality created the container for the working-through, which, in turn, included therapy with the defensive dissociative level of alters. Gerda said many times that this first adaptive structuring of the conscious self was critical to her ability to handle, and perhaps to survive, the pain and complexity of the working-through. (The alters, however, readily reminded me that I had missed their early attempts to leave me clues as to their existence. I might have begun contact with them sooner.)

The working-through stage, for Gerda, held a struggle with abandonment depression filled by extreme rage, guilt, terror, despair, and emptiness ("Everything is ashes. My life is nothing but ashes"). Despite an essentially supportive relationship with the mother in the present time, the longing for the inner, historical mother seemed inconsolable and endless. Suicide was a frequent concern, although she telephoned me infrequently, and only under great duress. Despite her suffering, she continued to be self-supporting and socially active throughout almost the entire process.

The pain of the working-through was directly related to the progress of the dissociative work. As the alters, in turn, released the portion of dissociated trauma each contained, the Host (and often other alters), who had not previously shared consciousness of the event, was shaken by this "new" knowledge, and struggled to handle it. In this way, the whole system, but the Host in particular, gradually absorbed perceptions and feelings that became part of the conscious life history. Since the dissociative defense was no longer required for a particular event, the alter who had held that experience no longer needed to be divided from the remainder of the system. As a result, a lost part of the self, split off to defend the greater self, returned as a flexible part of the whole. Although the greater self was shaken by the impact on consciousness of once-dissociated trauma, it also gained from more completeness. Protectors, who had guarded adaptive skills, Perpetrators, who had hoarded aggressive energy, Victim Children, who were loving and playful, and the Helper, who was wise and giving – all brought their attributes to the continuing integration of the self.

Something should be said about the complexities of the transference on the dissociative level. Each alter brings a separate issue of trust, mistrust, allegiance, opposition, or even total incomprehension to the therapist's acknowledgment of the alter's existence. Even the ISH, who intuitively understands the therapist from the beginning, learns about the complex unfolding of interrelationship over time. Other alters, however, see the therapist as an abuser or as a mother (or both, and sometimes to the point where the transference is hallucinatory). Most intense transference issues are worked through with separate alters, and then worked through once more on the level of the Host, who now carries the (now consciously manageable) transference issue of the integrated alter.

An ongoing issue for the therapist and patient relates to a shift in relationship that, with the process of therapy, is accentuated in MPD. *Each unification of alters into the system changes the nature of the self, and, therefore, the nature of the transference and the therapeutic alliance.* Even the character work must be redone somewhat, because *the person who is in therapy is not quite the same person as was there before the last integration.*

Something also needs to be said on the issue of countertransference, which parallels the diversity and intensity of transference. Briefly, the impact of both subjective countertransference (related solely to the therapist's own history) and patient-induced countertransference (the effect of the patient's projections on the therapist) is so formidable as to be almost diagnostic (at the very least, such reactions are probably indicators of significant abuse of the patient in the developmental years). The work evokes physical as well as mental states in the therapist and has a tendency to spill over into the therapist's social environment. The therapist experiences fascination, apprehension, exhilaration, and despair.

The therapist may develop one physical symptom or a kaleidoscope of discomfort. Pre-existing states may be exacerbated, or new physical problems may emerge that elude a satisfactory diagnosis and treatment. The therapist, overloaded with the data provided by the patient's alters and the technical challenge of work that is so frequently in crisis, may enter a state of stress that communicates itself to those around the therapist, verbally or nonverbally.

Until recently, the therapist's tendency to countertransference reactions has been exacerbated by a professional isolation parallel to the patient's personal isolation. There have been few professionals to turn to for guidance and support, and current pertinent literature only dates significantly from the 1980s. But the situation is changing rapidly, with the establishment of annual conferences on a high professional level, the journal *Dissociation*, and networking and additional conferences and publications on the local, national, and international levels.

Integration and the Termination Phase of Treatment

In Gerda's system, integration followed the orderly (not necessarily easy) process that occurs when the patient is highly motivated, and the therapist has acquired enough knowledge and skill to balance character work with trauma work.

The first alters who joined hands – as Gerda, (like "Sybil"; Schreiber 1973) described it – were the three Victim Children who had been sexually abused by the father. They became one representative child, Terri, who eventually stood for all the inner children abused by the father, and who learned to play and trust. Terri became a source of joy to the system, so that her integration at first was experienced as a loss. Terri integrated into Paulina, an unlikely combination that brought Gerda to tears. Gerda had wanted Terri to integrate immediately into her. The wisdom of the system had combined Terri's spontaneity and humor with Paulina's determination and pragmatism.

Subsequent integrations followed this pattern. Groupings of similar alters would merge as their knowledge was released to consciousness. and the remaining representative would integrate with an alter who demonstrated complementary characteristics. None of these integrations was clinically forced but occurred spontaneously as the need to dissociate parts of the self was diminished, and the self gathered its being together in a more balanced way.

In the final stages of unification, the multiple system had removed itself into single representatives of its primary subsystems: Child, Protector, Perpetrator, and Helper. The Host was now consciously accepting management of the self, practically and emotionally, in a more consistent way than ever before. The Child, mainly freed from the responsibility of bearing terrors no child should have to hold, was a source of pleasure and hope to the system. The Protector, a fiercely vigilant teenager, stayed around to watch over the Child and to keep the car in repair. The Perpetrator represented the role the patient would have assumed had she permanently aligned with the cult – that of a young priestess who had grown up largely ignorant of the world of consciousness, and who, in a sense, represented the "shadow side" of the self; she had struggled hard to relinquish her power, and only did so when she understood that love could exist in freely chosen, caring forms. The Helper gradually became a moral and ethical capacity and intuitive sense that permeated and guided the self.

The Inscape was fading. Gerda spoke less and less of the past, and even the representative alters ceased to appear. Her concerns were with her daily life and relationships. The Tunnel Folk had steadily crossed over to the Safe side. The parental introjects had lost their force: parts had been assimilated as positive identifications, and parts had been rejected from the system, suggesting the acquisition of a capacity for repression as an adaptive defense.

The tunnels collapsed like a house of cards. The old belief system of childhood had been replaced by a new belief in the self and the capacity for choice.

Criteria for the Achievement of Integration

Although the literature inclines to the hypothesis that integration is a larger matter than the merging of alters only, the criteria for integration tend to stress the completeness and permanence of that merging. In Gerda's case, issues connected with dissociation were of major concern, and her healing showed the following changes:

1. The absence of alternative personalities over a significant period and in pronounced times of stress

2. The management of feeling and conflict on a conscious, consistent level

3. The absence of Schneiderian symptoms (voices in the head, and so on)

4. Cessation of "lost time" other than normal distraction

5. Modification or cessation of such soft signs as headaches or ringing in the ears

6. The capacity for symbolic dreaming (where previously dreams tended to have abreactive quality — replicating a traumatic event or doing so in a thinly veiled form)

7. The acquisition of repression rather than dissociation as a major organizing defense of the psyche.

However, true integration is an achievement of the real self as well as of the whole self. The real self, as described by Masterson (1985), emerges with the resolution of the patient's personality disorder, as well as with the healing of the dissociative division of self. He cites the following as an adequate clinical working scheme for defining the capacities of the autonomous real self (pp. 26–27):

1. Spontaneity and aliveness of affect

2. Self-entitlement

3. Self-activation, assertion, and support

4. Acknowledgment of self-activation and maintenance of self-esteem

5. Soothing of painful affects

6. Continuity of self

7. Commitment

8. Creativity

9. Intimacy.

Conclusion

During the past few years, Gerda has relocated from the city and established herself in a sophisticated, semi-rural town. She secured a small business loan and set up a successful book-and-toy store. She commuted to her sessions (a drive of over an hour) twice, and then once, a week. The focus of therapy was on relationship, especially her deepening attachment to a young teacher and her residual wish to run away from relationship as dangerous. The couple, however, searched earnestly for closeness and commitment. They held each other and themselves to an agreement to stay and talk when they felt like running. The relationship has continued for three years, through both companionship and separation, and they are now married.

For over three years, Gerda has managed her life (which has included a number of crisis situations) without dissociating. Over two years ago, during a journey to another country, an inner child popped to the surface briefly (evoked by the echo of the continual journeys of her younger years), and then was gone.

What determines the healing of multiplicity? Time, which tests all things, will bring around unfinished business, or will simply present Gerda with the sorrows and pleasures that belong to the unity of the self. For now, it is enough to say that she has found herself, and she has also found, and entered into a committed relationship with, someone she loves and who loves her.

Candace Orcutt (1995b). In: J. F. Masterson & R. Klein (Eds.) Disorders of the Self: New Therapeutic Horizons – The Masterson Approach (pp. 227–254). New York: Brunner/Mazel. Copyright 1995 by Brunner/Mazel, Inc. Reprinted by permission of the publishers.

Bibliography

Allison, R. B. & Schwartz, T. (1980). *Minds in Many Pieces.* New York: Rawson, Wade.

American Psychiatric Association (1994). *Diagnostic and Statistical Manual of Mental Disorders*, 4th ed. Washington, DC: American Psychiatric Association.

Atwood, G. E. & Stolorow, R. D. (1979). *Faces in a Cloud: Intersubjectivity in Personality Theory.* New York: Jason Aronson (1993).

Balint, M. (1968). *The Basic Fault: Therapeutic Aspects of Regression.* London: Tavistock.

Bateson, G. (1970). A systems approach. *International Journal of Psychiatry*, 9: 242–244.

Beattie, M. T. (2005a). Consciousness and personality disorders. In: J. F. Masterson & R. Klein (Eds.), *The Personality Disorders Through the Lens of Attachment Theory and the Neurobiologic Development of the Self* (pp. 19–38). Phoenix, AZ: Zeig, Tucker & Theisen.

Beattie, M. (2005b) Early Development of Personality Disorders – Mother–Infant Dyadic Formation of the Infant Mind: The Psychological Dialectic. In: J. F. Masterson & R. Klein (Eds.), *The Personality Disorders Through the Lens of Attachment Theory and the Neurobiologic Development of the Self* (pp. 19–60). Phoenix, AZ: Zeig, Tucker & Theisen.

Berne, E. (1961). *Transactional Analysis in Psychotherapy.* New York: Grove Press.

Bowen, M. (1978). *Family Therapy in Clinical Practice.* New York: Jason Aronson.

Bowlby, J. (1969). *Attachment and Loss*, vol. 1, *Attachment.* New York: Basic Books.

Bradshaw, J. (1990). *Homecoming: Reclaiming and Championing your Inner Child.* New York: Bantam.

Brandchaft, B. (1989). Klein, Balint, and Fairbairn: a self-psychological perspective. In: D. W. Detrick & S. P. Detrick (Eds.), *Self Psychology: Comparisons and Contrasts* (pp. 231–258). Hillsdale, NJ: Analytic Press.

Braun, B. G. (1986). Introduction and issues in psychotherapy of multiple personality disorder. In: *Treatment of Multiple Personality Disorder.* Washington, DC: American Psychiatric Press.

Braun, B. G. & Sachs, R. G. (1986). The structure of the MPD's system of personalities. In: B. G. Braun (Ed.), *Dissociative Disorders 1986: Proceedings of the Third International Conference on Multiple Personality Disorder/Dissociative States.* Chicago, IL: Rush University Press.

Breuer, F. & Freud, S. (1895, reprinted 1955). *Studies on Hysteria.* J. Strachey (Ed. & Trans.). New York: Basic Books.

Bromberg, P. M. (1998/2001). *Standing in the Spaces: Essays on Clinical Process, Trauma, & Dissociation.* New York: Psychology Press.

Bromberg, P.M. (2006). *Awakening the Dreamer: Clinical Journeys*. Mahwah, NJ: The Analytic Press.

Bromberg, P. M. (2011). *The Shadow of the Tsunami and the Growth of the Relational Mind*. New York: Routledge.

Brown, D., Scheflin, A. W., & Hammond, D. C. (1998). *Memory, Trauma Treatment, and the Law*. New York: W. W. Norton.

Casey, J. F. & Wilson, L. (1991). *The Flock: The Autobiography of a Multiple Personality*. New York: Fawcett.

Clark, K.R. (1995). Season of light/season of darkness: the effects of burying and remembering traumatic sexual abuse on the sense of self. In: J. F. Masterson & R. Klein (Eds.), *Disorders of the Self: New Therapeutic Horizons* (pp. 255-279).

Comstock, C. M. (1991). The inner self helper and concepts of inner guidance: historical antecedents, its role within dissociation, and clinical utilization. *Dissociation*, 4: 165–177.

Daws, L. (Ed.) (2021). *Guardian of the Real Self: Selected Clinical Papers of James F. Masterson, MD*. Phoenix, AZ: Zeig, Tucker & Theisen.

Deutsch, H. (1965). *Neuroses and Character Types*. New York: International Universities Press.

Edelman, G. M. (2004). *Wider than the Sky: The Phenomenal Gift of Consciousness*. New Haven, CT: Yale University Press.

Eliot, T. S. (1933). The use of poetry and the use of criticism (lecture). MA: Harvard University Press.

Ellenberger, H. F. (1970). *The Discovery of the Unconscious: The History and Evolution of Dynamic Psychiatry*. New York: Basic Books.

Erickson, M. (1980). E. L. Rossi (Ed.). *Innovative Hypnotherapy by Milton H. Erickson: The Collected Papers of Milton H. Erickson on Hypnosis*. New York: Halsted.

Fairbairn, W. R. D. (1941). A revised psychopathology of the psychoses and psychoneuroses. *International Journal of Psycho-Analysis*, 22: 250–279.

Fairbairn, W. R. D. (1944). Endopsychic structure considered in terms of object-relationships. In *Psychoanalytic Studies of the Personality* (pp. 82–136). London: Routledge & Kegan Paul, 1952.

Fairbairn, R. D. (1946). Object-relationships and dynamic structure. *International Journal of Psycho-Analysis*, 27: 30–37.

Fairbairn, W. R. D. (1984). *Psychoanalytic Studies of the Personality*. London: Routledge & Kegan Paul.

Fonagy, P., Gergely, G., Jurist, E., & Target, M. (2002). *Affect Regulation, Mentalization and the Development of the Self*. New York: Other Press.

Freud, S. (1896). The aetiology of hysteria. *Collected Papers*, Vol. 1, 183–219. New York: Basic Books (1959).

Freud, S. (1900a). *The Interpretation of Dreams. Standard Edition*, Vols.4 & 5. London: Hogarth (1953).

Freud, S. (1905d). *Three Essays on the Theory of Sexuality. Standard Edition*, Vols. 7,

123–244. London: Hogarth (1953).

Freud, S. (1913). *Totem and Taboo. Standard Edition*, Vol. 12, 1–162. London: Hogarth (1955).

Freud, S. (1914). On narcissism: an introduction. *Collected Papers*, Vol. 4, 30–59. New York: Basic Books (1959).

Freud, S. (1914d). On the history of the psycho-analytic movement. *Collected Papers*, Vol. 1, 287–359. New York: Basic Books (1959).

Freud, S. (1915). Some character-types met with in psycho-analytic work. *Collected Papers*, Vol. 4, 318–344. New York: Basic Books (1959).

Freud, S. (1915d). Repression. *Collected Papers*, Vol. 4, 84–97. London: Hogarth (1959).

Freud, S. (1915). The unconscious. *Collected Papers*, 4, (pp. 98-136). London: Hogarth.

Freud, S. (1920g). *Beyond the Pleasure Principle. Standard Edition*, Vol. 18, 1–65. London: Hogarth (1955).

Freud, S. (1933a). *New Introductory Lectures. Standard Edition*, Vol. 22, 1–183. London: Hogarth (1964).

Gaston, L. (2015). *Within the Heart of PTSD: Amazing Stories of Gentle Psychotherapy and Full Trauma Recovery*. Bradenton, FL: BookLocker.

Gaston, L. (2017). Divergent change mechanisms in trauma-focused and non-trauma-focused therapies for post-traumatic stress disorder (PTSD). *International Journal of Victimology*, 14(34): 71–79.

Gay, P. (1998). *Freud, A Life for Our Time*. New York: W. W. Norton.

Gibran, L. (1923) *The Prophet*. York: Alfred A. Knopf.

Giovacchini, P. (1978). The psychoanalytic treatment of the alienated patient. In: J. F. Masterson (Ed.), *New Perspectives on Psychotherapy of the Borderline Patient* (pp. 1–19). New York: Brunner/Mazel.

Giovacchini, P. (1982). *A Clinician's Guide to Reading Freud*. New York: Aronson.

Glover, E. (1930). Grades of ego differentiation. *International Journal of Psycho-Analysis*, 11: 1–12.

Grotstein, J. S. & Rinsley, D. B. (Eds.) (1994). *Fairbairn and the Origins of Object Relations*. London: Guilford.

Guntrip, H. (1969). *Schizoid Phenomena, Object Relations, and the Self*. New York: International Universities Press.

Guntrip, H. (1971). *Psychoanalytic Theory, Therapy, and the Self: A Basic Guide to the Human Personality in Freud, Erikson, Klein, Sullivan, Fairbairn, Hartmann, Jacobson, & Winnicott*. New York: Basic Books.

Hamilton, E. (1942). *Mythology*. Boston, MA: Little, Brown.

Herman, J. L. (1992). *Trauma and Recovery: The Aftermath of Violence – From Domestic Abuse to Political Terror*. New York: Basic Books.

Hodges, A. (2014). *Alan Turing: The Enigma*. Princeton, NJ: Princeton University Press.

Hopkins, G. M. (1918, reprinted 1948). W. H. Gardner (Ed.) *Poems of Gerard Manley Hopkins*. New York: Oxford University Press.

Kavaler-Adler, S. (2014). *The Klein-Winnicott Dialectic: Transformative New Metapsychology and Interactive Clinical Theory*. London: Karnac.

Kernberg, O. F. (1967). Borderline personality organization. *Journal of the American Psychoanalytic Organization*, 15: 641–685.

Kernberg, O. F. (1978). Contrasting approaches to the psychotherapy of borderline conditions. In: J. F. Masterson (Ed.), *New Perspectives on Psychotherapy of the Borderline Adult* (pp. 75–104). New York: Brunner/Mazel.

Kernberg, O. F. (1994). Fairbairn's theory and challenge. In: J. S. Grotstein & D. B. Rinsley (Eds.), *Fairbairn and the Origins of Object Relations* (pp. 41–63). New York: Guilford.

Khan, M. M. R. (1963) The concept of cumulative trauma. *The Psychoanalytic Study of the Child*, 18(1): 286–306.

Khan, M. M. R. (1974, reprinted 1996). *The Privacy of the Self: Papers on Psychoanalytic Theory and Technique*. London: Karnac.

Klein, M. (1946). Notes on some schizoid mechanisms. *International Journal of Psycho-Analysis*, 27: 99–110.

Klein, R. (1989). Masterson and Kohut: comparison and contrast. In: D. W. Detrick & S. P. Detrick (Eds.), *Self Psychology: Comparisons and Contrasts* (pp. 311–328). Hillsdale, NJ: Analytic Press.

Klein, R. (1995). The self in exile: a developmental, self, and object relations approach to the schizoid disorder of the self: The Masterson Approach. In: J. F. Masterson & R. Klein (Eds.), *Disorders of the Self: New Therapeutic Horizons: The Masterson Approach* (pp. 1–178). New York: Brunner/Mazel.

Kluft, R. P. (1984). The phenomenology and treatment of extremely complex multiple personality disorder. Presented at the First International Conference on Multiple Personality Disorder/Dissociative States, Chicago, IL.

Kluft, R. P. (1988). The postunification treatment of multiple personality disorder: first findings. *American Journal of Psychotherapy*, 62(2): 212–228.

Knight, R. P. (1954). Borderline states. In: R. P. Knight & C. R. Friedman (Eds.), *Psychoanalytic Psychiatry and Psychology* (pp. 97–109). New York: International Universities Press.

Kohut, H. (1959). Introspection, empathy, and psychoanalysis – an examination of the relationship between mode of observation and theory. *Journal of the American Psychoanalytic Association*, 7: 459–483.

Kohut, H. (1971). *The Analysis of the Self: A Systematic Approach to the Psychoanalytic Treatment of Narcissistic Personality Disorder*. New York: International Universities Press.

Kohut, H. (1977). *The Restoration of the Self*. New York: International Universities Press.

Kris, E. (1956). The recovery of childhood memories in psychoanalysis. *Psychoanalytic Study of the Child*, 11: 54–88.

Laing, R. D. (1960). *The Divided Self*. New York: Random House.

Little, M. J. (1960). *Psychotic Anxieties and Containment: A Personal Record of an Analysis with Winnicott*. Northvale, NJ: Jason Aronson.

Loewenstein, R. (1990). Advanced topics in the treatment of MPD. Presented at the New Jersey Society for Study of Multiple Personality Disorder and Dissociation. Princeton, NJ.

Mahler, M. S., Pine, F., & Bergman, A. (1975). *The Psychological Birth of the Human Infant*. New York: Basic Books.

Masterson, J. F. (1967). *The Psychiatric Dilemma of Adolescence*. New York: Brunner/Mazel.

Masterson, J. F. (1972). *Treatment of the Borderline Adolescent: A Developmental Approach*. New York: John Wiley & Sons.

Masterson, J. F. (1976). *Psychotherapy of the Borderline Adult: A Developmental Approach*. New York: Brunner/Mazel.

Masterson, J. F. (1978). *New Perspectives on Psychotherapy of the Borderline Adult*. New York: Brunner/Mazel.

Masterson, J. F. (1981). *The Narcissistic and Borderline Disorders: An Integrated Developmental Approach*. New York: Brunner/Mazel.

Masterson, J. F. (1985). *The Real Self: A Developmental, Self, and Object Relations Approach*. New York: Brunner/Mazel.

Masterson, J. F. (1993). *The Emerging Self: A Developmental, Self, and Object Relations Approach to the Treatment of the Closet Narcissistic Disorder of the Self*. New York: Brunner/Mazel.

Masterson, J. F. (2000). *The Personality Disorders: A New Look at the Developmental, Self, and Object Relations Approach*. Phoenix, AZ: Zeig, Tucker &Theisen.

Masterson, J. F. (Ed.) (2005). *The Personality Disorders Through the Lens of Attachment Theory and the Neurobiologic Development of the Self: A Clinical Integration*. Phoenix, AZ: Zeig, Tucker, & Theisen.

Masterson, J. F., & Costello, J. L. (1980). *From Borderline Adolescent to Functioning Adult: The Test of Time*. New York: Brunner/Mazel.

Masterson, J. F. & Farley, J. P. (2005) Masterson supervision: 'nice guys finish last' – supervision of an individual with a schizoid disorder of the self. In: *The Personality Disorders Through the Lens of Attachment Theory and the Neurobiologic Development of the Self: A Clinical Integration* (pp. 167–184). Phoenix, AZ: Zeig, Tucker, & Theisen

Masterson, J. F. & Klein, R. (Eds.) (1989). *Psychotherapy of the Disorders of the Self: The Masterson Approach*. New York: Brunner/Mazel.

Masterson, J. F. & Klein, R. (Eds.) (1995). *Disorders of the Self: New Therapeutic Horizons – The Masterson Approach*. New York: Brunner/Mazel.

Masterson, J. F. & Orcutt, C. (1994). A theoretical and classical view of multiple personality disorder in the United States in the 1990s. *Kokoro no Rinsho (Clinical Mental Health)*, 13(4).

Masterson, J. F. & Rinsley, D. B. (1975). The borderline syndrome: the role of the mother in the genesis and psychic structure of the borderline personality. *International Journal of Psycho-Analysis*, 56: 163–177.

Masterson, J. F., Tolpin, M., & Sifneos, P. E. (1991). *Comparing Psychoanalytic*

Psychotherapies: Developmental, Self, and Object Relations; Short-Term Psychotherapy; Self Psychology. New York: Brunner/Mazel.

McWilliams, N. (2006). Some thoughts about schizoid dynamics. *Psychoanalytic Review*, 93: 1–24.

McWilliams, N. (2011). *Psychoanalytic Diagnosis: Understanding Personality Structure in the Clinical Process.* New York: Guilford.

Ogden, T. H. (1994). The concept of internal object relations. In: J. S. Grotstein & J. B. Rinsley (Eds.), *Fairbairn and the Origins of Object Relations* (pp. 88–111). London: Guilford.

Orcutt, C. (1989a). Confrontation of hysterical transference acting out. In: J. F. Masterson and R. Klein (Eds.) *Psychotherapy of the Disorders of the Self: The Masterson Approach* (pp. 231–240). New York: Brunner/Mazel.

Orcutt, C. (1989b). Progressive interventions based on the developmental paradigm. In: J. F. Masterson & R. Klein (Eds.), *Psychotherapy of the Disorders of the Self: The Masterson Approach* (pp. 110–146). New York: Brunner/Mazel.

Orcutt, C. (1989c). Psychotherapy with a borderline adolescent: from clinical crisis to emancipation. In: J. F. Masterson & R. Klein (Eds.), *Psychotherapy of the Disorders of the Self: The Masterson Approach* (pp. 185–196). New York: Brunner/Mazel.

Orcutt, C. (1995a). Early trauma and the developing self. In: J. F. Masterson & R. Klein (Eds.), *Disorders of the Self: New Therapeutic Horizons: The Masterson Approach* (pp. 181–254). New York: Brunner/Mazel.

Orcutt, C. (1995b). Integration of multiple personality disorder in the context of the Masterson Approach. In: J. F. Masterson & R. Klein (Eds.) *Disorders of the Self: New Therapeutic Horizons – The Masterson Approach* (pp. 227–254). New York: Brunner/Mazel.

Orcutt, C. (1998). Death, trauma, and personality disorder: thoughts on the inability to mourn. *Frontières*, 10(3).

Orcutt, C. (2012a). *Trauma in Personality Disorder: A Clinician's Handbook – The Masterson Approach.* Bloomington, IN: AuthorHouse.

Orcutt, C. (2012b). A patient with manifest narcissistic and developmental trauma. In: *Trauma in Personality Disorder: A Clinician's Handbook – The Masterson Approach* (pp. 73–98). Bloomington, IN: AuthorHouse.

Orcutt, C. (2017). Schizoid fantasy: refuge or transitional location? *Clinical Social Work*, 46(1): 42–47.

Orcutt, C. (2018). The False Memory Inquisition. *Clio's Psyche*, 24(3): 332–339.

Ovid (2004). *Metamorphoses* (C. Martin, Trans.). New York: W. W. Norton.

Pearson, J. (2005). Representations of reality: the analytic quest for the unnarrated self. In: J. F. Masterson (Ed.), *The Personality Disorders through the Lens of Attachment Theory and the Neurobiologic Development of the Self* (pp. 203–230). Phoenix, AZ: Zeig, Tucker & Theisen.

Prince, M. (1906). *Dissociation of a Personality.* New York: Longman, Green.

Putnam, F. W. (1989). *Diagnosis and Treatment of Multiple Personality Disorder.* New York: Guilford.

Putnam, F. W. (1992). Discussion: are alter personalities fragments or figments? *Psychoanalytic Inquiry*, 12, 95–111.

Putnam, F. W. (2016). *The Way We Are: How States of Mind Influence our Identities, Personality, and Potential for Change*. New York: International Psychoanalytic Books.

Reed, S. K. (2005). Psychotherapy of the disorder of the self with trauma. In: J. F. Masterson (Ed.), *The Personality Disorders through the Lens of Attachment Theory and the Neurobiologic Development of the Self* (pp. 145–166). Phoenix, AZ: Zeig, Tucker & Theisen.

Rodman, F. R. (2003). *Winnicott: Life and Work*. Cambridge, MA: Da Capo Press.

Ross, R. (1989). *Multiple Personality Disorder: Diagnosis, Clinical Features, and Treatment*. New York: Wiley.

Rubens, R. L. (1994). Fairbairn's structural theory. In: J. S. Grotstein & D.B. Rinsley (Eds.), *Fairbairn and the Origins of Object Relations* (pp. 151–173). London: Guilford.

Sandford, C. (1997). *Bowie: Loving the Alien*. New York: Time Warner.

Schore, A. N. (2004). The effects of a secure attachment relationship on right brain development, affect regulation, and infant mental health. *Infant Mental Health Journal*, 22: 201–269.

Schore, A. N. (2009). Relational trauma and the developing right brain: an interface of psychoanalytic self psychology and neuroscience. *Self and Systems: Annals of the New York Academy of Science*, 115: 189–203.

Schore, A. N. (2014). The right brain is dominant in psychotherapy. *Psychotherapy*, 51(3): 388–397.

Schreiber, F. R. (1973). *Sibyl*. New York: Warner.

Schwartz, R. C. (1995). *Internal Family Systems Therapy*. New York: Guilford.

Seinfeld, J. (1991). *The Empty Core: An Object Relations Approach to Psychotherapy of the Schizoid Personality*. Northvale, NJ: Jason Aronson.

Short, B. L. (2005). From concrete truth to symbolic reality – transference and the language of change. In: J. F. Masterson (Ed.), *The Personality Disorders through the Lens of Attachment Theory and the Neurobiologic Development of the Self* (pp. 61–79). Phoenix, AZ: Zeig, Tucker & Theisen.

Silberstein, S. (1995). Safety first: approaching treatment of the schizoid disorder of the self. In: J. F. Masterson & R. Klein (Eds.), *Disorders of the Self: New Therapeutic Horizons: The Masterson Approach* (pp. 143–160). New York: Brunner/Mazel.

Sizemore, C. C. & Pittillo, E. E. (1997). *I'm Eve*. New York: Doubleday.

Stern, D. (1985). *The Interpersonal World of the Infant: A View from Psychoanalysis and Developmental Psychology*. New York: Basic Books.

Strozier, C. (2001). *Heinz Kohut: The Making of a Psychoanalyst*. New York: Farrar, Straus & Giroux.

Sutherland, J. D. (1989a). *Fairbairn's Journey into the Interior*. London: Free Association Books.

Sutherland, J. D. (1989b). Fairbairn's achievement. In: J. S. Grotstein & D. B. Rinsley

(Eds.), *Fairbairn and the Origins of Object Relations* (pp. 17–33). New York: Guilford (1994).

The Troops for Truddi Chase (1987). *When Rabbit Howls*. New York: E. P. Dutton.

van der Hart, O. (2016). Pierre Janet, Sigmund Freud, and dissociation of the personality. In: E. F. Howell & S. Itzkowitz (Eds.), *The Dissociative Mind in Psychoanalysis: Understanding and Working with Trauma* (pp. 44–56). New York: Routledge.

van der Kolk, B.A. (2014). *The Body Keeps the Score: Brain, Mind, and Body in the Healing of Trauma*. New York: Viking.

Watkins, J. G. & Watkins, H. H. (1997). *Ego States: Theory and Therapy*. New York: W. W. Norton.

Willoughby, R. (2005). *Masud Khan: The Myth and the Reality*. London: Free Association Books.

Winnicott, D. W. (1941). The observation of infants in a set situation. In: *Through Paediatrics to Psycho-Analysis* (pp. 52–69). New York: Basic Books (1975).

Winnicott, D. W. (1945). Primitive emotional development. In: *Through Paediatrics to Psycho-Analysis* (pp. 145–156). New York: Basic Books (1975).

Winnicott, D. W. (1951). Transitional Objects and Transitional Phenomena. In: *Through Paediatrics to Psycho-Analysis* (pp. 229–242). New York: Basic Books (1975).

Winnicott, D. W. (1952). Psychoses and child care. In: *Through Paediatrics to Psycho-Analysis* (pp. 219–242). New York: Basic Books (1975)

Winnicott, D. W. (1954). Metapsychological and clinical aspects of regression within the psycho-analytical set-up. In: *Through Paediatrics to Psycho-Analysis* (pp. 278–294). New York: Basic Books.

Winnicott, D. W. (1955). Clinical varieties of transference. In: *Through Paediatrics to Psycho-Analysis* (pp. 295–299). New York: Basic Books (1975).

Winnicott, D. W. (1956). Primary maternal preoccupation (1956). In: *Through Paediatrics to Psycho-Analysis* (pp. 300–305). New York: Basic Books (1975).

Winnicott, D. W. (1960). Ego distortion in terms of true and false self. In: *The Maturational Processes and the Facilitating Environment* (pp. 140–152). New York: Basic Books (1965).

Winnicott, D. W. (1965). *The Maturational Processes and the Facilitating Environment: Studies in the Theory of Emotional Development*. New York: International Universities Press.

Winnicott, D. W. (1967). The location of cultural experience. *International Journal of Psycho-Analysis*, 48: 368–372.

Winnicott, D. W. (1975). *Through Paediatrics to Psycho-Analysis*. New York: Basic Books (first published 1958 by Basic Books under the title *Collected Papers: Through Paediatrics to Psycho-Analysis*).

Index

Karnac Books, founded in 1950 and relaunched in 2020, publishes seminal and contemporary texts on psychotherapy and psychoanalysis. It continues its long tradition of exploring the intricacies of these disciplines, providing space for the best writers on the complexities of the mind.